IMAGES
of America

MIDDLETOWN TOWNSHIP
DELAWARE COUNTY

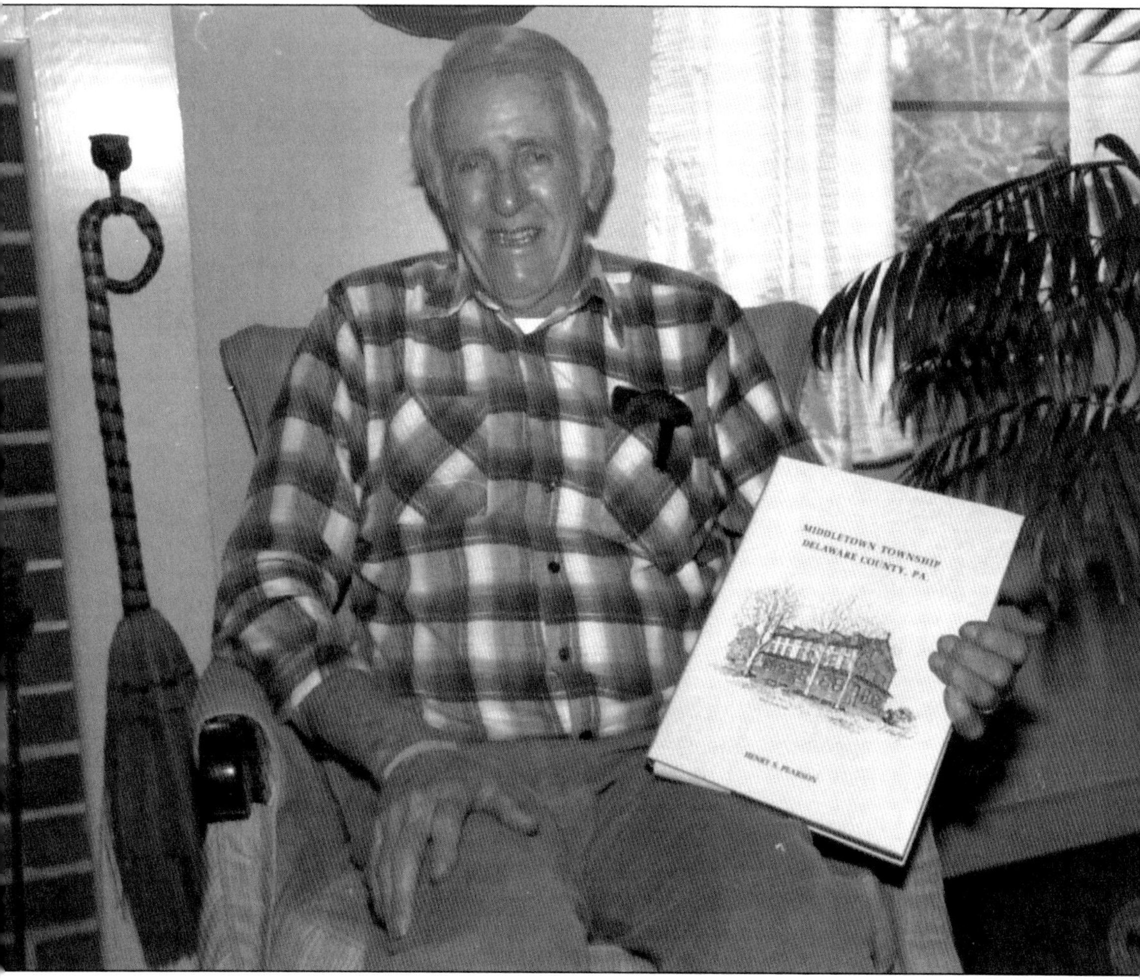

Henry S. Pearson is holding one of the 2,000 copies of his 1985 self-published book *Middletown Township, Delaware County, PA*. Henry began collecting old photographs and other ephemera relating to the township's history in 1977 by going door to door and talking with longtime township residents, most of whom were Henry's friends and neighbors. Much of the text in this book is based on Henry's continuing research, undertaken until his death in 1999. (Town Talk Newspapers.)

On the Cover: Residents of Middletown pose on Election Day 1930 in Lima. Pictured are, from left to right, Jessie Baker, Isaac Pennington, Lydia Ann Baker, James J. Skelly, unidentified, David Fury, and John Pedlow. Lydia Ann Baker was 100 years old at the time this photograph was taken; she passed away four years later. Her home was at 27 South Pennell Road. In 2011, it is the location of the district justice office. (Middletown Township Historical Society's Henry S. Pearson Collection.)

IMAGES *of America*

MIDDLETOWN TOWNSHIP
DELAWARE COUNTY

Mary Anne Eves

ARCADIA PUBLISHING

ISBN 978-0-7385-7538-4

Published by Arcadia Publishing
Charleston, South Carolina

Printed in the United States of America

Library of Congress Control Number: 2010942413

For all general information, please contact Arcadia Publishing:
Telephone 843-853-2070
Fax 843-853-0044
E-mail sales@arcadiapublishing.com
For customer service and orders:
Toll-Free 1-888-313-2665

Visit us on the Internet at www.arcadiapublishing.com

To my father, William J. "Hi" Eves, who taught me to love history.

Contents

Acknowledgments

As I put this book together, I tried to keep track of everyone who helped with photographs and information. If I left any of you out, please forgive me. Thanks go to Barbara Anderson; Betsy Barnes and the staff at the Middletown Free Library; Suzanne Davis; Steve Derby at Riddle Memorial Hospital; Carolyn Doerfler; Paul Dougherty, Ruth Ross, and the Aston Township Historical Society; Bruce Downing; Kay Ferrari; Gary Grove; Jim Hannigan and Carl Vairo at Williamson School; Pam Harper; Ann Herring and Mary Jane Kachelries at the Lima United Methodist Church; Dave Irving; Margie Johnson at the Delaware County Historical Society; Keith Lockhart, creator of delawarecountyhistory.com; Meredith Merino, Susan Suplee, and the staff at the Middletown Township Building; Steve and Sue Mescanti; Betsy Ney at the Tyler Arboretum; Noreen Shredenschek at the Middletown Presbyterian Church; Stuart Spisak; J. Karl Thomas; Maria Thompson; Larry Weathers Jr.; Nancy Webster; and David Williams.

INTRODUCTION

Since the photographs in this book are from the second half of the 19th and the 20th centuries, the introduction is devoted to the pre-photographic history of Middletown Township. Colonial townships are dated from the appointment of their first officer. On the third day of the first week of the 10th month in 1686, the court of common pleas of Chester County, Pennsylvania, appointed a constable for Middletown Township. Up to and through 1751, the Julian calendar was used in England, Wales, Ireland, and the British colonies. On the Gregorian calendar, that date is December 3, 1686. Middletown Township was part of Chester County until September 26, 1789, when the southern part of Chester County became Delaware County.

Most areas, when they develop, are either agricultural or industrial. From the beginning of European settlement, southeastern Pennsylvania, Middletown Township included, had both. This was in part because of the geography and in part because of the Quaker ethic of not amassing too much money. Quakers who made money in agriculture were expected to invest those funds in new businesses in their townships. Many Quaker farmers eventually became mill owners. Later, as the Quaker mill owners made money, they reinvested it in agriculture. The main reason this region survived economic depressions, wars, and other natural and manmade disasters was because of the strength of this economic diversification.

Middletown's eastern border is Ridley Creek, and its western border is Chester Creek. Both creeks were lined with mills, although there was a greater number on the more powerful and deeper Chester Creek. Mills were more than just buildings. They were often at the center of what became towns, and they were usually important transportation hubs. A mill was generally built where a smaller stream came into the main stream. At that point the smaller stream would deposit silt in the main stream, creating a shallow spot that allowed the main stream to be easily forded. Fords created crossroads, and crossroads grew into villages.

A support system was needed to operate mills. In the case of gristmills, the most common type in Middletown, a blacksmith had to be close to make and sharpen the chisels used to carve the grindstones and to shoe the horses that pulled the wagons of grain. A wheelwright and harness maker had to be there to maintain the wagons. A barrel maker was needed to make the containers that held the ground grain. These people needed homes, so most mills had a cluster of worker housing around them. Additionally, there had to be temporary housing, such as taverns, where farmers and teamsters could eat and sleep while waiting for the grain to be ground. There were also inns, which offered higher quality accommodations, where mill owners could conduct business with their clients. All this associated activity surrounded the many mills here in 18th-century Middletown.

Generally, where wheat can be grown in America, indeed around the world, there can only be two crops planted and harvested each year. But the growing conditions in the lower Delaware Valley allowed for three crops each year. Therefore, the mills had more work annually producing flour than mills elsewhere. It was not until the beginning of the 20th century that more wheat was produced on the Great Plains than here. Eventually, textile mills became second in number to gristmills in Middletown, particularly along the lower half of Chester Creek beginning at Lenni.

Much of the information we have on early-19th-century southeastern Pennsylvania comes from records created by the 1798 Direct Tax Act, sometimes called the Glass Tax, because part of that tax was levied on glass windowpanes. The tax assessments still survive for Delaware County, giving volumes of details on homes, businesses, and associated outbuildings. Additional information comes from a group of businessmen who, in 1826, prepared a creek-by-creek report called the Statistical Account of Mills of Delaware County. They were not only listing the mills that existed in 1826, but also other places along the creeks where new mills could be built. In the fall of 1843, the area had one of the worst floods that Delaware County has ever seen. Dozens of lives were lost, most mills were seriously damaged, and some were completely destroyed. After the 1843 flood, a report was made detailing what mills had been standing before the flood, what was lost, and what was being rebuilt. The second worst flood in terms of damage was caused by Hurricane Agnes in the fall of 1972.

These and other documents show that in the first half of the 19th century, not so much in Philadelphia, but within 30 miles outside the city (and mostly in Delaware County), there were more mills, and they produced more in total than all the other mills in the United States at that time. Only in the 1850s, when the large textile mills in Lowell, Massachusetts, began to operate, was there any kind of competition for our textile mills.

But by that point, mill technology had advanced from waterpower to steam power. A number of the local mills moved into Chester to be close to the Delaware River for easy transport, but many stayed here and retooled. In Middletown, the remaining mills, although small, were known to produce products of high quality. In addition to the mills, farming and dairy production remained a constant in Middletown for over 300 years. This trend continued up through World War II, when the nationwide economy slowly changed from agriculture and manufacturing to service industries.

The roads and other locations referred to in the captions are for the most part 21st-century citations for readers' reference. For example, Cumberland Cemetery did not exist when the Middletown Meeting split and the Orthodox Friends built their 1835 meetinghouse south of the present-day cemetery.

Much of the information in this introduction came from historian Nancy Webster's research. All historians in the Delaware Valley are indebted to Nancy for her diligent work over the past 40 years. The information on the 19th-century schools comes from Keith Lockhart's title searches. David Williams and Stuart Spisak were very helpful in dating photographs based on the automobiles pictured.

Special thanks go posthumously to Dr. Anna Broomall who, from 1900 to 1922, compiled a series of scrapbooks containing photographs, newspaper clippings, and handwritten notes on historic buildings around Delaware County. This invaluable resource is now in the collection of the Delaware County Historical Society.

Unless otherwise identified, the images in this book are from the Middletown Township Historical Society's Henry S. Pearson Collection.

Abbreviations when used for photograph credits are as follows: ATHS, Aston Township Historical Society; DCHS, Delaware County Historical Society; DCIS, Delaware County Institute of Science; Hagley, Hagley Museum and Library; LUMC, Lima United Methodist Church; MHAC, Media Historic Archives Commission; MTFL, Middletown Free Library; and PHSAA, Penncrest High School Alumni Association.

One

Black Horse

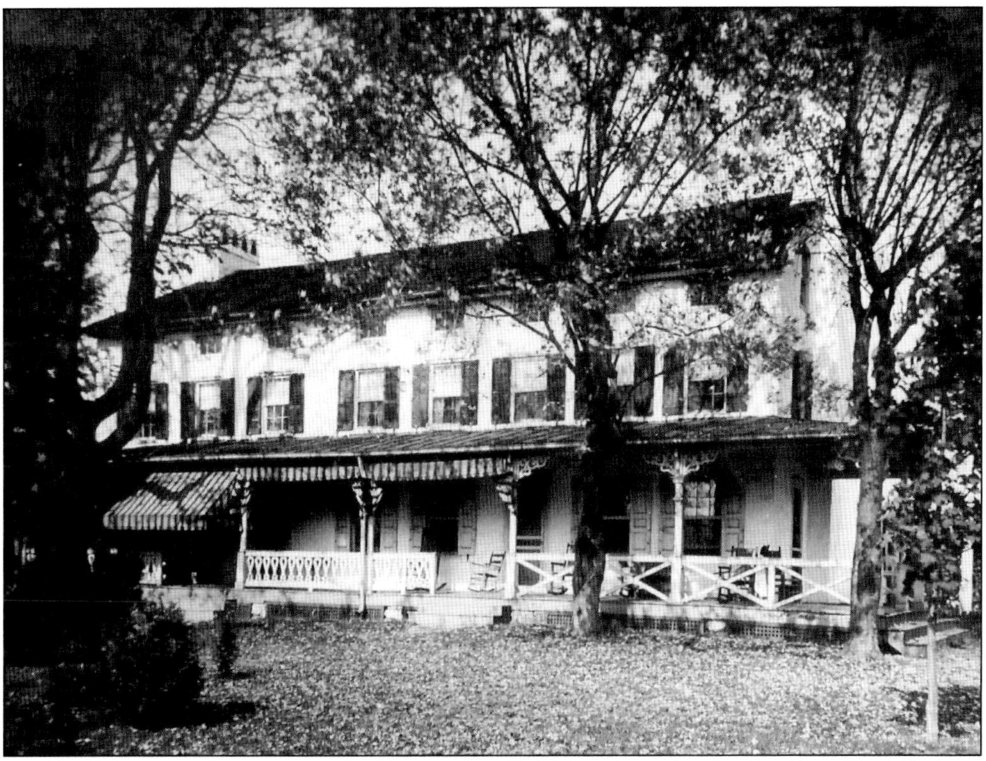

For 200 years, the area around the intersection of Baltimore Pike (US Route 1) and Middletown Road (PA Route 352) was called "Black Horse." In 1737, William Noblit built the Black Horse Inn on the northeast corner of the intersection. Noblit was granted a license to operate the structure as an inn in 1739. The inn, pictured here around 1895, was purchased in 1908 by Swarthmore attorney Alan Cunningham. It was torn down in 1939 for the construction of the "cloverleaf" interchange. From then on, locals have called the area "the cloverleaf."

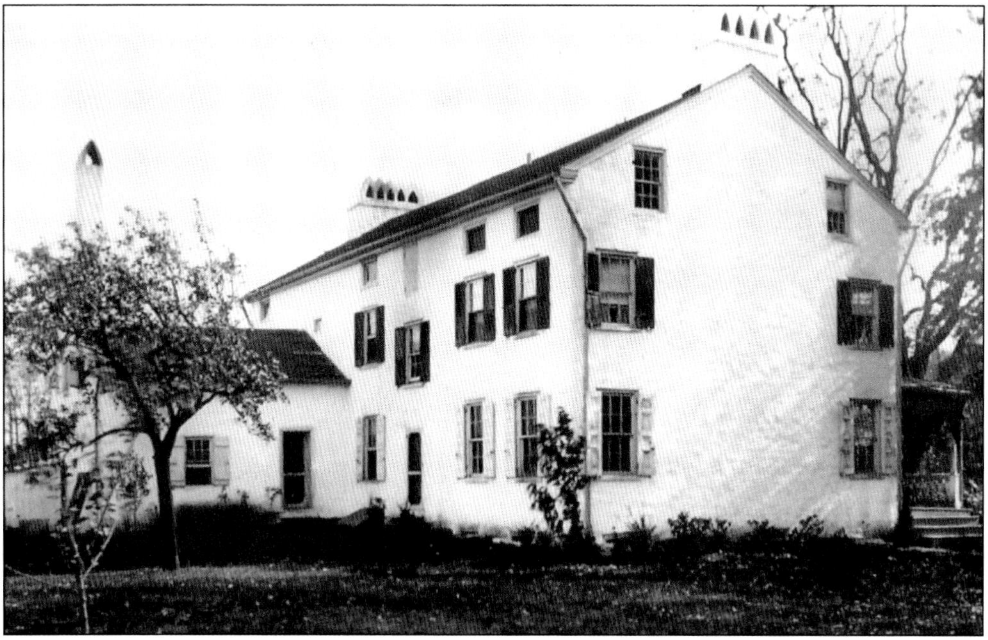

The rear of the original 1739 structure is pictured around 1918. Cunningham practiced law in Wilmington, Delaware, where he also served as assistant district attorney. In 1895, he joined the staff of the Philadelphia *Public Ledger*, a daily newspaper, as an editorial writer, and later became managing editor and associate editor. Upon retiring from the paper, he bought the property and used it as his summer retreat and as a working farm.

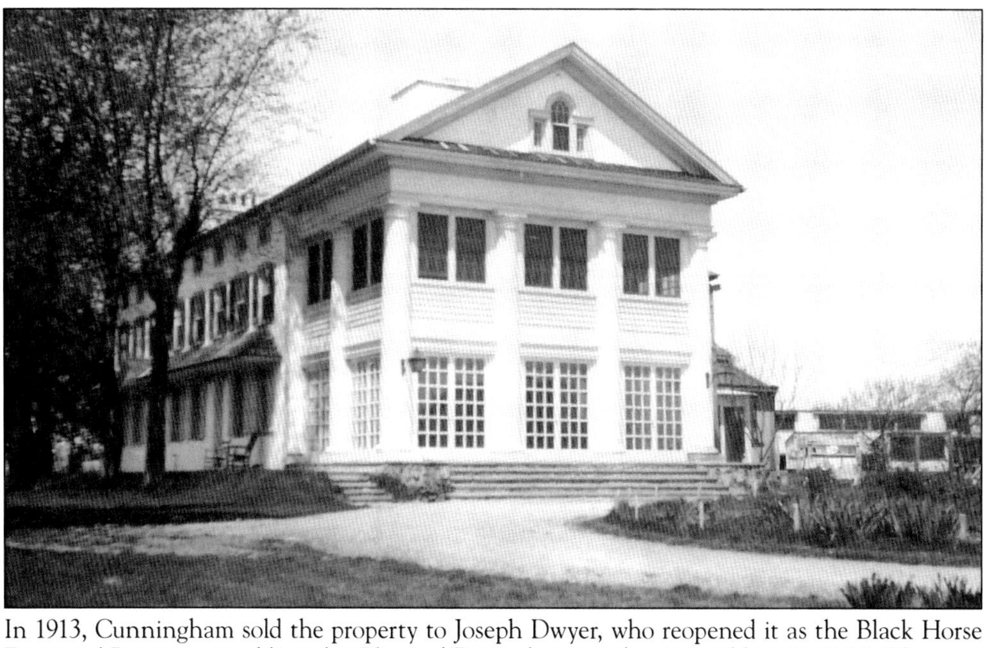

In 1913, Cunningham sold the property to Joseph Dwyer, who reopened it as the Black Horse Farm and Restaurant, adding the Classical Revival sunporch, pictured here in 1915. The pent roof of the original structure can be seen just past the last column on the left. The restaurant closed in 1935. The building then became a substation of the state highway patrol until it was demolished in 1939 for the cloverleaf interchange.

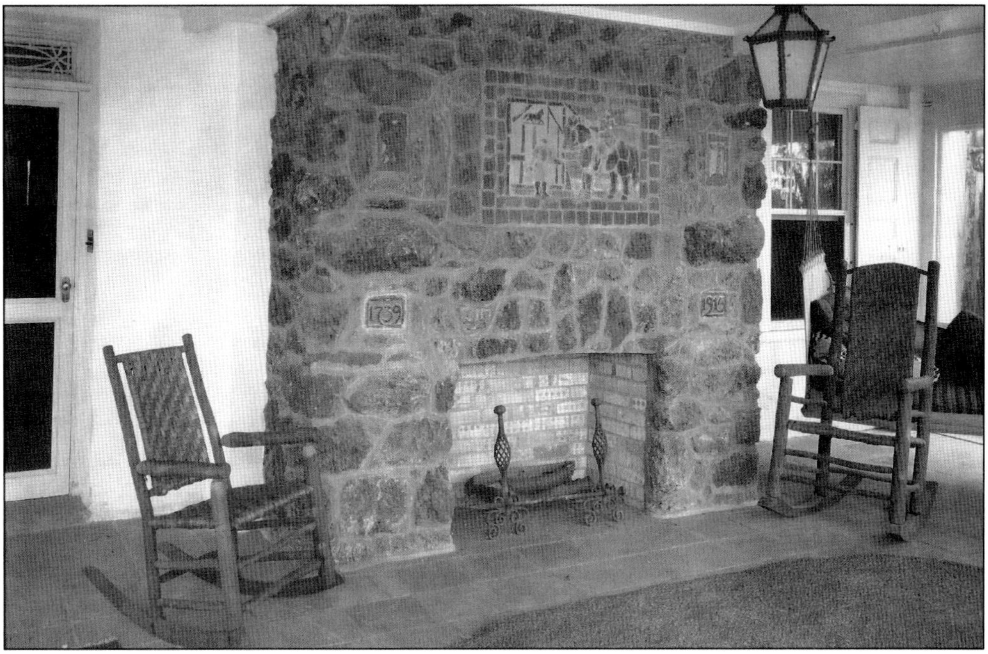

The hearth inside the restaurant's tearoom was decorated with tiles from the Moravian Pottery and Tileworks in Doylestown, Pennsylvania. The scene is of a rider arriving at the Black Horse Inn. The inn's distinctive black horse weather vane stands atop a pole at the left. Flanking the hearth are date stones marked "1739" and "1915." The inn was opened in 1739, and the addition was made in 1915.

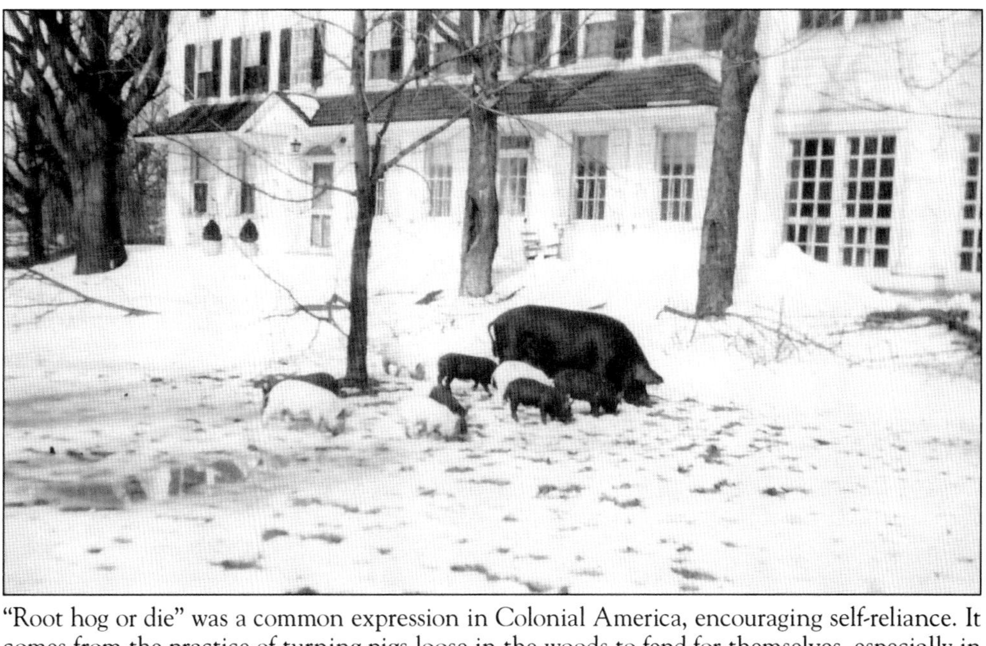

"Root hog or die" was a common expression in Colonial America, encouraging self-reliance. It comes from the practice of turning pigs loose in the woods to fend for themselves, especially in the winter when animal feed was scarce. In the 18th century, the inn grounds included a cattle market and 100 acres of grazing land, but it had been reduced to 55 acres when Cunningham purchased it.

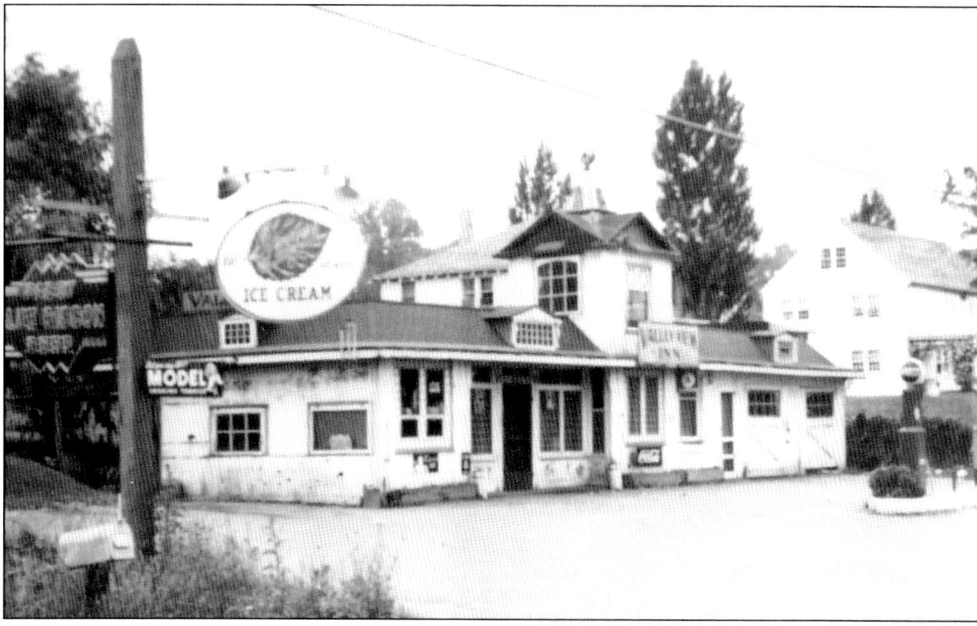

Pictured about 1937, the Valley View Inn was on Old Baltimore Pike, just west of the entrance to Elwyn Institute. Pres Lawrence ran the combination lunchroom and gas station. He was also a justice of the peace. While in high school, Allen Miller worked there pumping gas, and after graduation he opened a car repair shop in the garage on the left. The building was torn down in the 1960s.

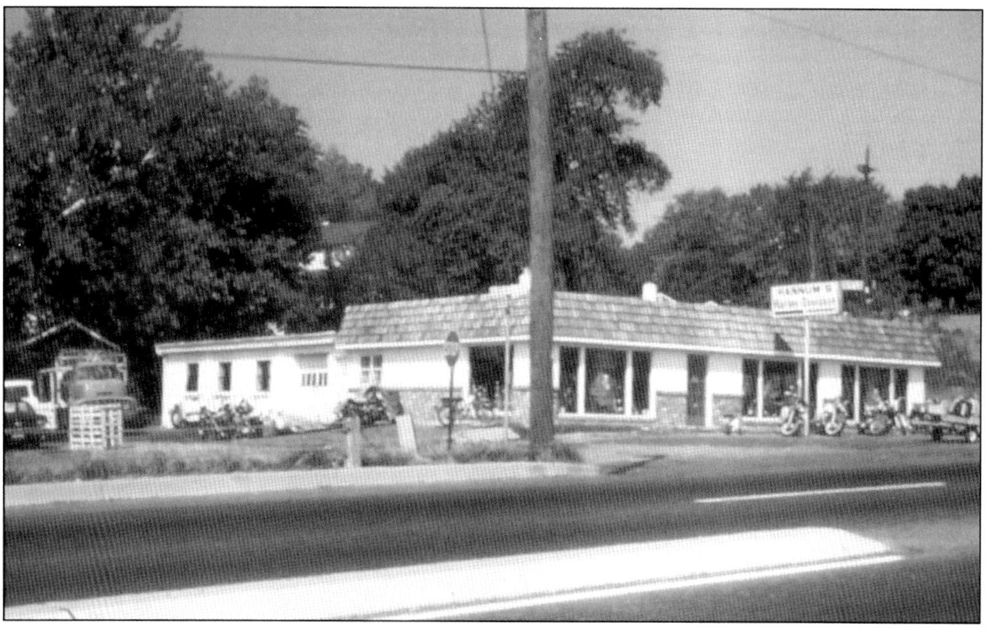

Hannum's Harley-Davidson was opened on the northwest corner of the cloverleaf in 1959. In 1954, Tom Hannum Jr. convinced his father to sell his automotive business and purchase a Harley-Davidson dealership. Hannum's H-D opened on Chester Pike in Crum Lynne, Pennsylvania, in 1954. Five years later, needing more room for their growing business, they moved to Middletown. (Paul Dougherty/ATHS.)

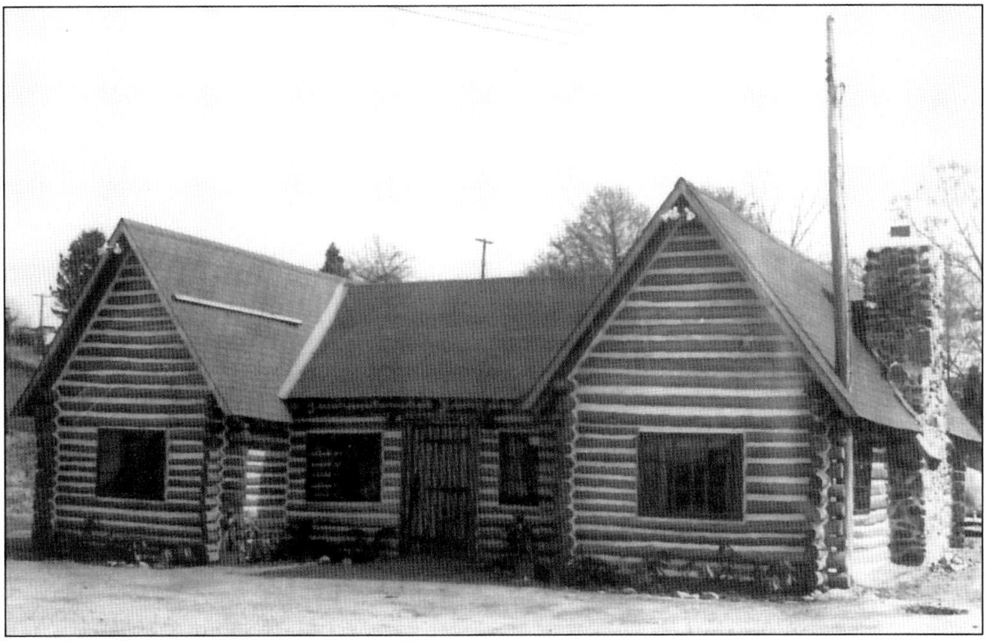

The Log Cabin Inn was located east of Black Horse on the south side of Baltimore Pike. The original building was of hand-hewn logs on all four sides, as well as the trusses and rafters. It was constructed in 1948 by Richard Schultz and his father and mother, Ernest and Emma Zerlando. "A lot of sweat went into it," Shultz recalled. "We drove the nails, set the mortar blocks and stone, you name it." In 1951, a dining room was added to the right of the original cabin, and in 1968, a banquet room was added on the left. The photograph below was taken in 1985. Two years later, in 1987, Shultz's son Richard II took over as proprietor. In the summer of 1993, the restaurant was destroyed in a five-alarm fire and never rebuilt. Granite Run Buick GMC currently occupies the site.

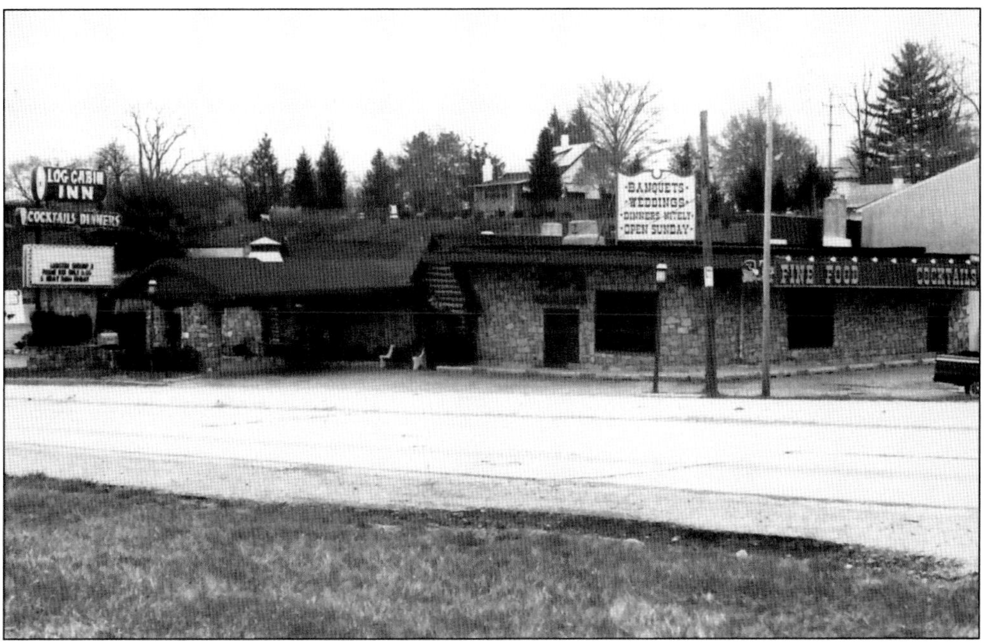

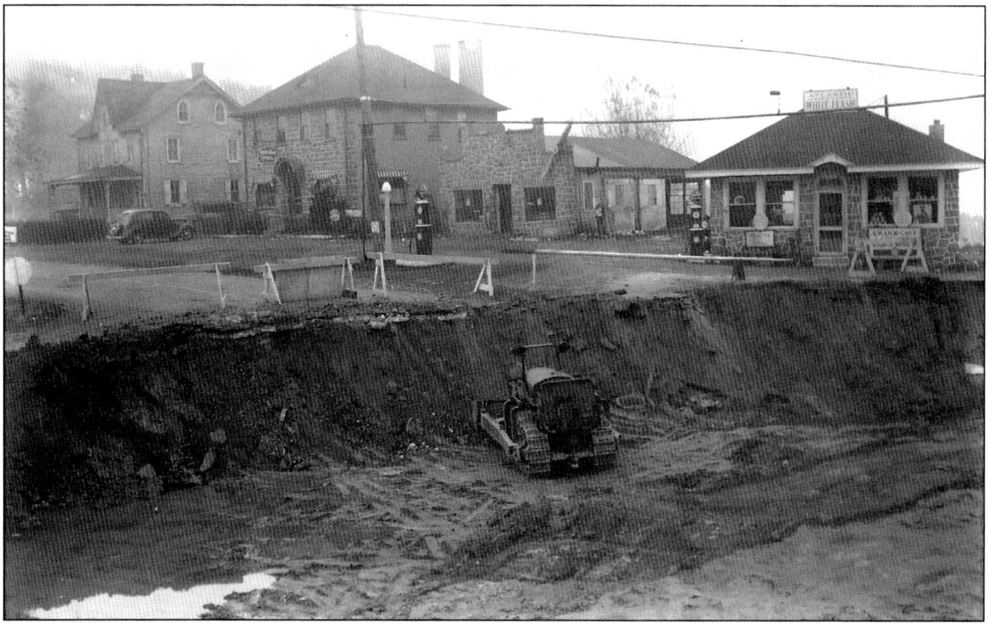

Beginning in 1939, Baltimore Pike was expanded to four lanes from Ridley Creek west to the railroad bridge in Wawa. The roadbed was lowered about 40 feet at Black Horse to create the cloverleaf interchange. The two buildings on the right in the image above were torn down. The square stone building, D'Ignazio's Clover Leaf Inn, was raised and moved 400 feet to the southwest corner of the new intersection. The original building was raised above lower additions that were added in the 1940s and 1950s, as shown in the photograph below from the early 1960s. After serving the dining needs of the region for 30 years, the Clover Leaf Inn was destroyed by fire in October 1967. Rather than rebuild on this site, the D'Ignazios opened a new restaurant, Len's Place, a half mile south on Baltimore Pike in October 1968. (Above, DCHS; below, Bonnie D'Ignazio.)

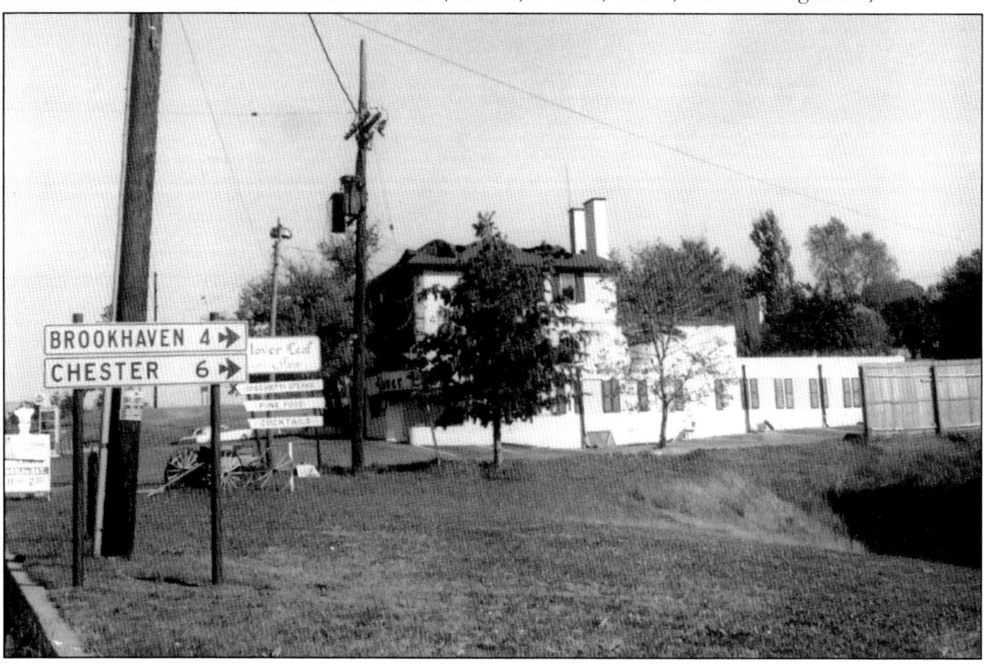

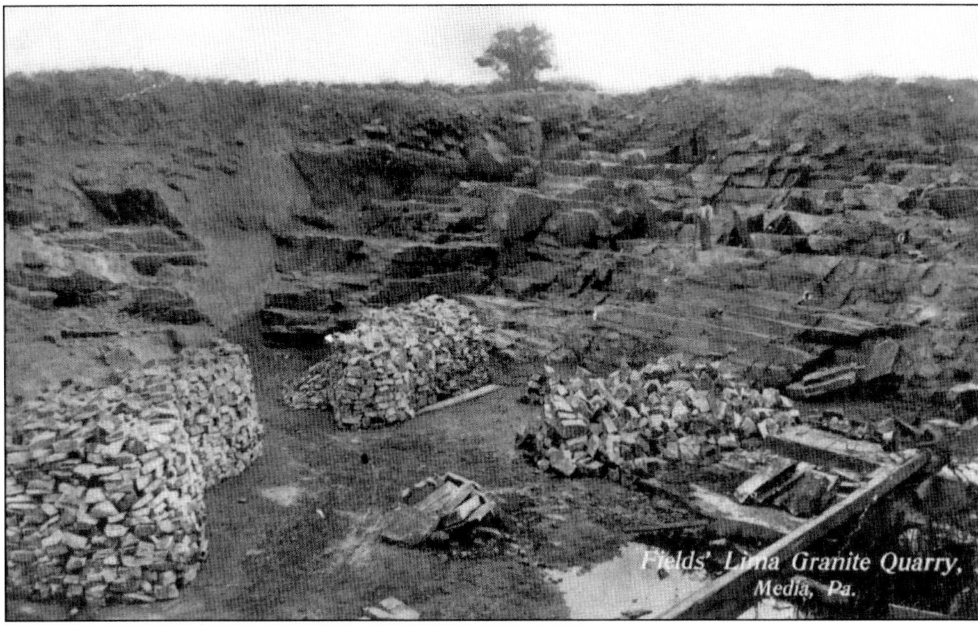

Lima Quarry is shown on maps as early as 1875. The granite was used for building stone in many of the homes, businesses, churches, and other structures in the area. Ben Fields was the owner in the early 1900s, and Granite Run Mall is now on this site. One end of the mall is slightly higher than the other because it would have cost too much to remove the granite below. (Larry Weathers Jr.)

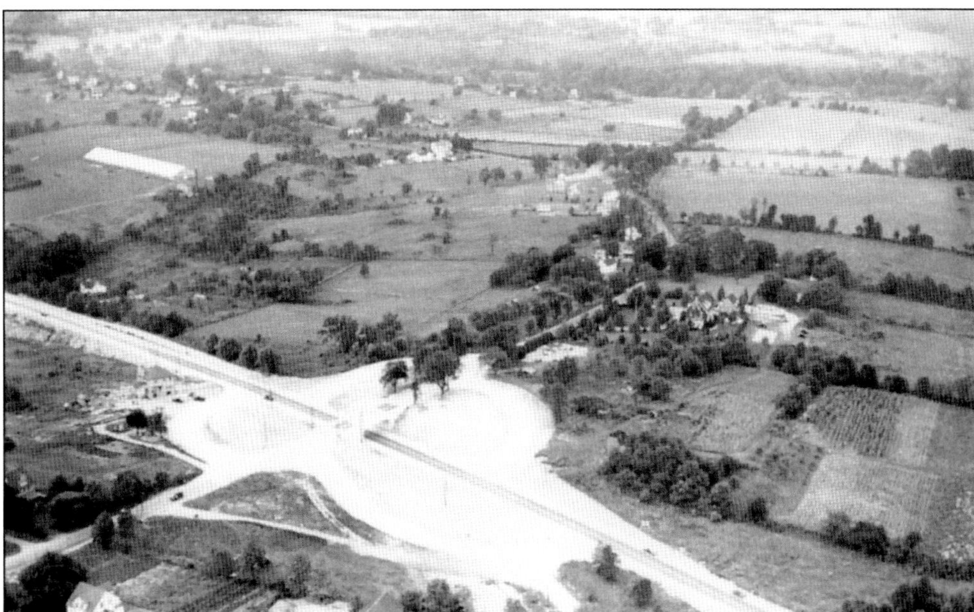

The completed cloverleaf interchange is seen here in 1941. The greenhouse visible in the upper left was operated by Casper Nullen and his father beginning in 1929. They grew 17,000 long stem roses at a time. In 1943, they took on a partner and became Nullen and Rolf. Later, Fred Muller raised cut roses here solely for the Penn Fruit chain of supermarkets. This is now the site of Granite Run Mall. (DCHS.)

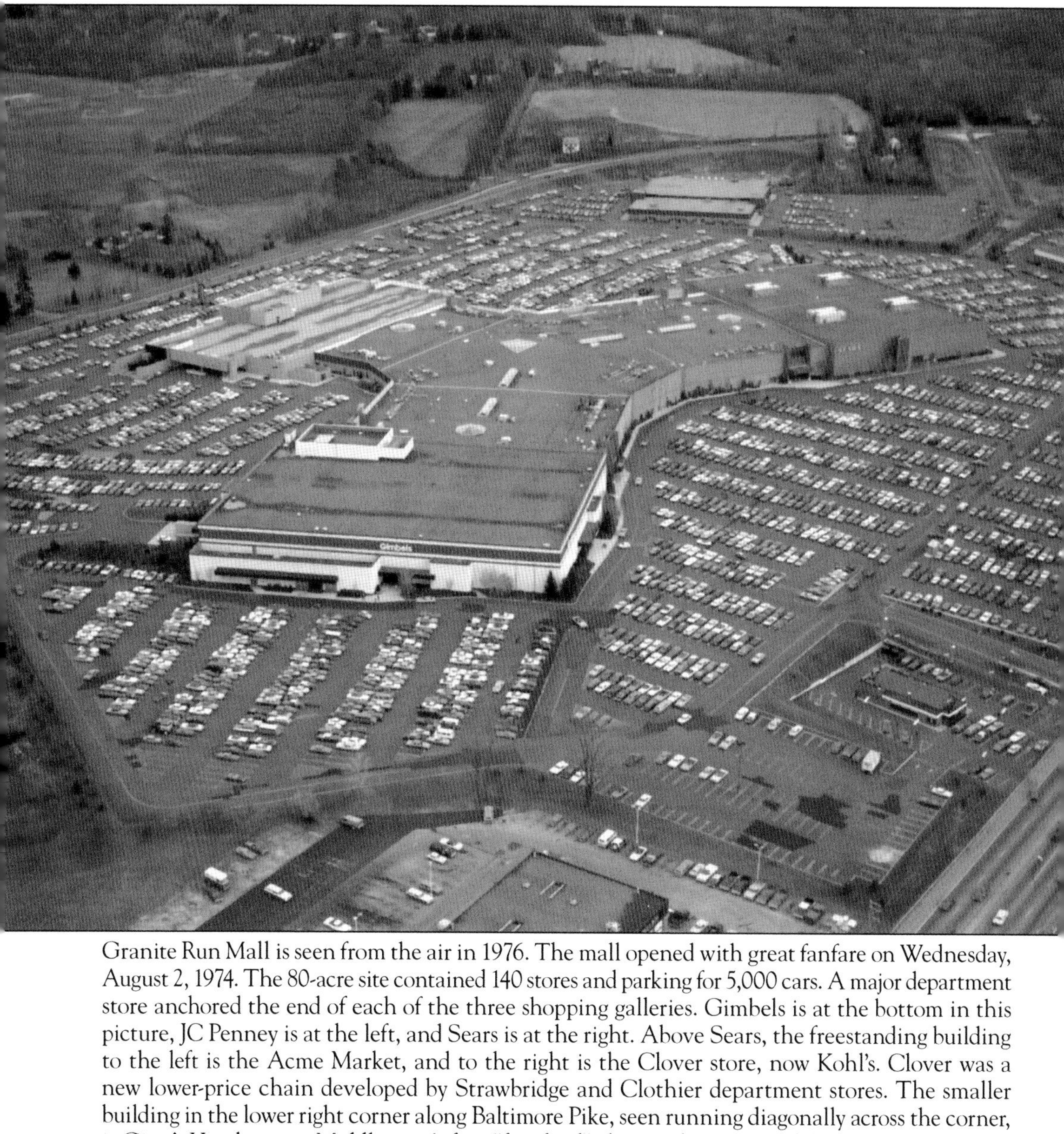

Granite Run Mall is seen from the air in 1976. The mall opened with great fanfare on Wednesday, August 2, 1974. The 80-acre site contained 140 stores and parking for 5,000 cars. A major department store anchored the end of each of the three shopping galleries. Gimbels is at the bottom in this picture, JC Penney is at the left, and Sears is at the right. Above Sears, the freestanding building to the left is the Acme Market, and to the right is the Clover store, now Kohl's. Clover was a new lower-price chain developed by Strawbridge and Clothier department stores. The smaller building in the lower right corner along Baltimore Pike, seen running diagonally across the corner, is Gino's Hamburgers, Middletown's first "fast food" chain. The corner of the building visible in the center along the bottom of this photograph was Walsh Ford. Eventually, that building would house the AMC Movie Theaters and several restaurants.

Two

LIMA

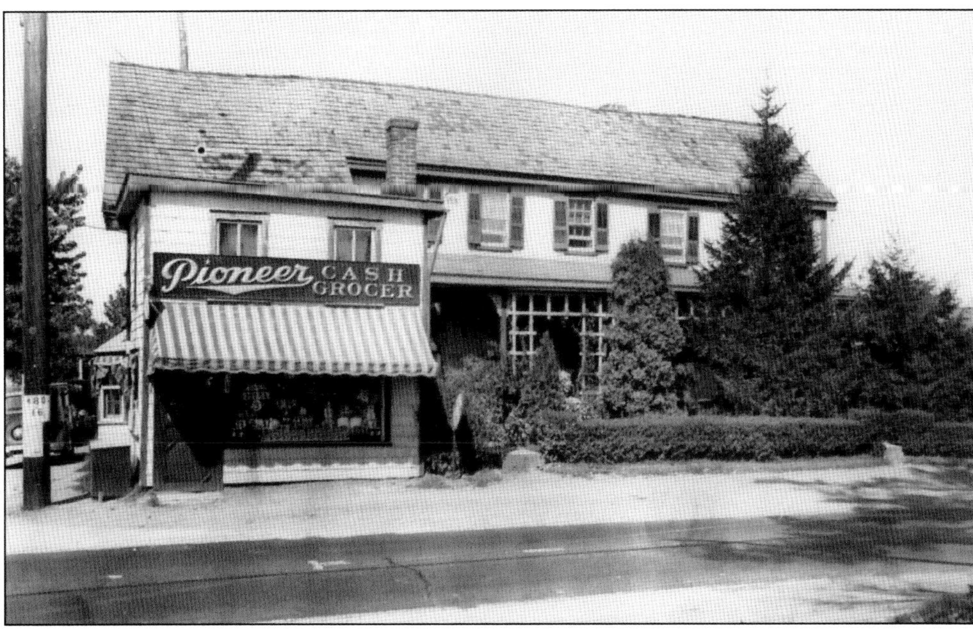

Lima grew along Pennell Road (PA Route 452) between the intersections of Baltimore Pike (US Route 1) and Middletown Road (PA Route 352). The Pineapple Tavern stood on the northeast corner. It is seen here as a grocery store in the early 1900s. The tavern was opened in 1806 by Philip Yarnall, and shortly thereafter, the crossroads was nicknamed "Wrangletown" because of all the fights that broke out inside. (Larry Weathers Jr.)

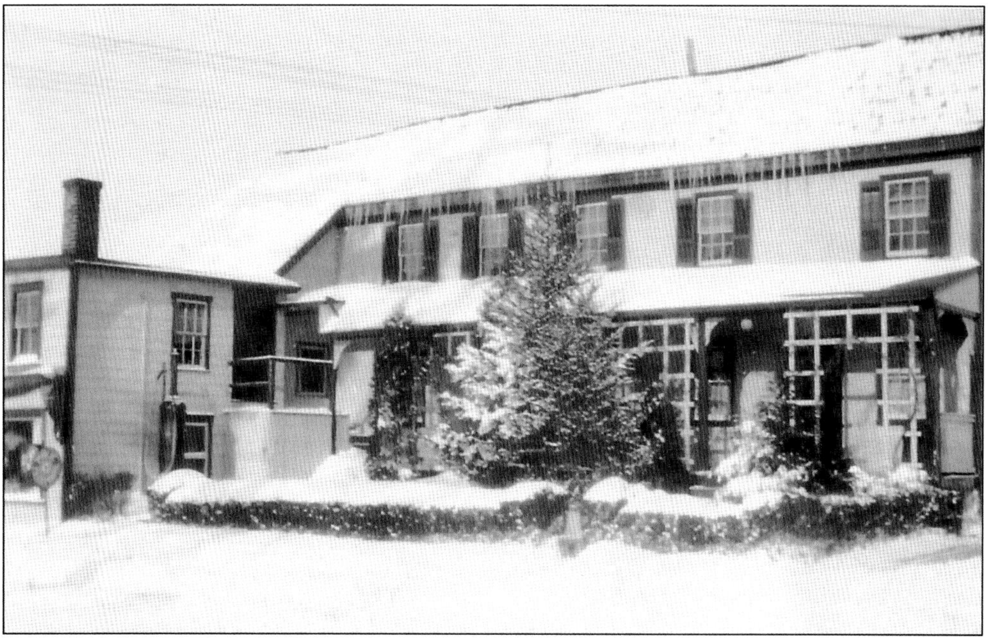

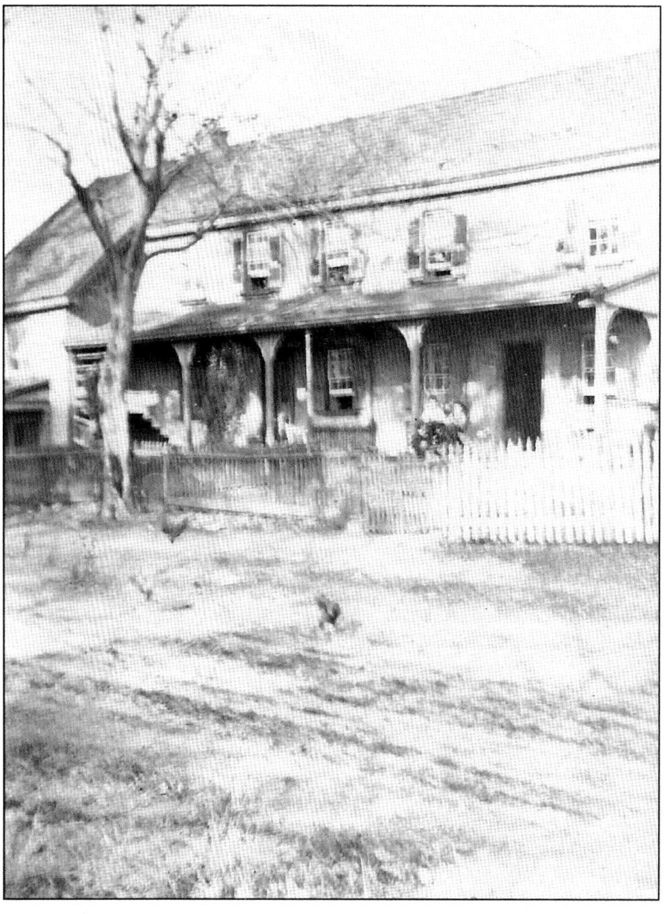

In describing the Pineapple Tavern, Ashmead's 1884 *History of Delaware County* reads, "The sale of whiskey at this place was extensive . . . at night and on rainy days, a number of men from the neighborhood would gather, and, as whiskey was cheap, there would soon be a noisy crowd, usually ending in a broil. The men, seated round a table with a dirty pack of cards, would sing a song composed by a local jingler of rude verses, one of which, for it had a dozen or more stanzas, was, *Wrangletown we will pull down, The sign-board we will alter; And if we had Joe Yarnall here, We would hang him with a halter.*" Joseph Yarnell was the proprietor of the tavern when these verses were written. The photograph above was taken about 1935, the photograph at left in 1905. (Above, Larry Weathers Jr.; left, DCHS.)

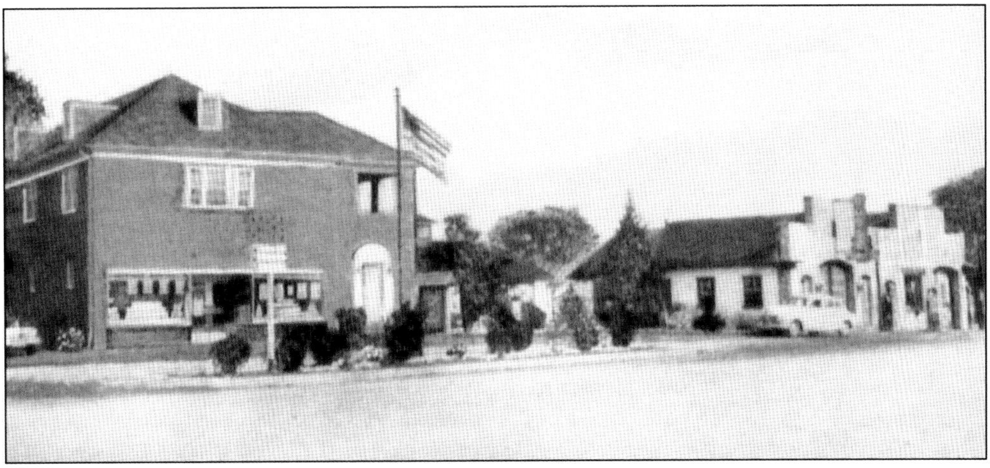

In 1908, James J. Weathers purchased the former Pineapple Tavern and operated a grocery store on the premises. In 1939, when Baltimore Pike was widened, that building was demolished and the family built a new store with an apartment above for the sisters Ann and Marion Weathers, who ran the store from 1939 to its closing in 1975. Below, in the interior of the new Weathers Market, is cashier Renee Westcott; butcher Alphonso "Fons" Weathers stands at the meat counter. Westcott's husband was killed in Germany during World War II. His name is on the Middletown War Memorial, to the right of the American flag, above. It was built in 1942, but moved for more roadwork on the pike in the 1960s. The memorial is now in front of the township building on Pennell Road. (Above, Keith Lockhart; below, Larry Weathers Jr.)

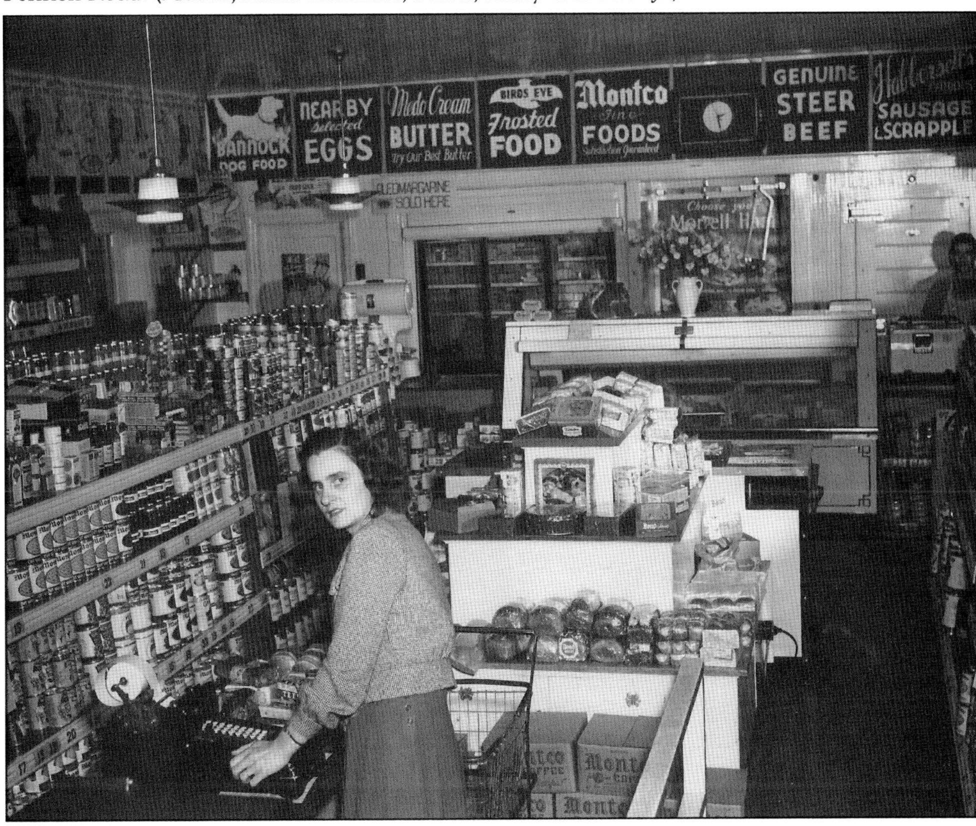

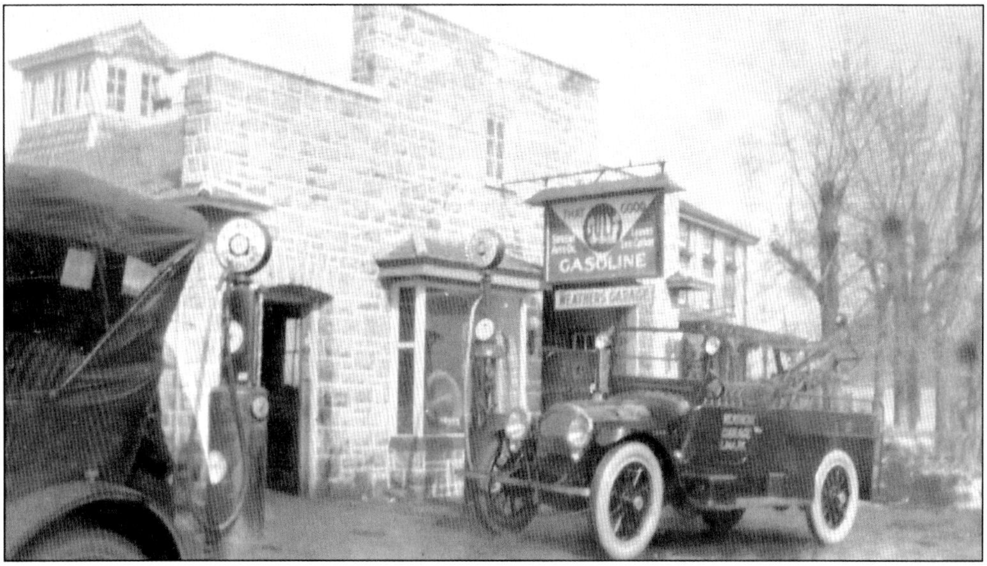

Around the age of 10, Lawrence "Lar" Weathers left Lima School to work at Wawa Dairy Farm and the family grocery store. Later, he worked at Turner's Wheelwright shop and Harry Springer's Garage, both at Baltimore Pike and Pennell Road. In 1920, he started an automobile repair shop in the barn at today's Weathers Motors. A new garage, above, was built in 1922 and became a Dodge dealership in 1933. (Larry Weathers Jr.)

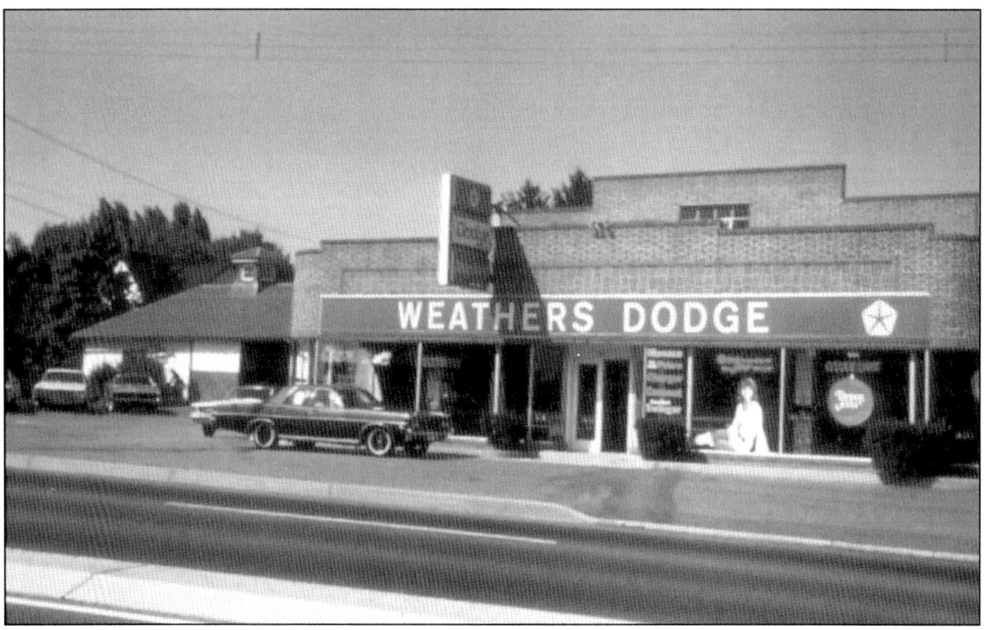

In 1939, a new showroom was added in front of the garage. In 1961, Larry Weathers Jr. took over the dealership, and in 2007, Larry Weathers III became the manager. In the summer of 2009, Weathers Dodge was one of the 789 dealerships eliminated by Chrysler in their bankruptcy reorganization. The family regrouped and continues to sell and service all makes and models of automobile as Weathers Motors. (Paul Dougherty/ATHS.)

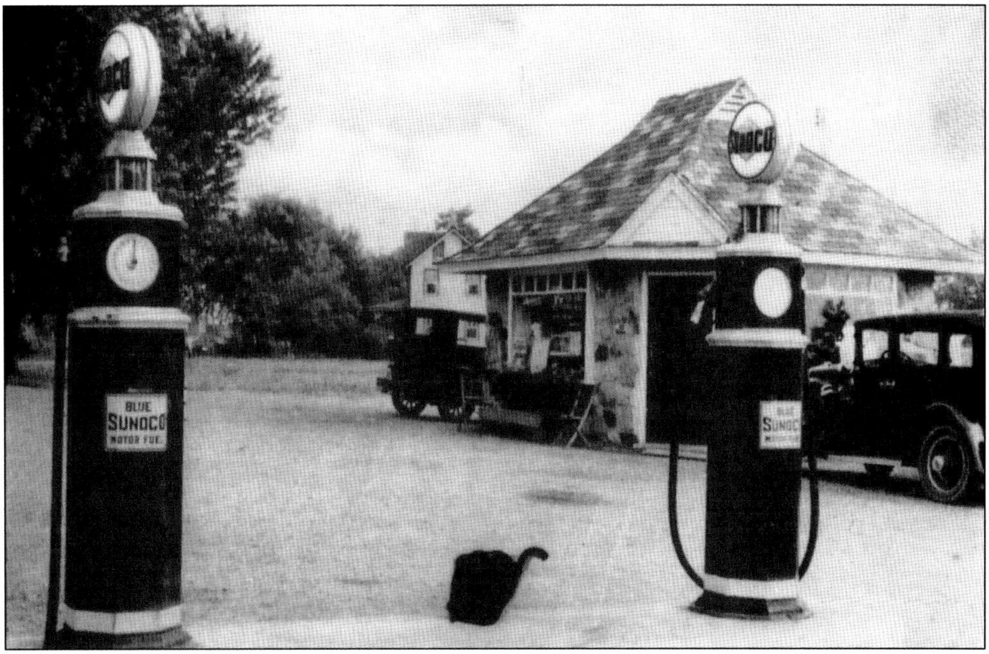

Bill Mellen's Sunoco gas station was on the southwest corner of Baltimore Pike and Pennell Road. Mellen's Chevrolet dealership was on the northwest corner. Around 1950, Mellen had a second-story apartment added to the gas station where he lived until his death in 1955. His son Bill Jr. then took over the gas station and Chevrolet dealership until they were closed in the late 1950s or early 1960s. (Paul Dougherty/ATHS.)

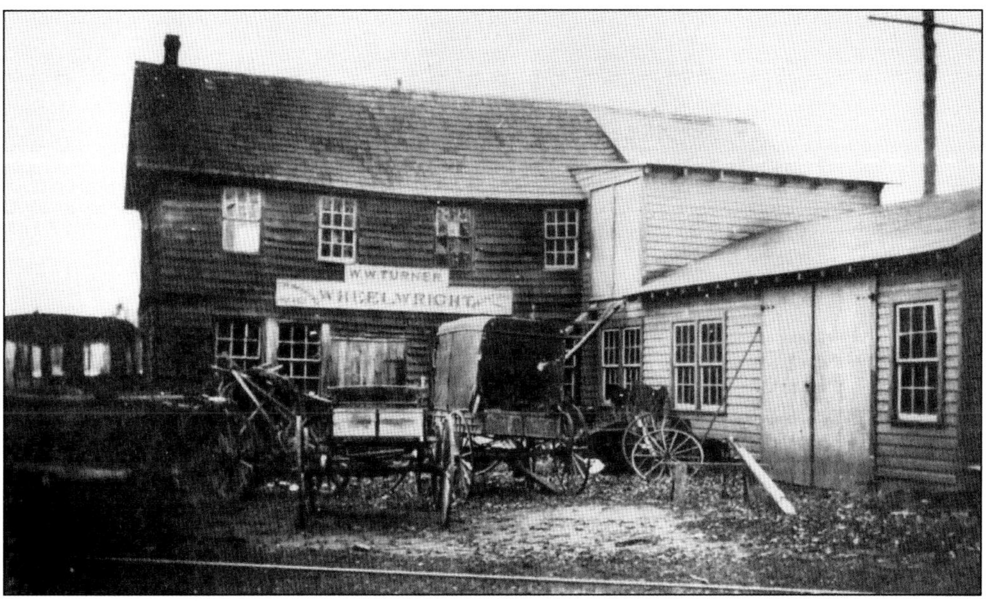

Before Mellen's Chevrolet dealership, another kind of service facility for wheeled transports occupied the southwest corner of Baltimore Pike and Pennell Road. W.W. Turner's Wheelwright shop, pictured here around 1900, made wooden and metal wheels for carriages and wagons. This photograph was donated to the Pearson Collection by Clarence Raezer, whose father learned the wheelwright trade from Turner in the early 1900s.

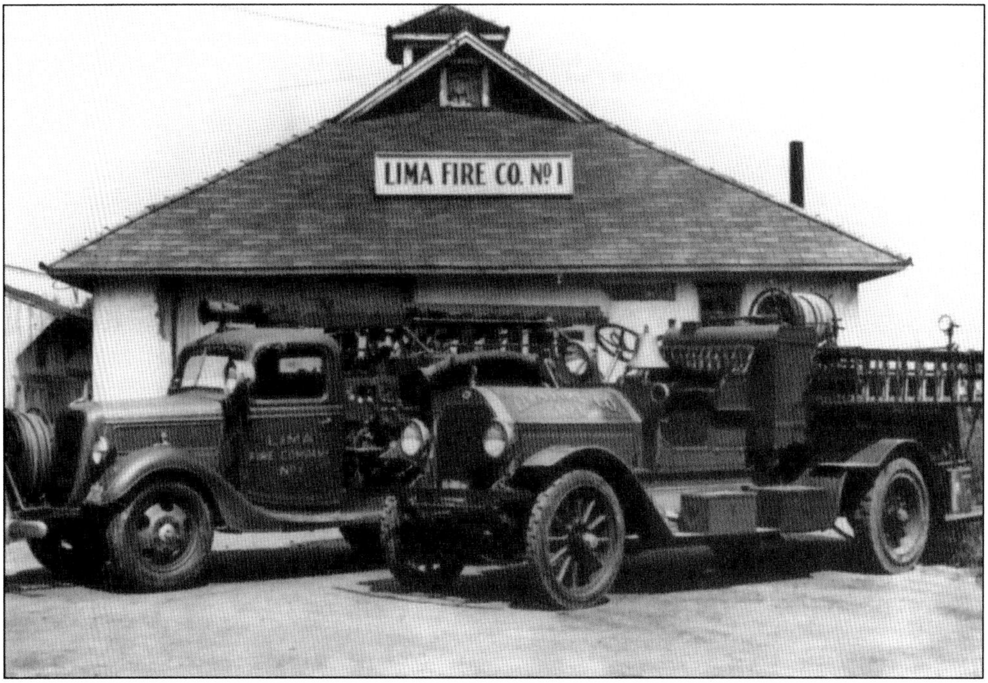

The all-volunteer Lima Fire Company No. 1 was chartered in March 1945. Parked in front of the first firehouse, a garage owned by James McHoul off Oriole Avenue, now Carlson's Auto Body, is a 1937 Ford pumper (left) purchased from the Claymont, Delaware, Fire Company and a 1917 Seagraves (right) purchased from the Media Fire Company. The current Lima firehouse is on the southwest corner of Baltimore Pike and War Admiral Lane. Construction of this building began in 1953, and it was occupied in May 1954. The Ladies Auxiliary was formed in July 1947. They ran card parties, held bingo games, and assisted at carnivals, chicken barbeques, and dinners, all to help fund the purchase of new equipment and maintain the building. In 1972, the ambulance division was created, and the building was expanded to house the additional equipment (Above, Larry Weathers Jr.)

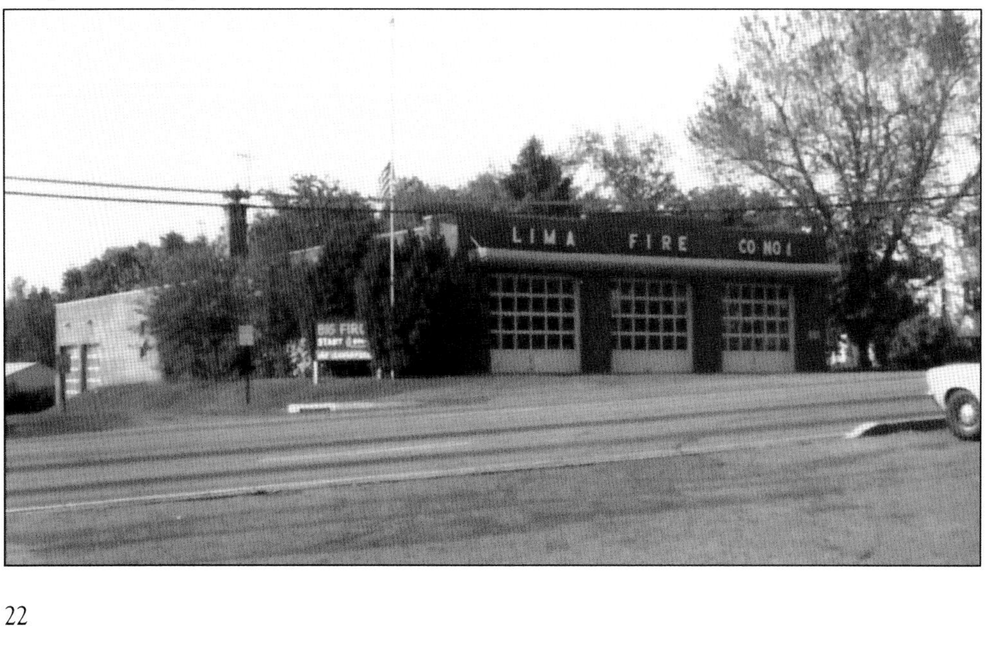

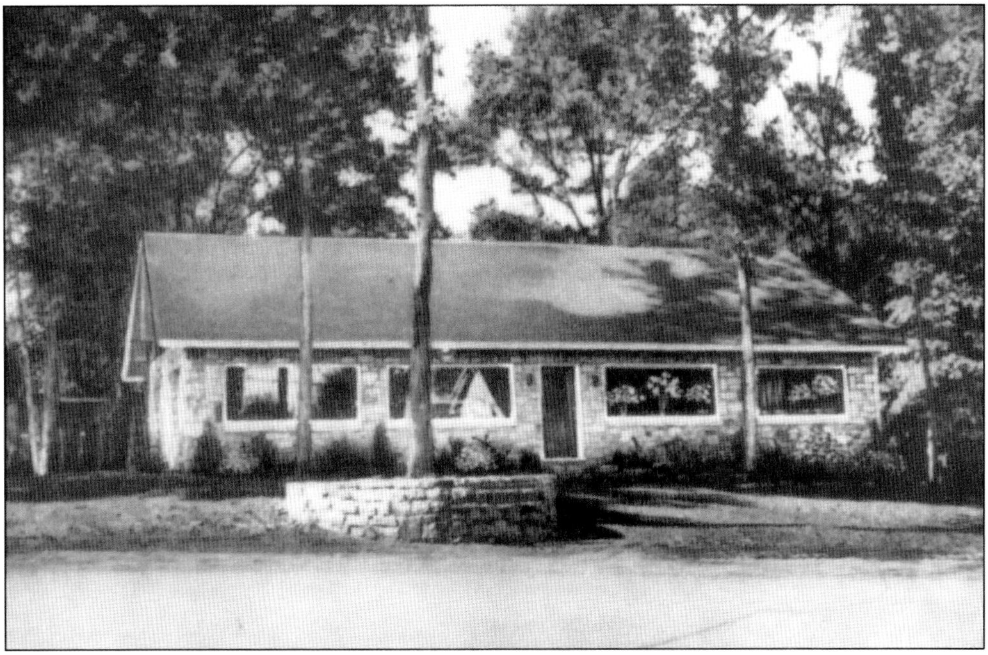

Lima Farms Restaurant was located on the north side of Baltimore Pike, east of Oriole Avenue. They were famous for their pies, especially coconut custard, and their Sunday dinners, which drew crowds from all around. The owner, Raymond King, lived in an old log cabin behind the restaurant that was at one time, according to the postcard below, offered as a honeymoon cabin. Ray owned all the land along Oriole Avenue north from Baltimore Pike except the last lot at the corner of Middletown Road. He raised cattle on the land. Oriole Avenue would be laid out in 1920. A 1934 map shows six houses and 20 lots on the west side and 22 lots on the east side. The first house built was for Ray's daughter. This area was once known as Lima Heights. (Below, Keith Lockhart.)

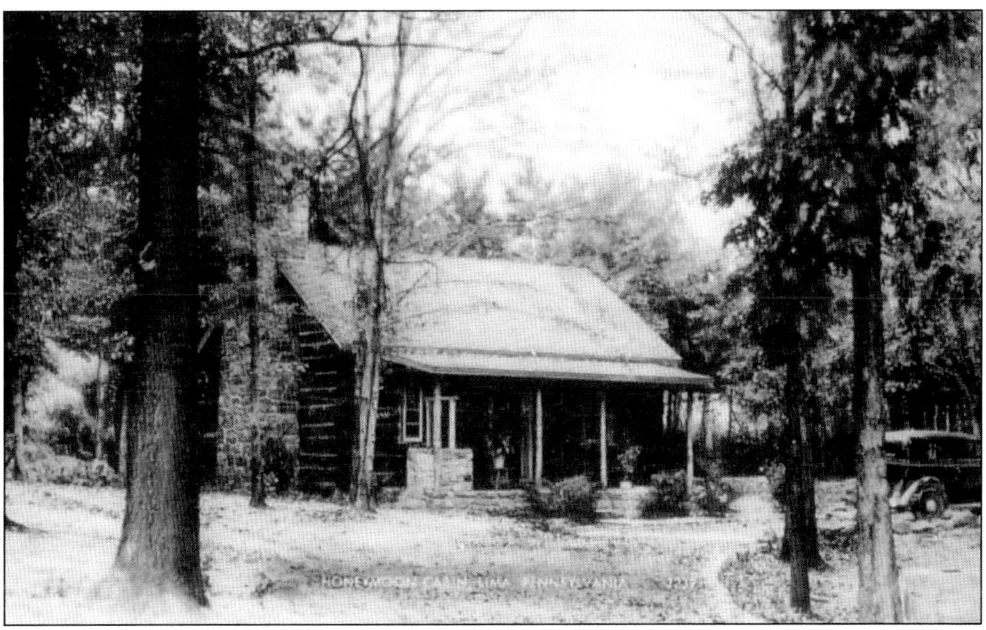

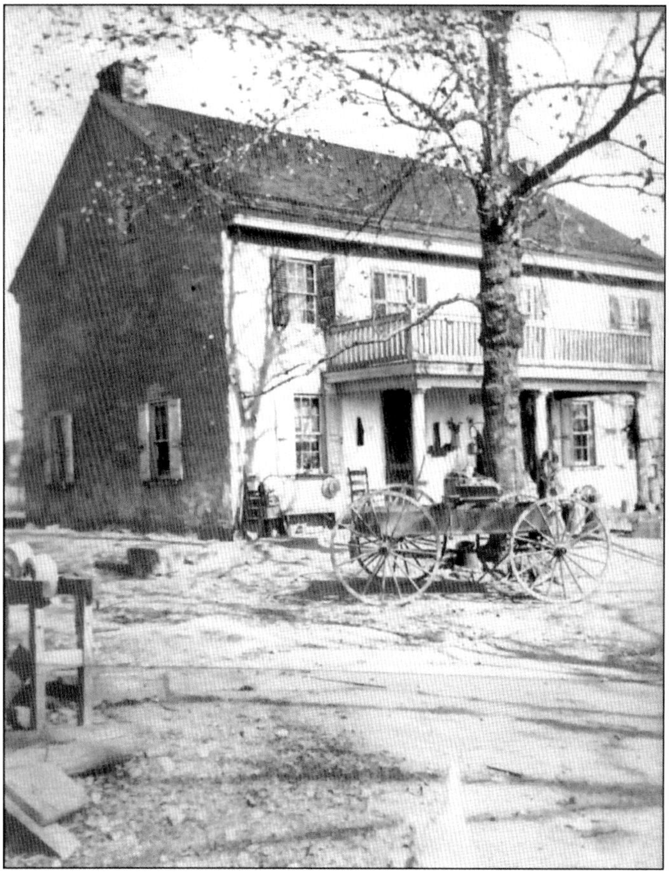

The 1784 farmhouse seen in this 1914 photograph was built by Samuel Hibberd and stood on the south side of Baltimore Pike. In 1909, Samuel D. Riddle purchased the farm. Riddle, who died in 1951, owned woolen mills inherited from his father, Samuel Riddle, along Chester Creek. But he is best known as a sportsman and breeder of champion racehorses. Riddle Memorial Hospital (below) was created by Riddle's bequest. His will stipulated that the residue of his estate, approximately $2.5 million, be used to provide a new hospital for the Media area. He also left the 72-acre Hibberd site for the location of the hospital. The hospital charter was issued in November 1956, ground breaking took place in September 1960, and the hospital opened in February 1963, with 144 beds and 16 bassinets. (Left, DCHS.)

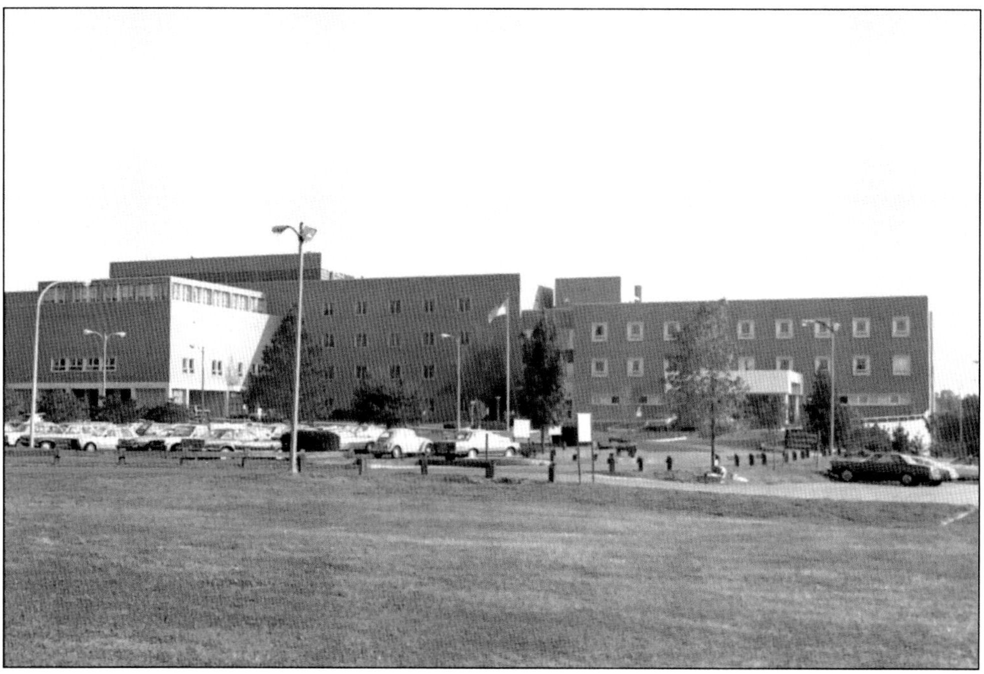

The Twin Pines, on the southeast corner of Baltimore Pike and Pennell Road, was a popular gathering place in Lima through World War II. The hot dog stand was operated by Penrose "Penny" Worrell and his brother. Penny was also the Middletown Township tax collector for many years. Eventually, the Wonder brothers bought the business, but they let it fall into disrepair after they moved to Springfield. It was torn down in the 1950s. (Paul Dougherty/ATHS.)

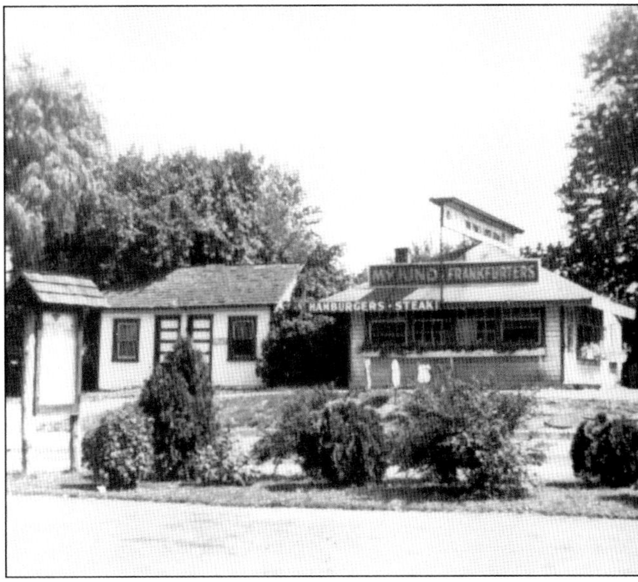

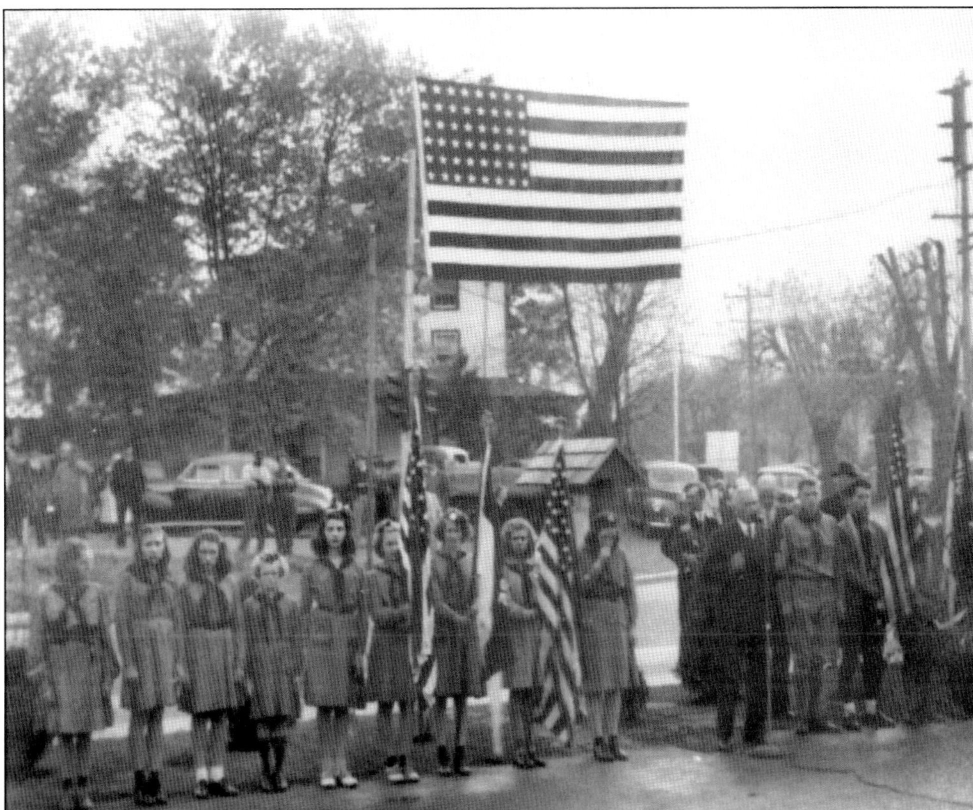

Local Girl Scout and Boy Scout troops are pictured here in front of the Twin Pines for a ceremony during World War II. Delaware County judge George Welsh is speaking. Among the Girl Scouts, Doris Reed is fourth from the left, June Whitmore is fifth from the left, and Jean Weathers is to the far right. The Boy Scouts are Lloyd Master (left) and ? Whitmore. (Paul Dougherty/ATHS.)

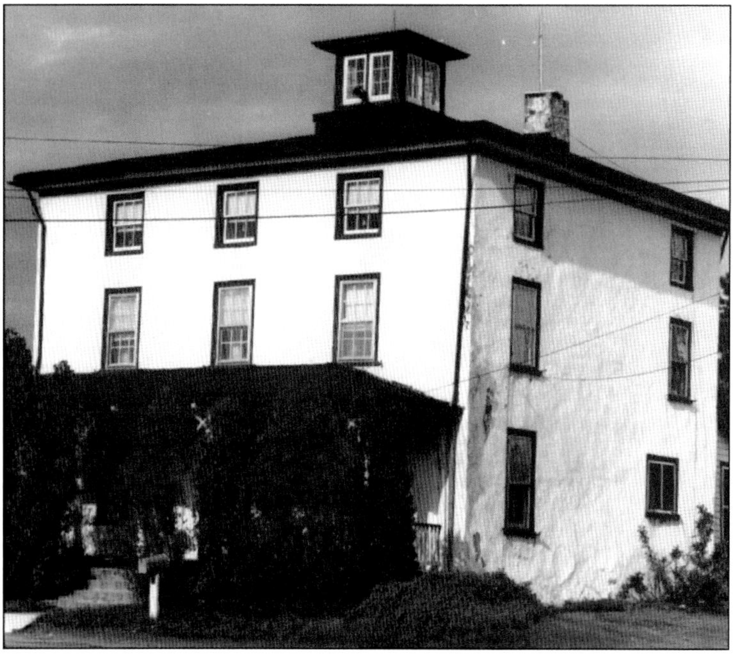

This house on Pennell Road, with its distinctive widow's watch, was next to the Twin Pines. For most of the 20th century, Penny Worrell and his family lived here. It was built in the mid-1800s by S. Ivison. Samuel D. Riddle purchased all but 15 acres of the Ivison farm in the early 1900s. This property was sold in 1986 and the house was demolished. (DCHS.)

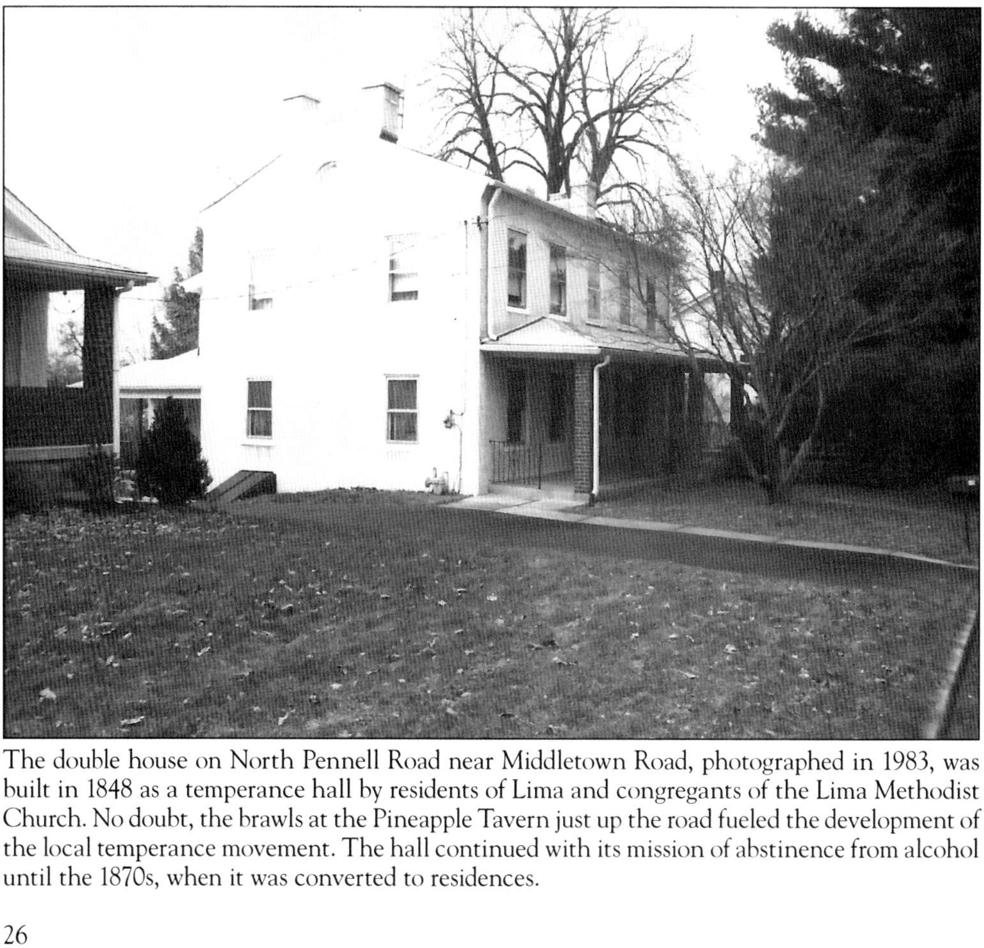

The double house on North Pennell Road near Middletown Road, photographed in 1983, was built in 1848 as a temperance hall by residents of Lima and congregants of the Lima Methodist Church. No doubt, the brawls at the Pineapple Tavern just up the road fueled the development of the local temperance movement. The hall continued with its mission of abstinence from alcohol until the 1870s, when it was converted to residences.

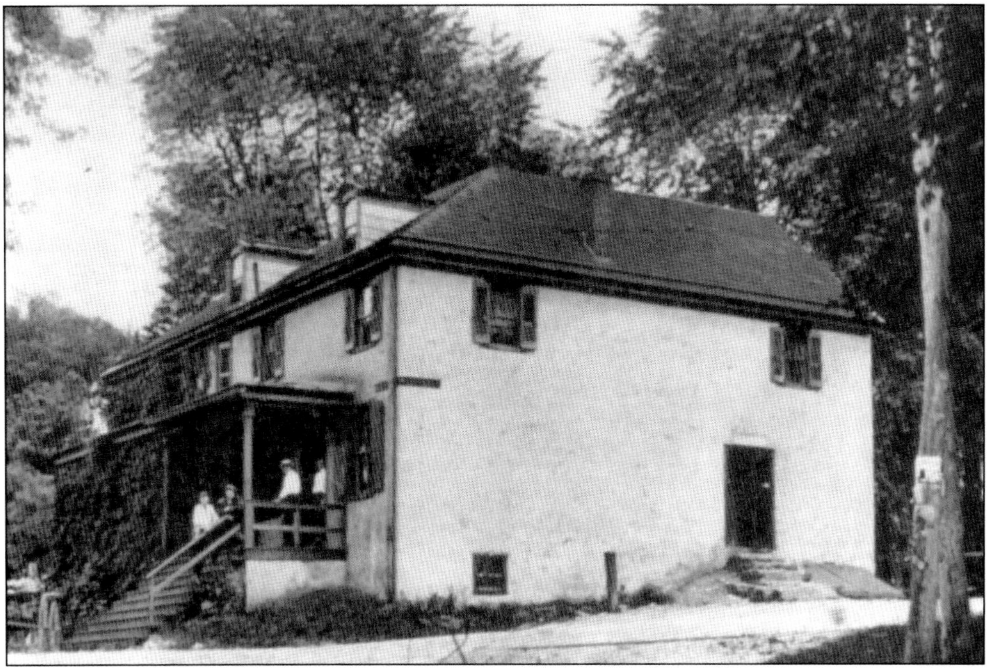

The Lima Store (seen above in 1915), on the southeast corner of Pennell and Middletown Roads, was built by Dr. Richard Gregg in 1829. It had several proprietors over the decades. By 1832, the Lima Post Office was located in the building then known as Hamor's Store. In 1833, it was sold to John Van Leer and Issac Chamel. Robert Hoopes bought it in 1836 and ran it until 1868, when his son Homer Hoopes took over. Then came William M. Thomas, and in 1882, it was operated by Albert Ogden. The last owner-operator of the store was Ed Lewis, who lived in the house just behind the store on North Pennell Road. It was closed in 1963 (below) and demolished by the Pennsylvania Department of Transportation to make way for an enlarged intersection. The property's barn still stands along the south side of Middletown Road.

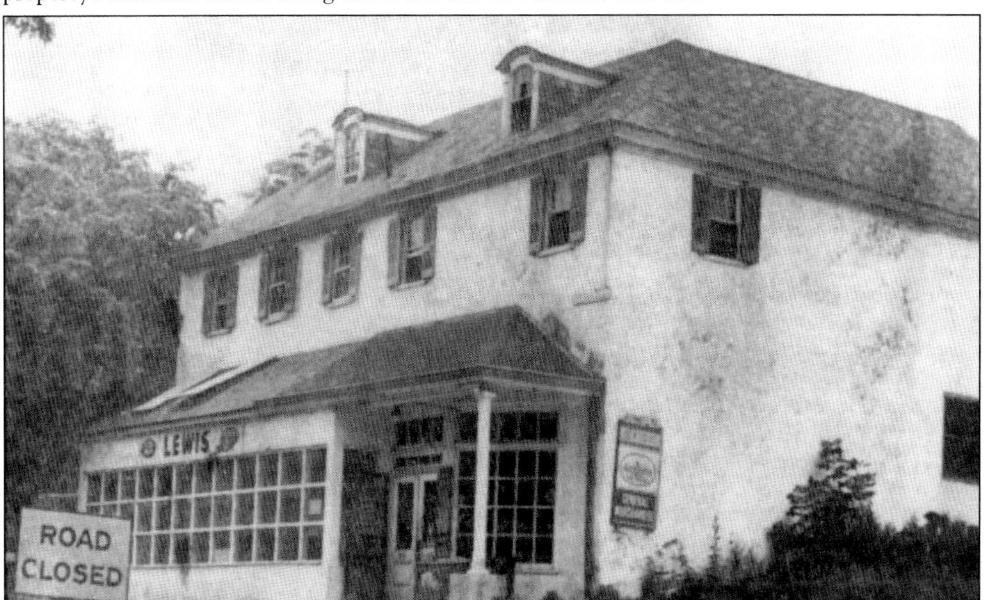

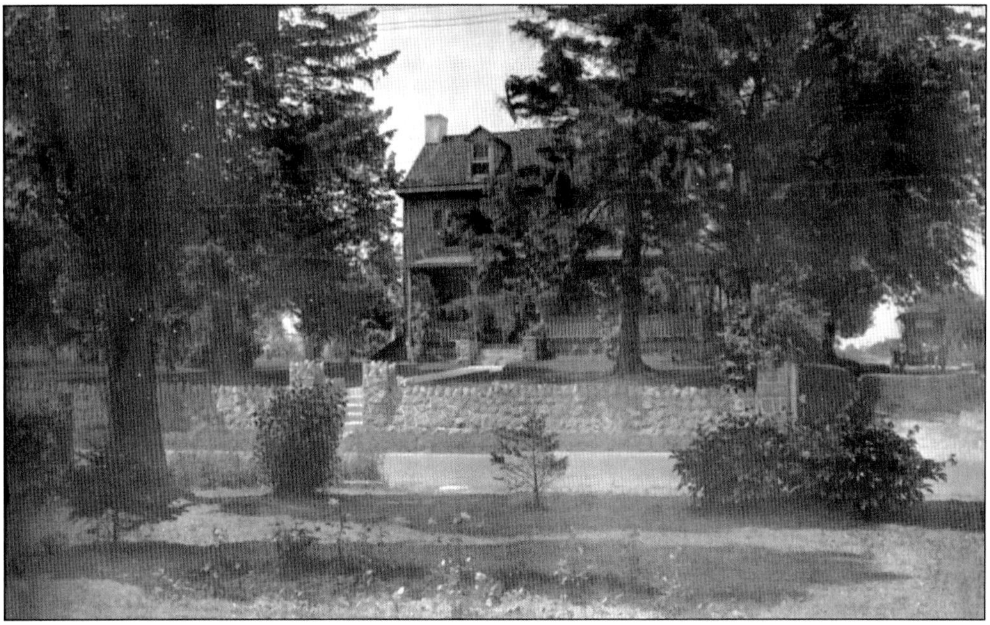

The house above, photographed around 1915, still stands at the northwest corner of Middletown Road and Van Leer Avenue. It was built about 1834, when John Van Leer subdivided the area. In 1875, it was owned by Mrs. N. Passmore, in 1912 by Hessie Miller, and in 1934 by Thomas Fields. It was purchased in 1951 by Doris and Harry "Skip" Clower. The stone house below stood on the south side of Middletown Road, opposite Van Leer Avenue. It was built in 1870 from stone found on the property. In 1912, it was owned by the Fields family, who called it Idle Moments. The 55-acre site included the Lima Quarry. In 1934, the property was owned by A.H. Gehris and was known as Shadybrook Farm. The land was sold to create Granite Run Mall. (Above, Susan Clower Mescanti.)

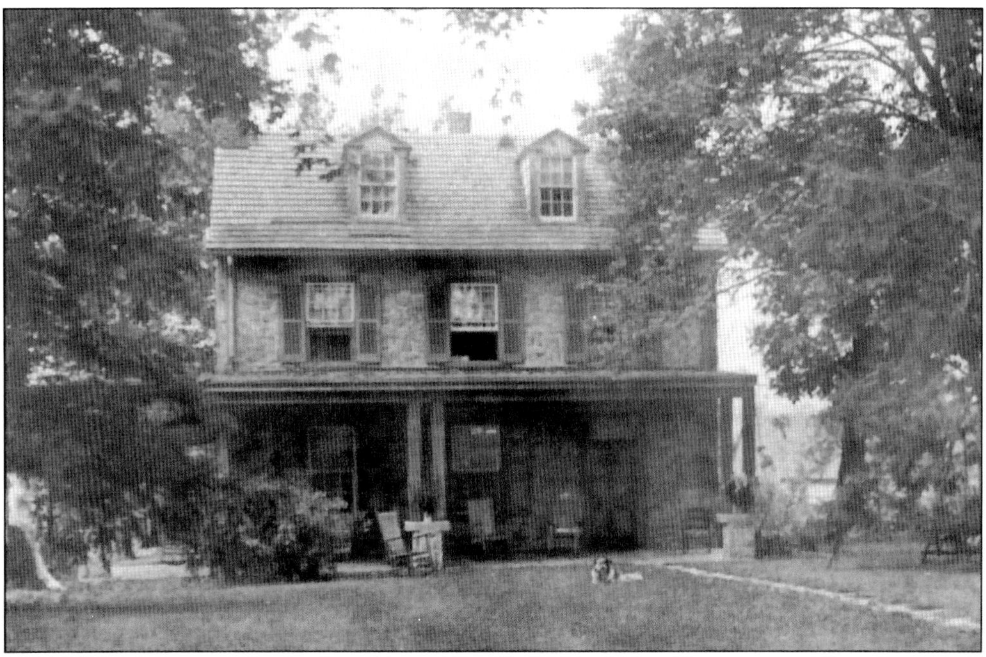

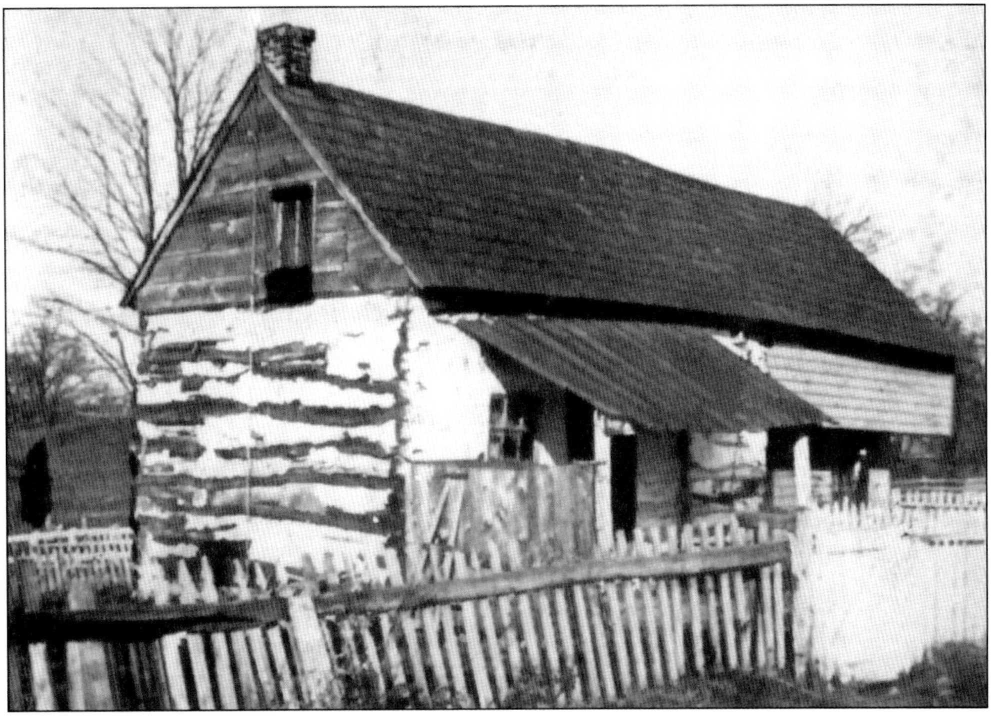

The intersection of Barren Road and Van Leer Avenue holds two of the township's extant log cabins that are still visible as log cabins. Many houses were built around a family's original log house until the logs were no longer visible. This one, on the northwest corner, was built in the late 1830s by E. Saunders. (DCHS.)

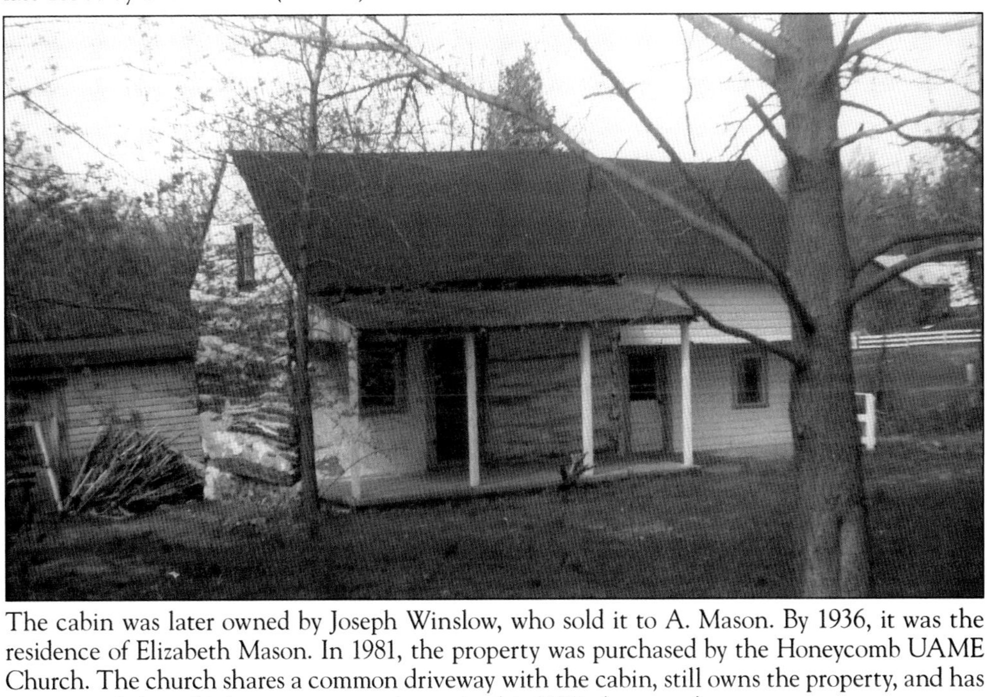

The cabin was later owned by Joseph Winslow, who sold it to A. Mason. By 1936, it was the residence of Elizabeth Mason. In 1981, the property was purchased by the Honeycomb UAME Church. The church shares a common driveway with the cabin, still owns the property, and has maintained the cabin's appearance as it was in this 1982 photograph.

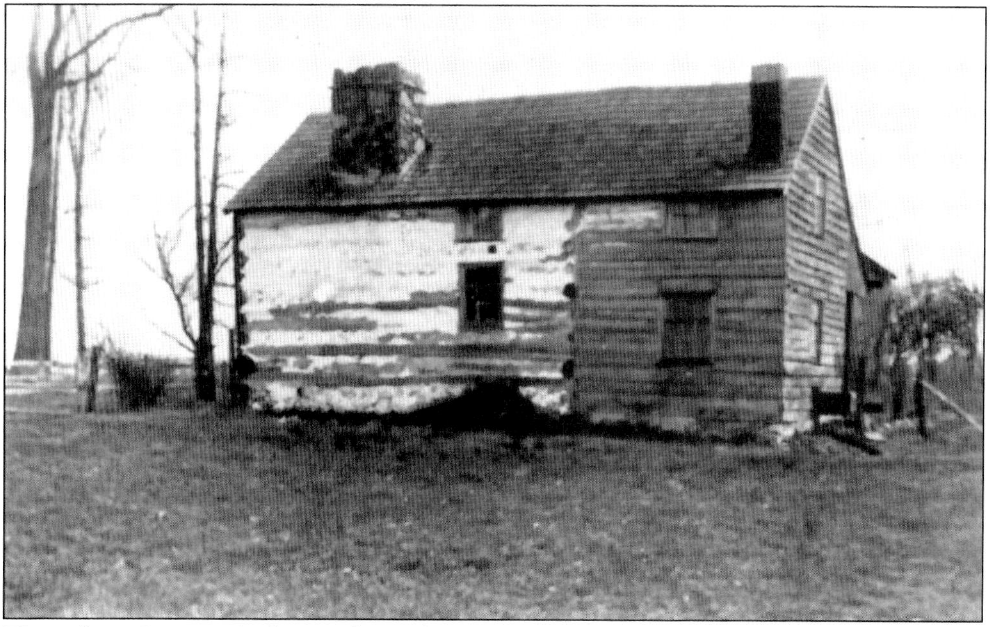

This cabin, photographed around 1910 by Dr. Anna Broomall, is on the southwest corner of Barren Road and Van Leer Avenue. It was also built in the late 1830s. In 1875, it was owned by E. Morre and in 1905 by George Green. It was purchased around 1915 by Jack Moor from Green's widow. (DCHS.)

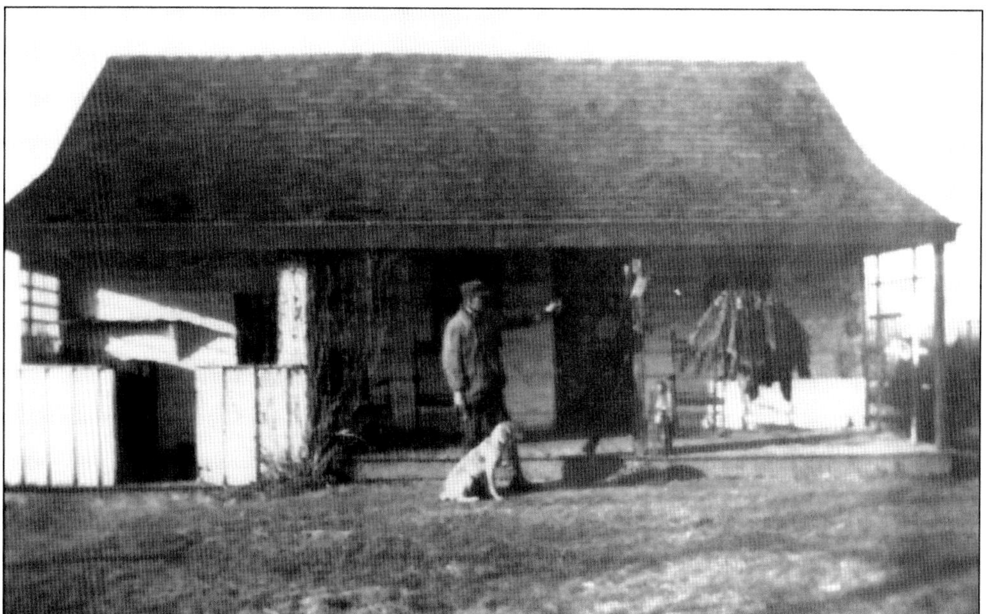

Jack Moor is pictured here in 1917 in front of the cabin. Jack, who worked in Aston, was well known for the pony cart he used into the 1950s to get back and forth around the area. On payday, Jack would take the pony cart to a local tavern for a few drinks. If Jack had a little too much, no problem—the pony knew the way home.

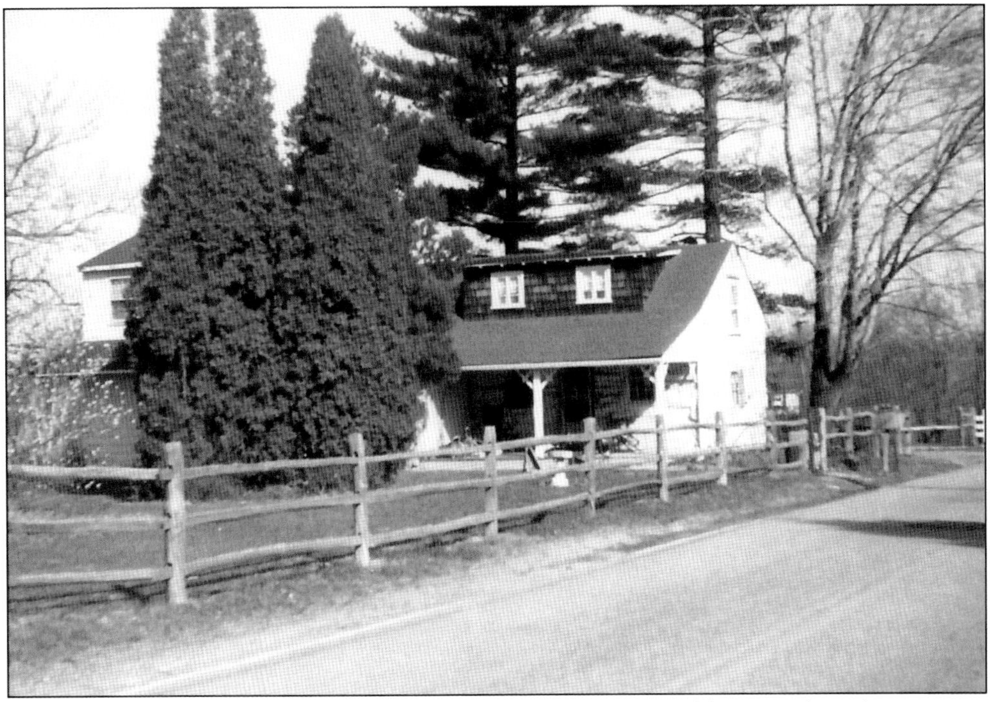

In 1965, the Umberger family bought the property and added an addition to the cabin, seen on the left behind the trees on the south side. The Umbergers raised their family on the property, and as of 2011, Esther Umberger still lives in the house and maintains the log cabin, as well as the Moor barn and outbuildings.

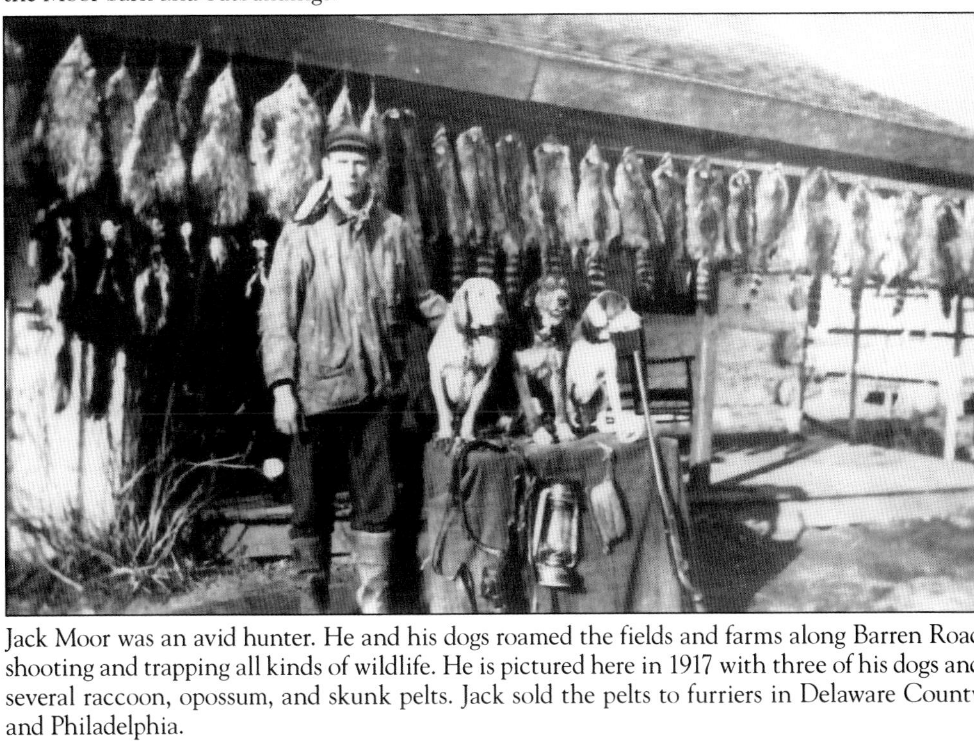

Jack Moor was an avid hunter. He and his dogs roamed the fields and farms along Barren Road shooting and trapping all kinds of wildlife. He is pictured here in 1917 with three of his dogs and several raccoon, opossum, and skunk pelts. Jack sold the pelts to furriers in Delaware County and Philadelphia.

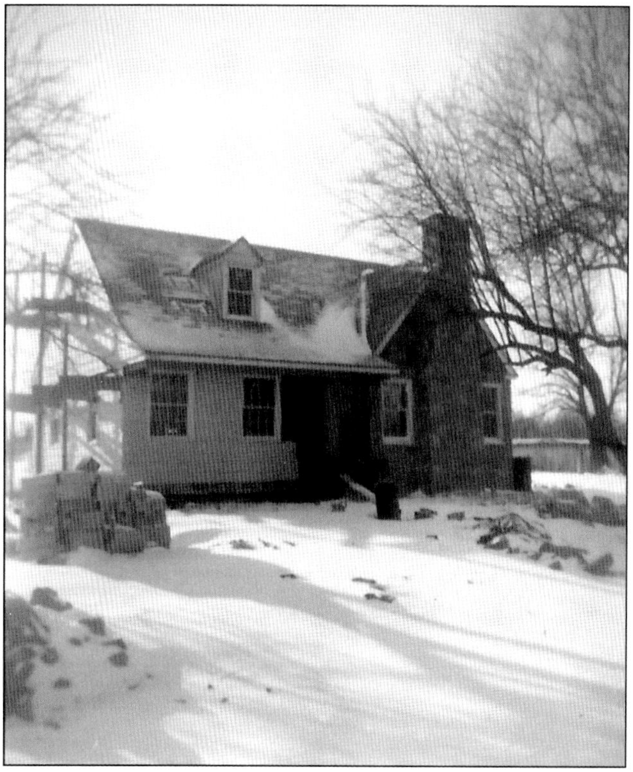

This is the William J. "Hi" Eves residence on the south side of Barren Road west of Van Leer Avenue. Eves bought the apple orchard on his great aunt Clara Pratt's farm in 1954. Eves and his father were carpenters who designed and built the house on weekends and evenings with the help of coworkers. The exterior was finished by the fall of 1954 so work could be done on the interior into the winter of 1955. Jack Moor would come over in the morning on the weekends and build a fire in the fireplace so the inside would be warm when Eves and his father came out from Media to work. (Mary Anne Eves.)

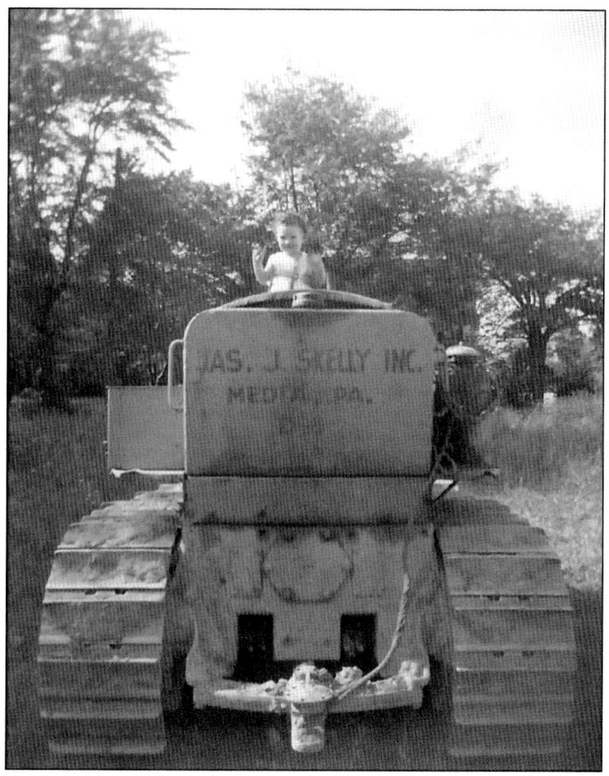

Mary Anne Eves sits on a James J. Skelly bulldozer at the house in 1954. Skelly is pictured on the cover of this book. Founded in 1903 in Glen Mills, James J. Skelly Company, General Contractors and Road Builders moved to Lima in 1909 and to Media in 1920. Skelly built many of the roads throughout Delaware County in the early 20th century. Eves's grandfather, John A. Tracy of Media, was a heavy machinery operator for the Skelly company. (Mary Anne Eves.)

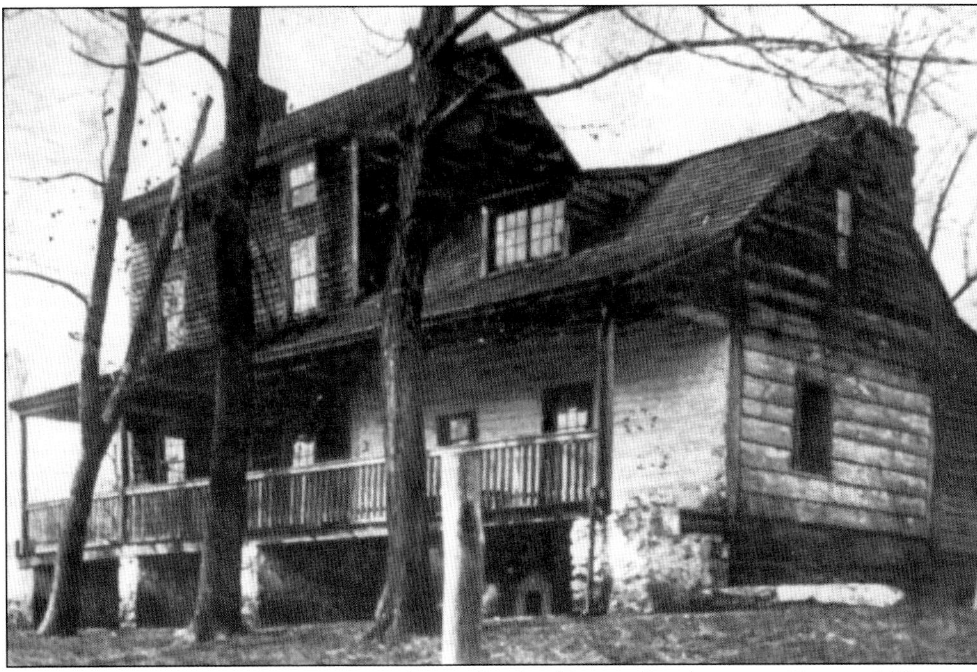

This cabin, photographed in 1905, is on the north side of Painter Road opposite Hunting Hills Lane. It was built in the early 19th century on the John Smedley farm. In 1900, Ambrose Smedley, John's son, sold it to William Eves of Media. Eves renamed it Century Farm in honor of the new century. In 1934, Eves sold the property to his daughter Letitia and her husband, Samuel N. Rhodes. (DCHS.)

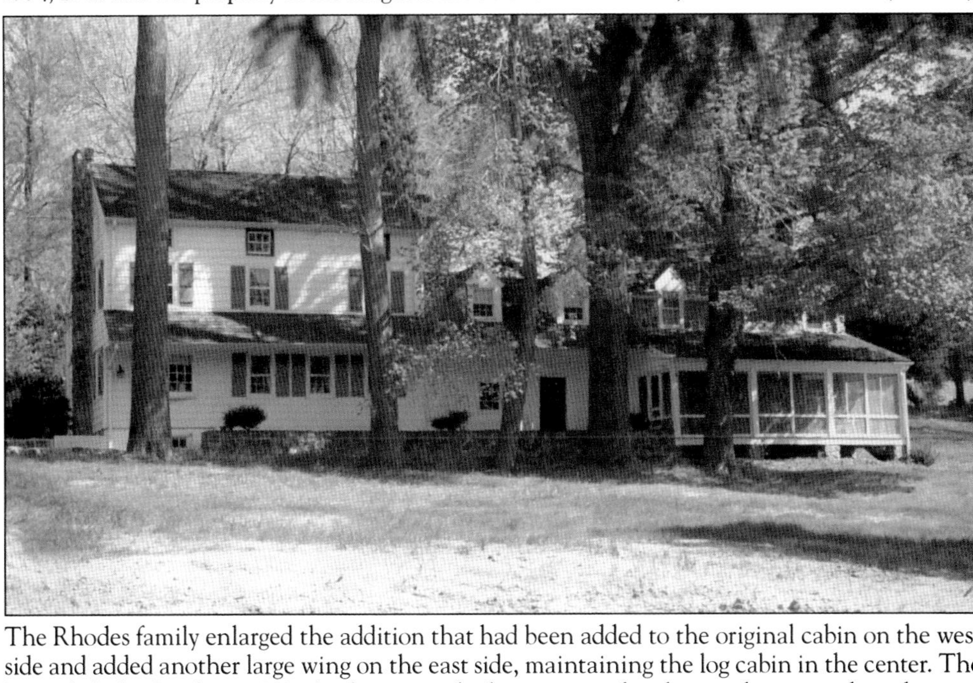

The Rhodes family enlarged the addition that had been added to the original cabin on the west side and added another large wing on the east side, maintaining the log cabin in the center. The house left the family in 1982. At that time, the large corner fireplace and cast iron hearth crane were still intact in the cabin section. The cabin is no longer visible due to additions made by later owners.

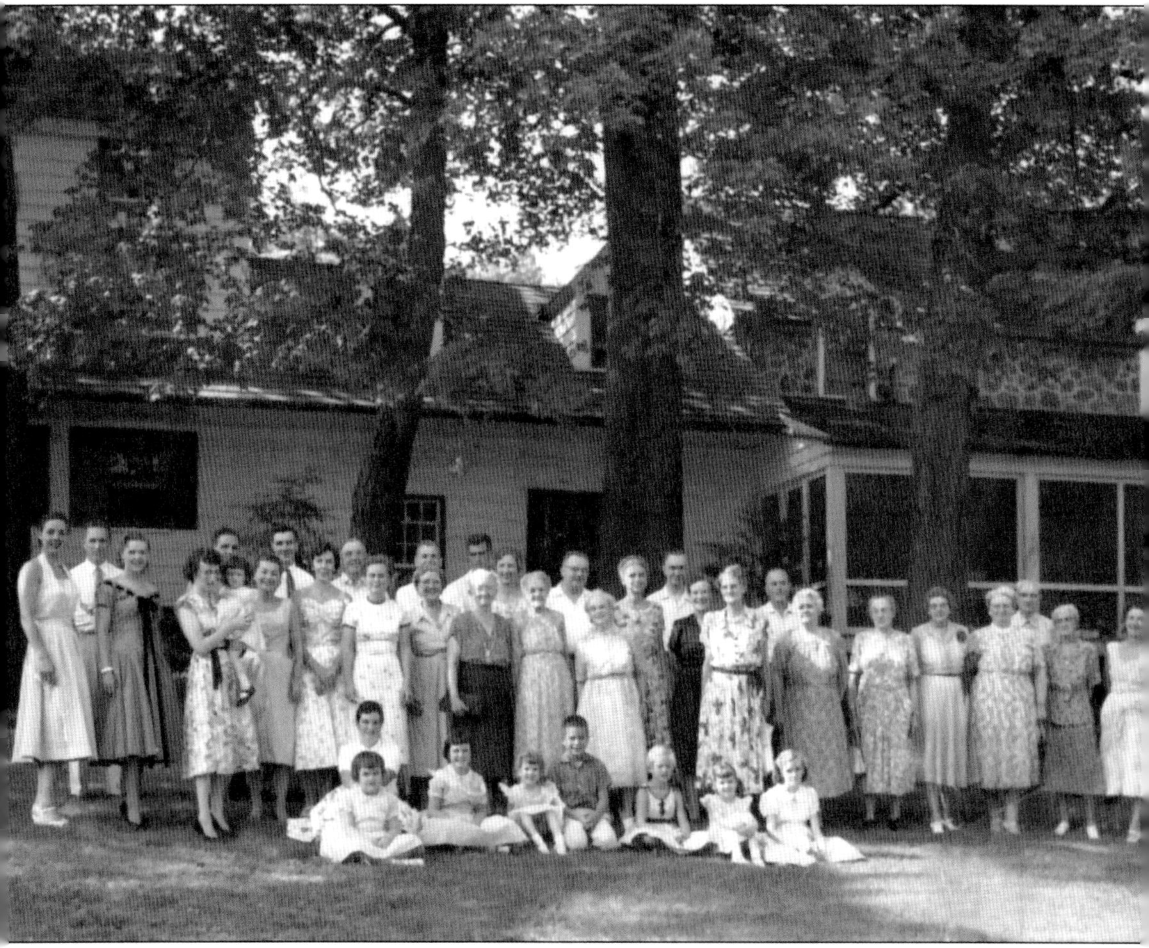

This photograph was taken in 1955 at an Eves-Rhodes family reunion. The guests stand in front of the original cabin. The horizontal square-hewn logs are seen just as they were in the 1905 photograph. Pictured here are, from left to right, (standing) Renee Fury Grace Laughead, Robert Mahan, Elaine Rhodes, Ann Tracy Eves, Jack Turner, Mary Anne Eves, William J Eves, Mary Eves Petree, Hiram P. Eves, Roberta Rhodes Mahan, Samuel N. Rhodes Jr., Mina Travers Eves, Jennie Bowers, Catherine Eves Fury, Ernie Grace, Lydia Williamson Eves, Pennell Fury, Clara Williamson Pratt, Letitia Eves Rhodes, two unidentified, Florence Yeatman, Samuel N. Rhodes Sr., Reba ?, Elsie Marshall Smith, Gladys Williams, Louise Marshall, Fred Crawford, Dora Crawford, and Mary Hibbard; (seated) Beth Turner Rorke, Rue Turner Baronsky, Letitia Turner Mayo, Sandy Rhodes Fogt, Scott Mahan, Kathy Mahan Green, Jeanette Haupt, and unidentified. (Mary Anne Eves.)

Three

Wawa and Darlington

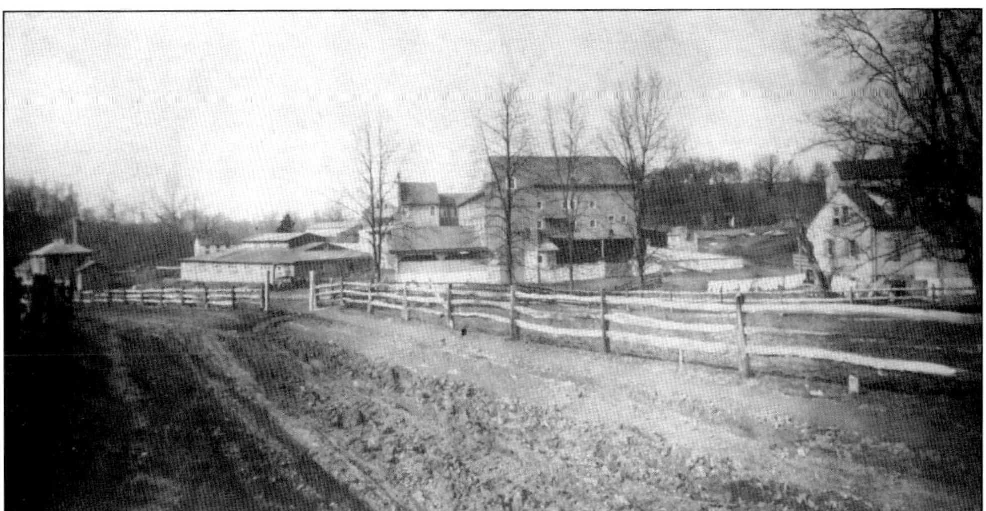

The neighborhood of Wawa lies along Baltimore Pike south of Lima, bordered on the south by Chester Creek. In the early 18th century, mills lined Chester Creek, but by the early 19th century, Wawa had become a dairy center. In 1900, George Wood bought Rocky Run Dairy Farm and two adjacent farms. Wawa Dairy Farm opened in 1902 to sell milk bottled under sanitary conditions from cows certified as healthy and disease free. (Hagley.)

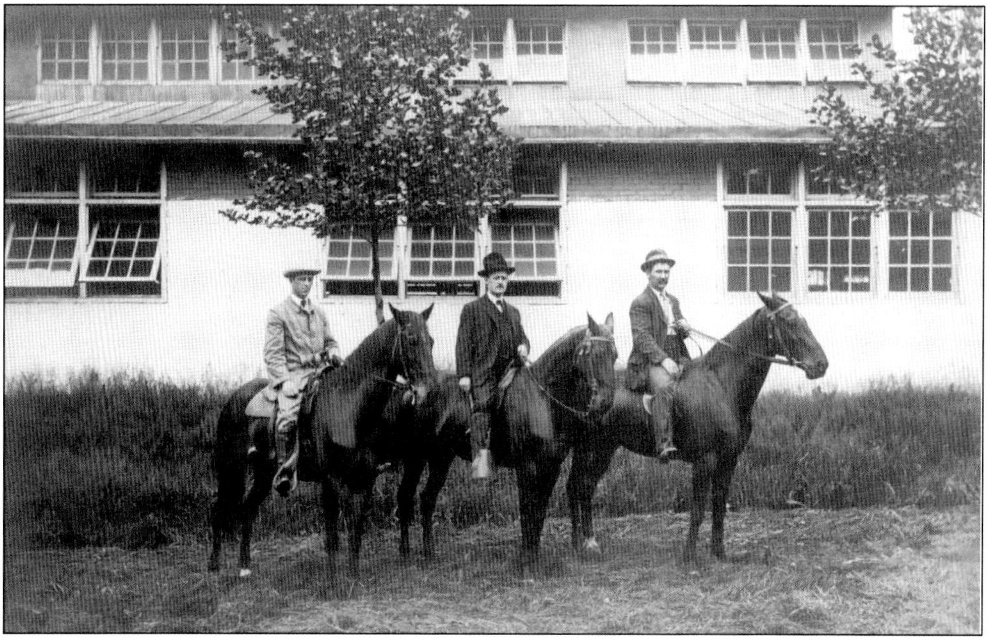

Certification begins with the cows, their feed, and the field conditions. It was up to these men to monitor those conditions and to be sure that standards were being met. The 1915 photograph above includes, from left to right, C.H. Rife, the herdsman; R.L. Smith, the superintendent; and Edward McCardle, the farm boss. Workers in the photograph below are, from left to right, (first row) two unidentified, Mel Johnson, unidentified, Tom Graham, three unidentified, and Edgar McCardle; (second row) Charlie Taylor, John Goodwin, Mr. Schofield, Mr. Schofield, Julius West, five unidentified, and C.H. Rife; (third row) six unidentified, George Graham, and Harry Farber; (fourth row) four unidentified, Harry Hartranft, unidentified, Mr. Blakson, John Heuston, and three unidentified; (fifth row) all unidentified except third from left, Mr. Heil.

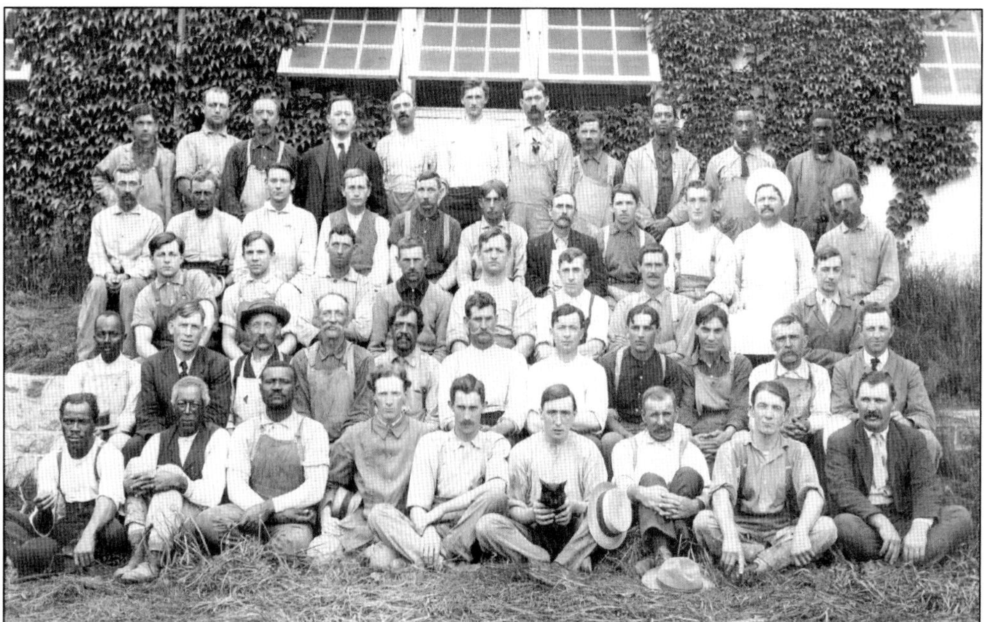

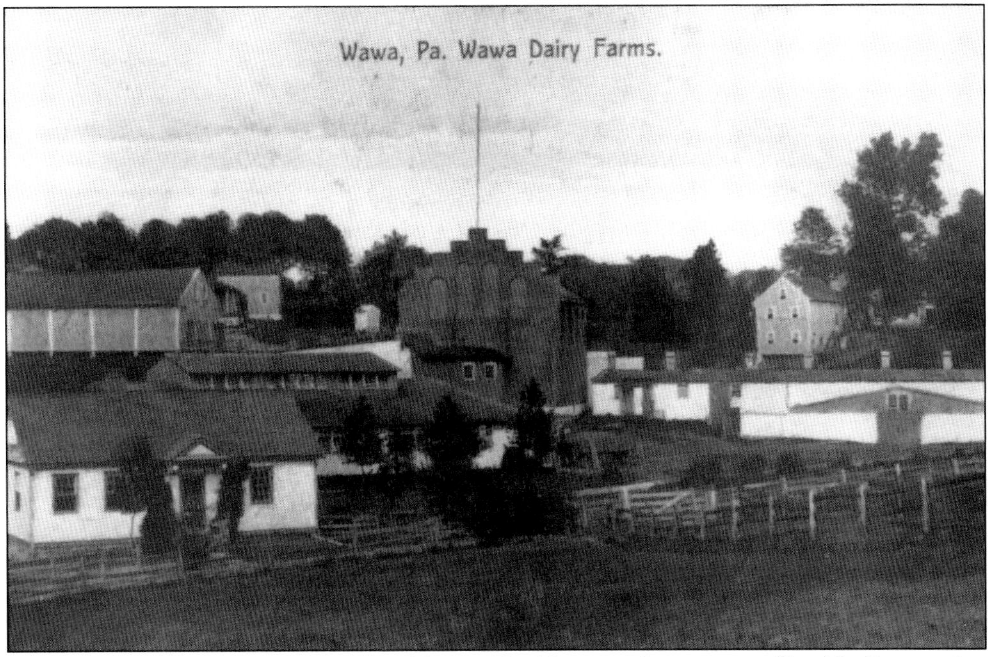

In the 1910s, Wawa added numerous additional buildings in the interest of health. During this period, drinking milk became popular among all segments of the population, not just children and the sick. But along with this came fears of disease spread by contaminated milk, especially tuberculosis. In 1914, Philadelphia required all milk sold in the city to be pasteurized unless it was certified. (Keith Lockhart.)

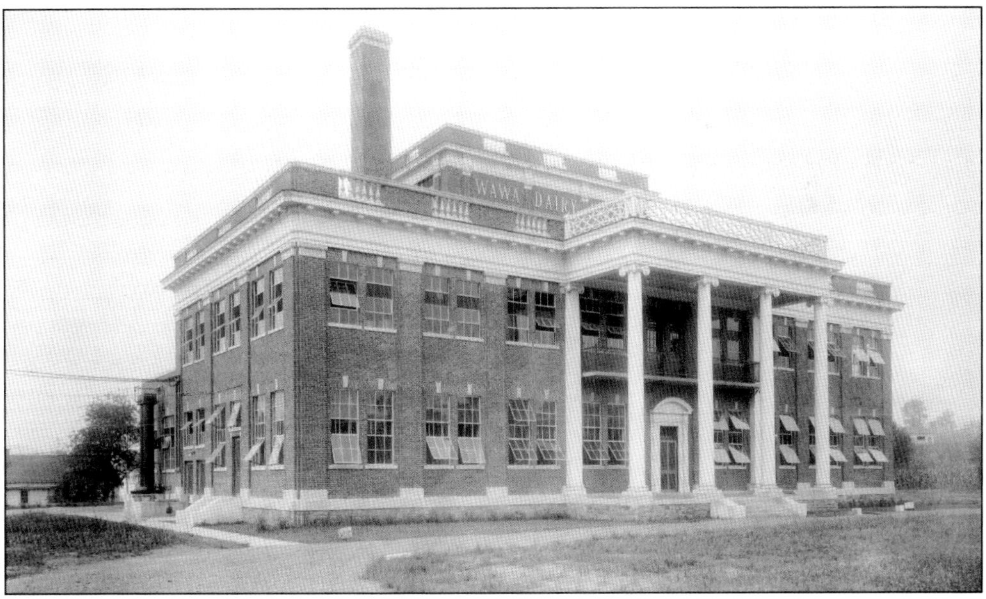

Throughout the 1920s, Wawa increased its share of the region's fresh milk market by adding cream to its product line. In 1928, health laws called for separate plants to process pasteurized and certified dairy products. Wawa opened this building that year on the northeast corner of Baltimore Pike and Valley Road, ingeniously combining the two plants within a single structure. The building is still in use by Wawa in 2011. (Hagley.)

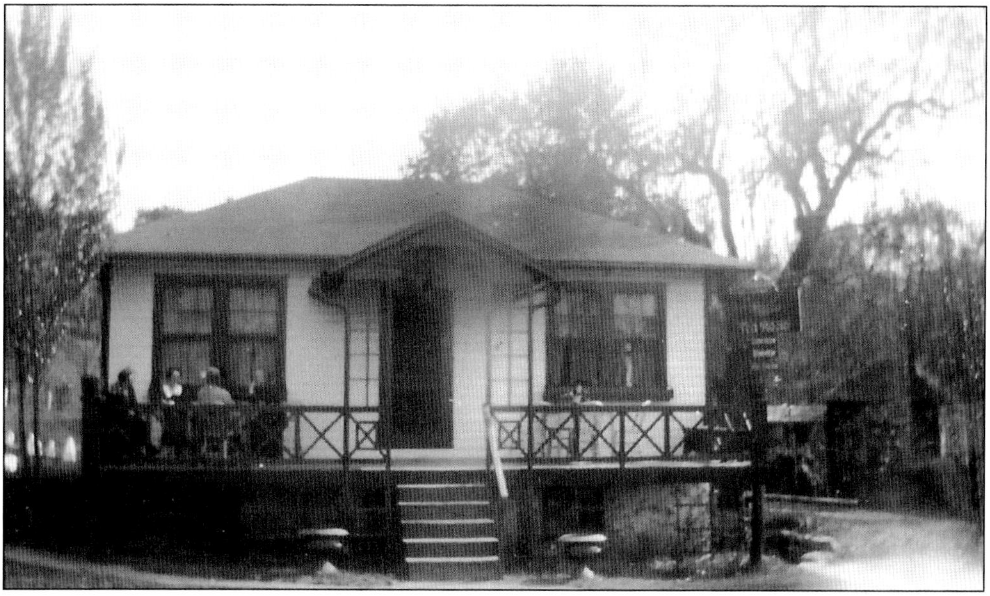

Katherine Willcox operated the Wild Goose Tea Room on the south side of Baltimore Pike opposite Valley Road. In the 1921 view above, patrons are on the outdoor dining porch. Over time, Willcox expanded the building and the business to a full-service restaurant and banquet facility. In 1963, she sold the business to Jack Kelly. Kelly sold it in 1968 to John Meyers, who operated it as the Lobster Pot and Steak House. In 1995, the property was purchased by the Franklin Mint. The restaurant was abandoned and eventually demolished.

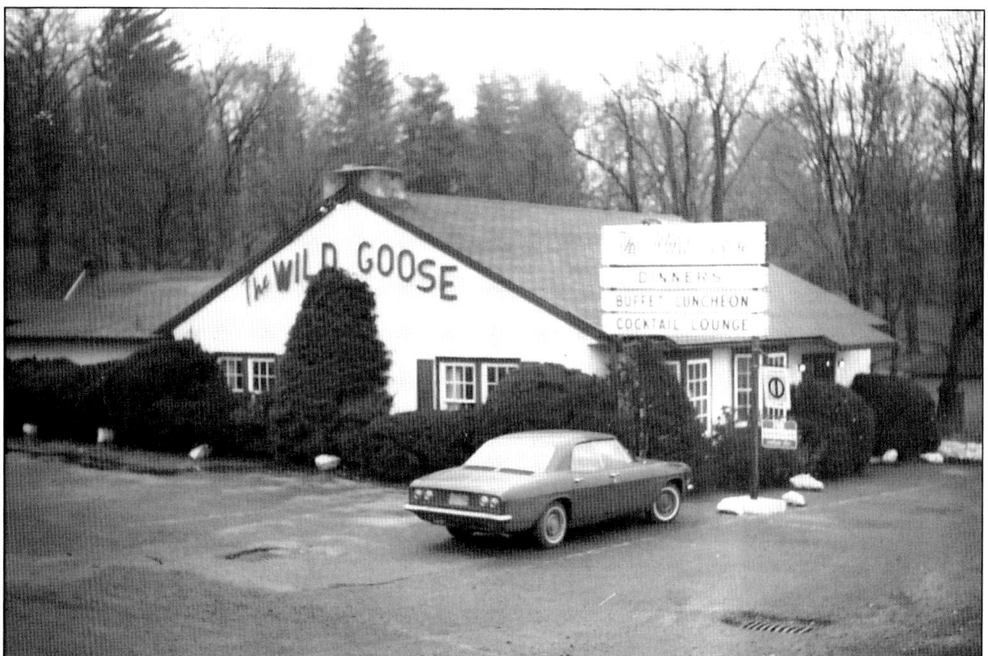

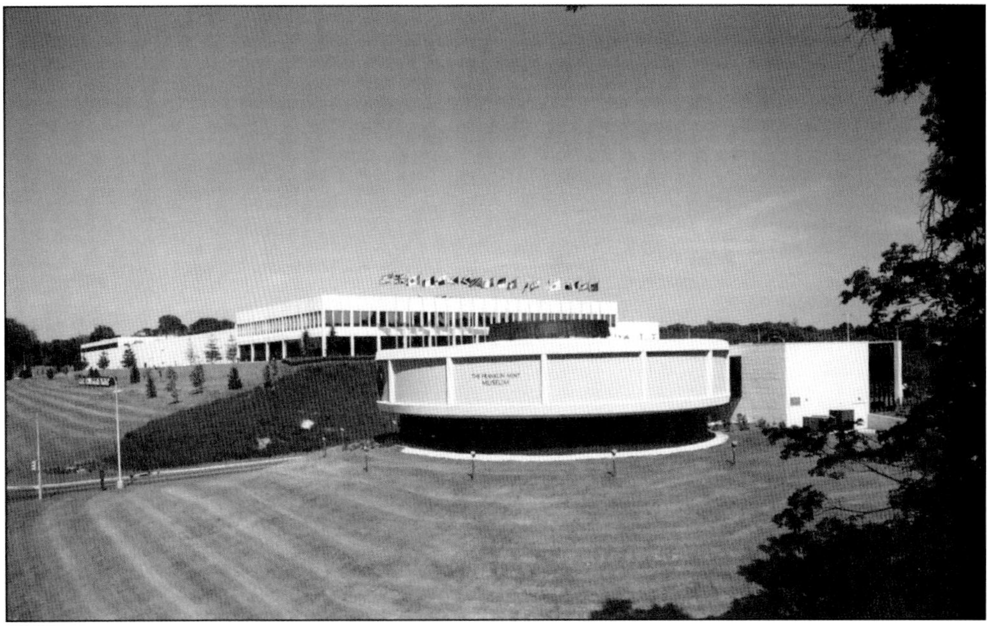

Founded in 1964 by entrepreneur Joseph Segel, the Franklin Mint was built in Wawa on the south side of Baltimore Pike at Valley Road in 1976. It was the world's largest private mint in the mid-1980s, coining currency for nearly 20 sovereign nations. Eventually, they expanded into collectible die-cast objects, fine books and jewelry, and porcelain figures. The business was sold in 1980, and this facility was closed by the mid-1990s.

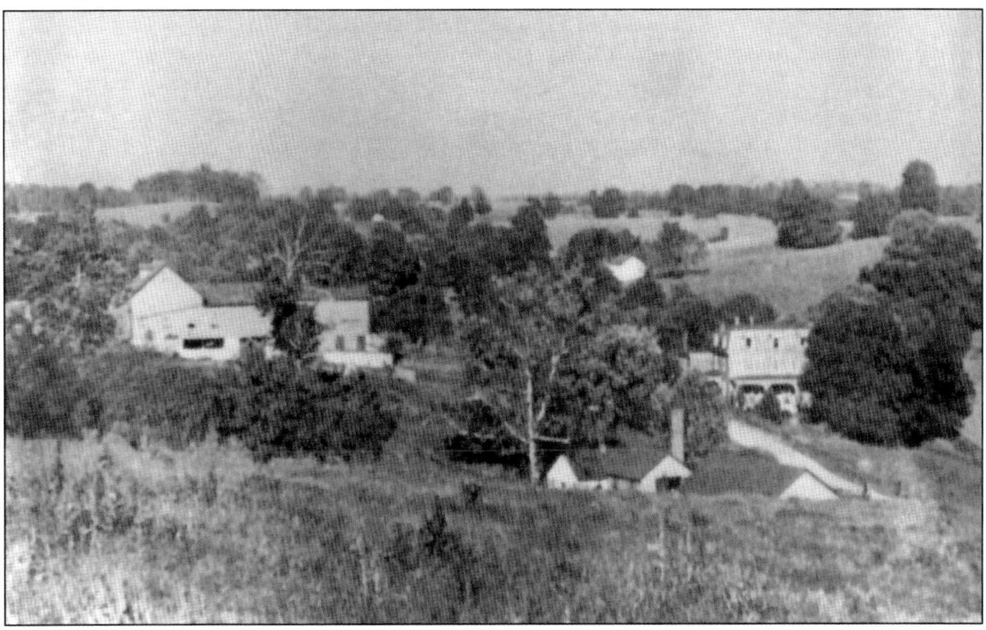

A half-mile north of Baltimore Pike among the meanders of Chester Creek lays the hamlet of Darling, Pennsylvania. For close to 200 years, Darlington Road linked several dairy farms owned and operated by six generations of the Darlington family. Jesse Darlington settled in Middletown in 1795 and shipped fresh-churned butter to shops in Delaware and Chester Counties and Philadelphia, first by horseback and then by wagon as the roads were improved.

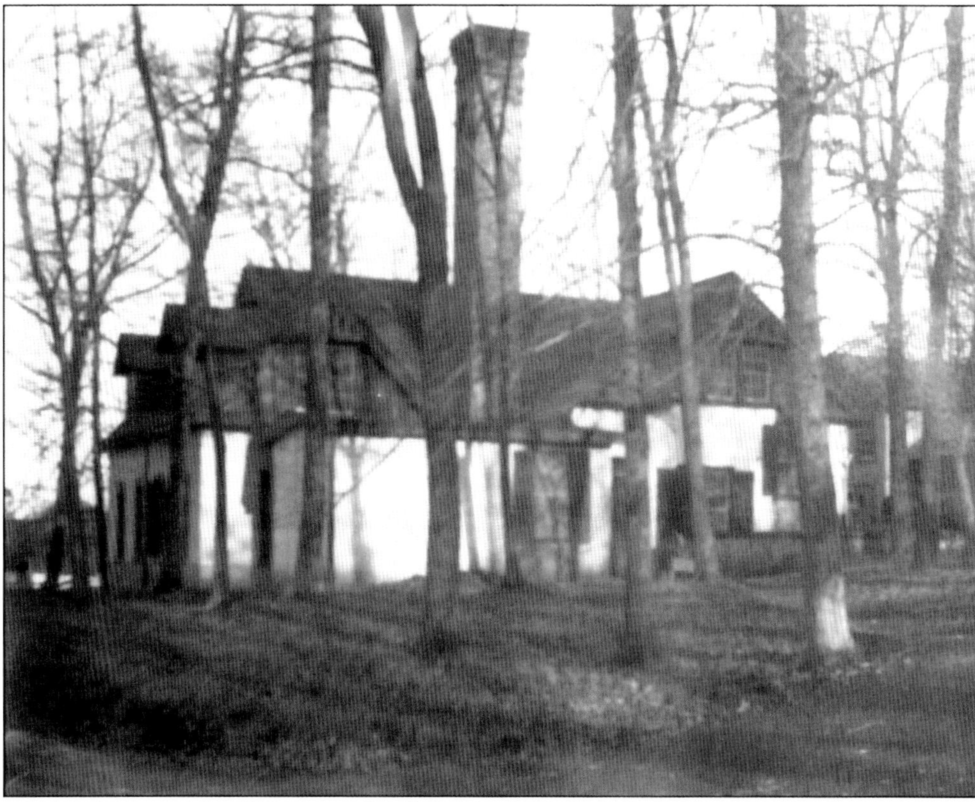

The Darlingtons were the first in the Philadelphia market to pack their butter in ice to keep it fresh and hard during shipping. Beginning in 1858, Darlington's Cornucopia Dairies shipped butter by rail to Philadelphia, New York, Baltimore, and Washington, where it was served at the White House. About that time, butter sold for $1 a pound in winter and 75¢ in summer. The creamery building is shown here around 1895.

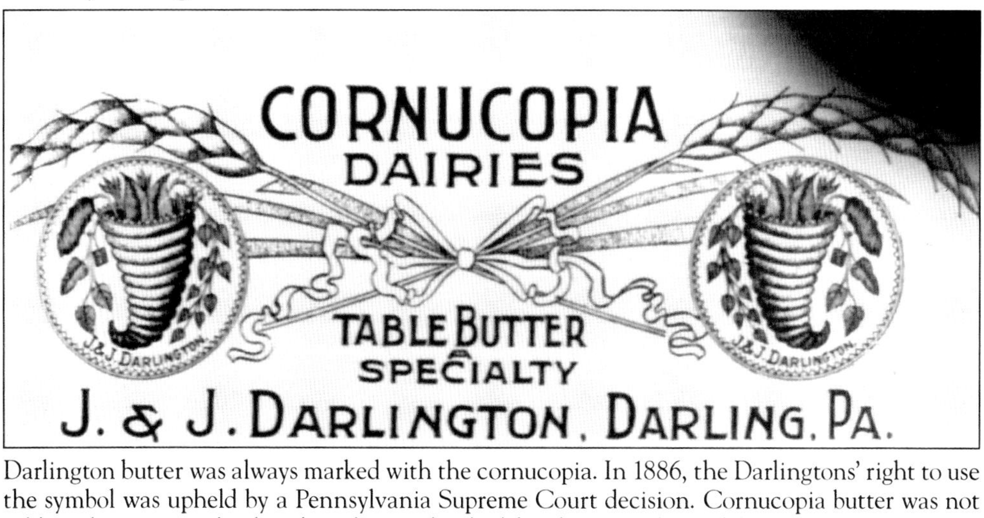

Darlington butter was always marked with the cornucopia. In 1886, the Darlingtons' right to use the symbol was upheld by a Pennsylvania Supreme Court decision. Cornucopia butter was not sold on the open market but directly to individual families. Members of these families testified as to the quality of Darlington butter and its association with the cornucopia symbol. In 1966, the dairy was sold to the Calbusera brothers, who continued to operate it until 1969. (DCHS.)

Four

Elwyn, Glen Riddle, and Lenni

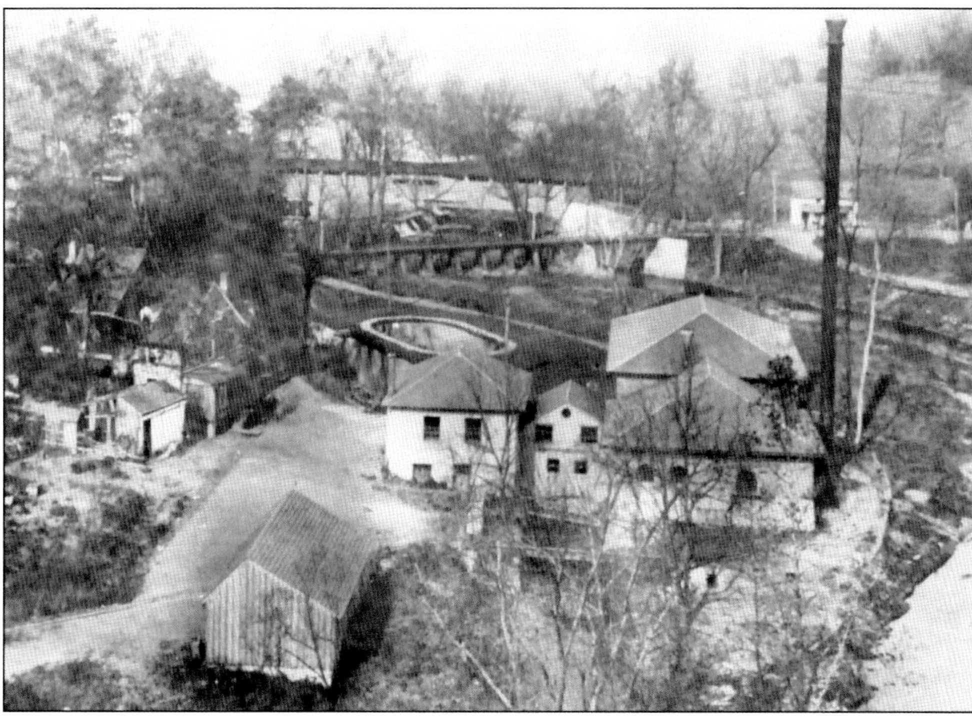

The Media Water Works, pictured around 1900, is on the west bank of Ridley Creek, the eastern boundary of Middletown Township. This photograph was taken from the Philadelphia and West Chester Railroad bridge. Rising up the hill to the south and west of the water works, the area known as Elwyn is centered around the intersections of Middletown Road (PA Route 352), Elwyn Road, and Glen Riddle Road.

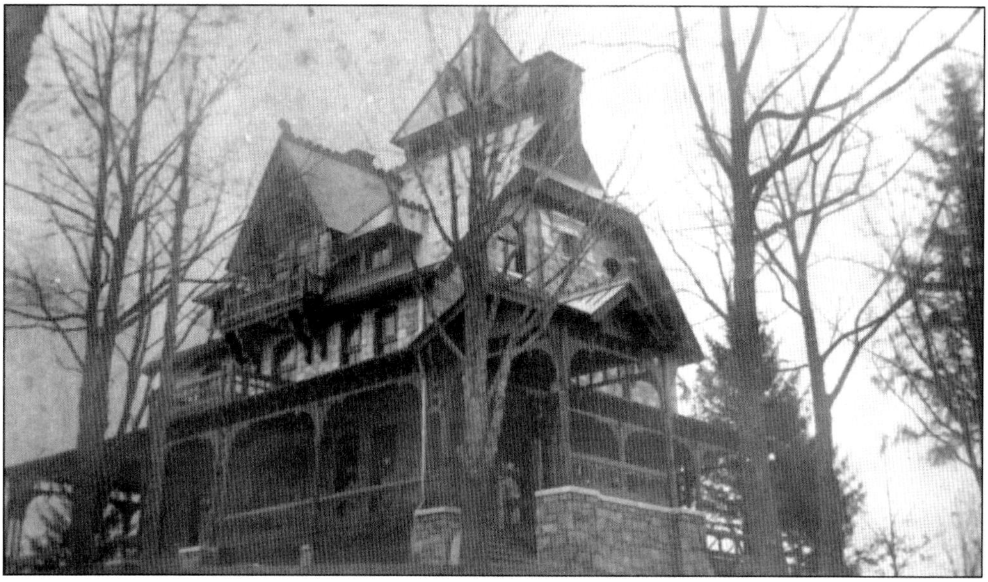

This exuberant Victorian mansion, called Clothier Hill, was the summer residence of Conrad F. Clothier of the Strawbridge and Clothier department store family. Built in 1883 on Indian Lane above Ridley Creek, it was designed by Philadelphia architect James H. Windrim. In the 1950s, it was owned by Mrs. Howard B. Steigelman, Clothier's granddaughter. In the 1970s, the top two stories were removed, creating a single-story stone house. (DCIS.)

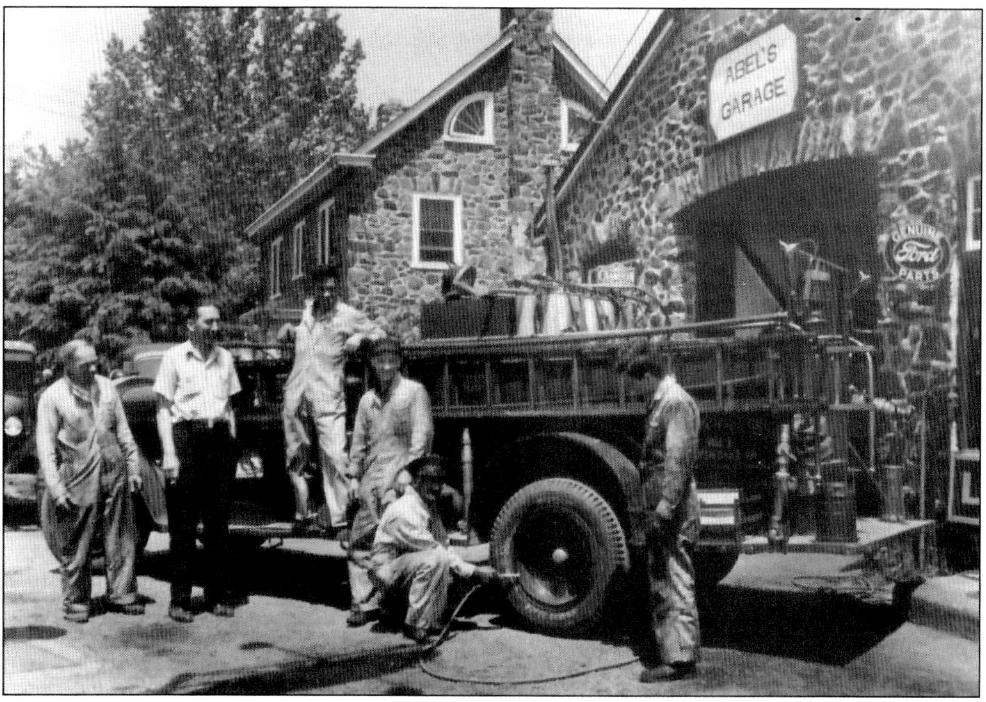

Abel's Garage was on the northeast corner of Middletown Road and Elwyn Avenue. Pictured here in the early 1940s are, from left to right, Larry Wagner, Carlton Abel, Vic Starr, Bob Scull, Ernie Miller, and Jack Lambdin. The Abels' home is to the left of the garage. These buildings were torn down in 1976 to make way for an Exxon gas station.

The Fairlamb house stood on the northwest corner of Middletown and Glen Riddle Roads. Dr. Anna Broomall's notes read, "The square brick house near the high carriage road over the Philadelphia and West Chester Railroad was built by Salkeld Larkin of Upper Chichester for his daughter Susan, when she married John Fairlamb about 1854." (DCHS.)

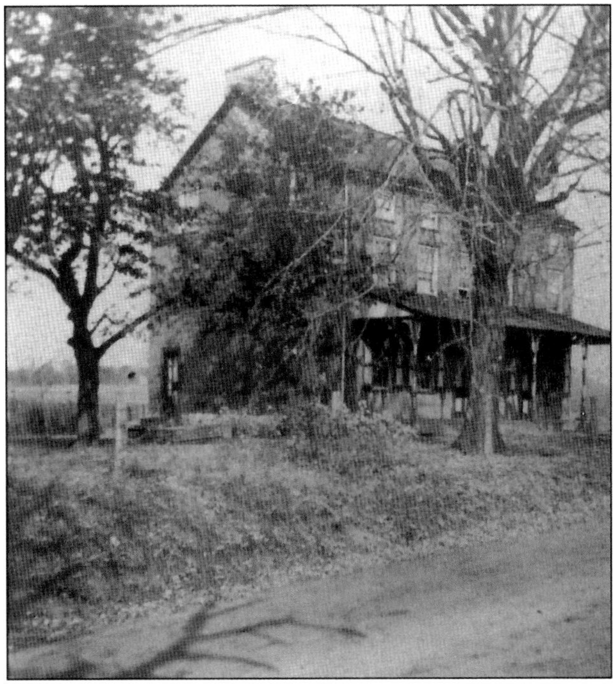

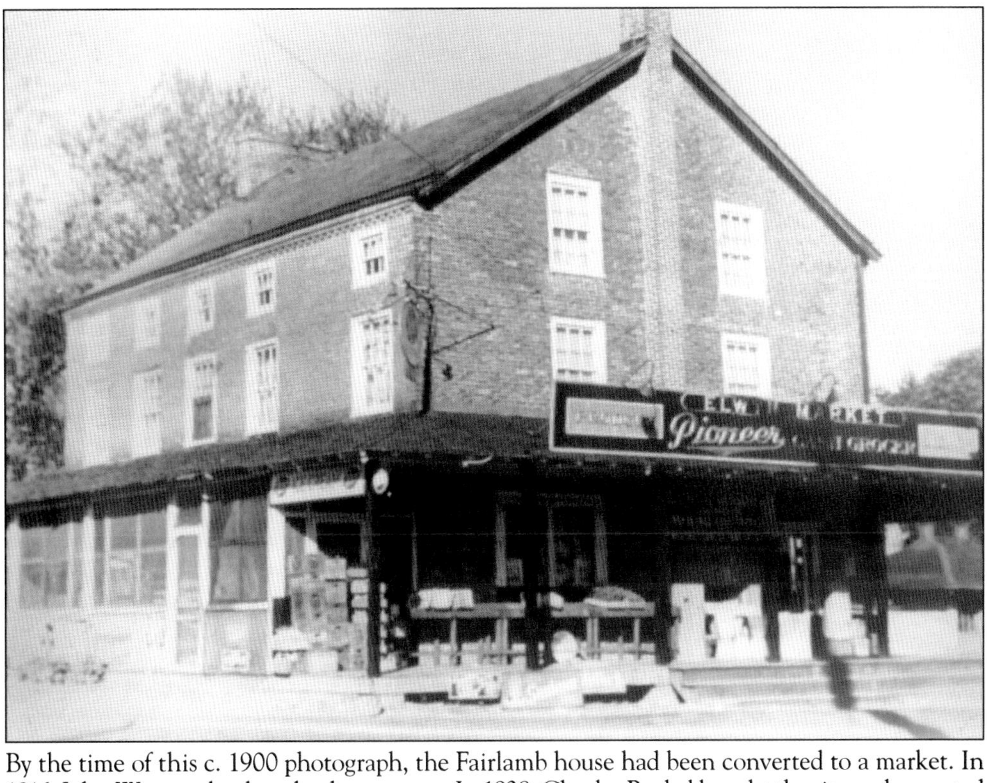

By the time of this c. 1900 photograph, the Fairlamb house had been converted to a market. In 1916, John Wanamaker bought the property. In 1938, Charles Beckel bought the site and operated the Elwyn Market. In 1961, Beckel had the Fairlamb house torn down and built the "modern" shopping center that exists on the site in 2011.

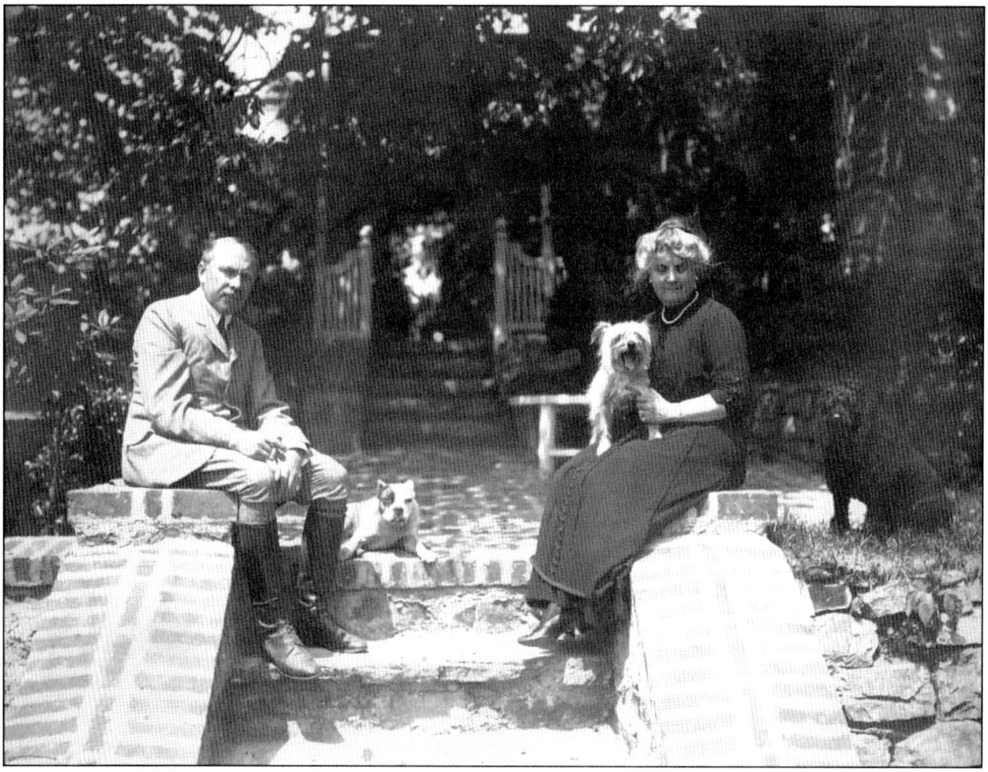

Horseman Samuel D. Riddle poses with his wife, Elizabeth, in front of their home at Glen Riddle Farm on Glen Riddle Road. Riddle's grandfather, also Samuel, emigrated from Belfast in the early 1820s and for about 20 years operated mills he leased from the owners. In 1843, he purchased mills at Pennsgrove on Chester Creek. In 1854, the area was renamed Glen Riddle to prevent residents' mail from being delivered to Pennsgrove, New Jersey.

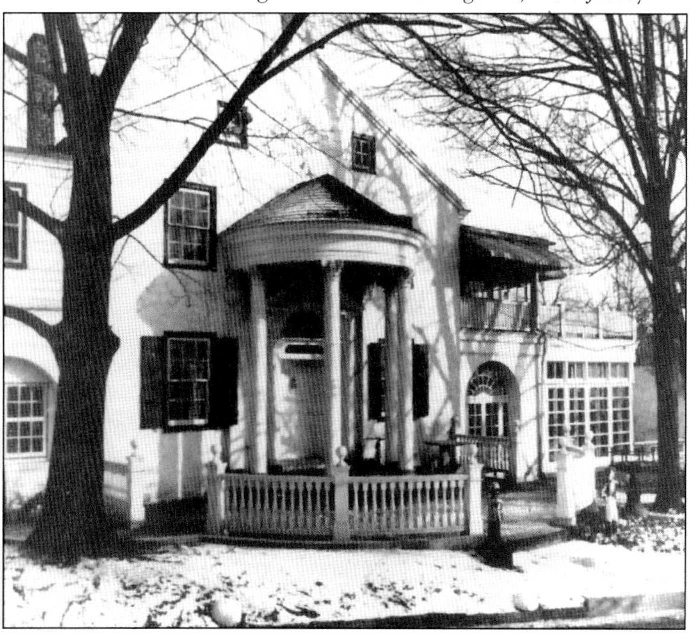

Samuel D. Riddle inherited the mills and land from his father and continued to increase the size of the estate. At the time of his death in 1951, Glen Riddle Farm encompassed most of the land from Mount Alverno Road to Baltimore Pike between Pennell and Middletown Roads, with the exception of a few road-front properties. Riddle added additions to the left and right of the original farmhouse, along with this classical portico entrance.

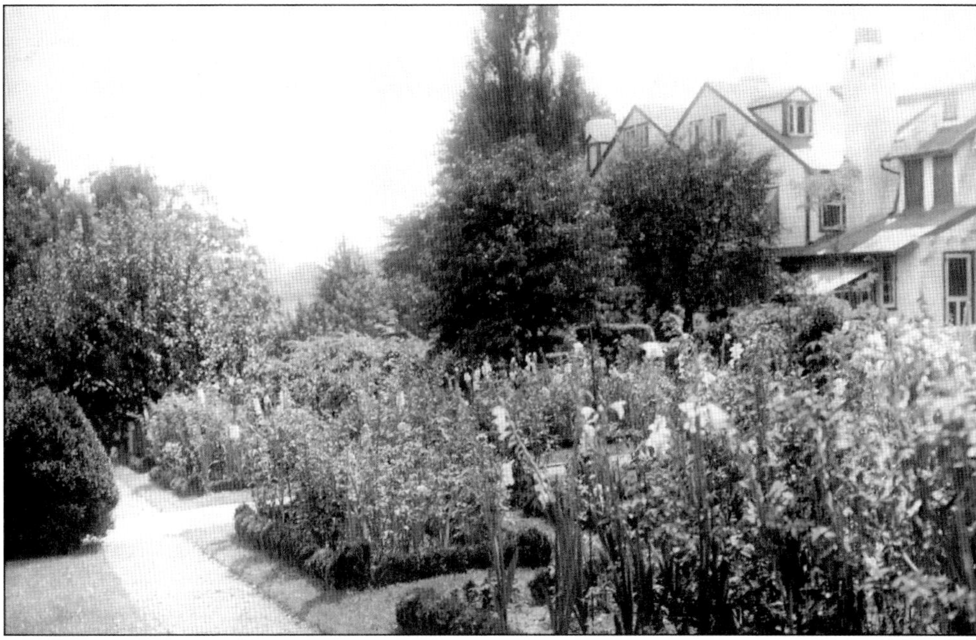

These views of the estate were taken in the early 1930s. Here, farm buildings rise behind the cutting gardens. In addition to the dozens of farm hands, animal handlers, and managers, Riddle had a full staff of house servants, cooks, gardeners, and drivers. Once a year, the local farmers were invited to a breakfast hosted by the Riddles. In 1915, guests in attendance numbered 2,000.

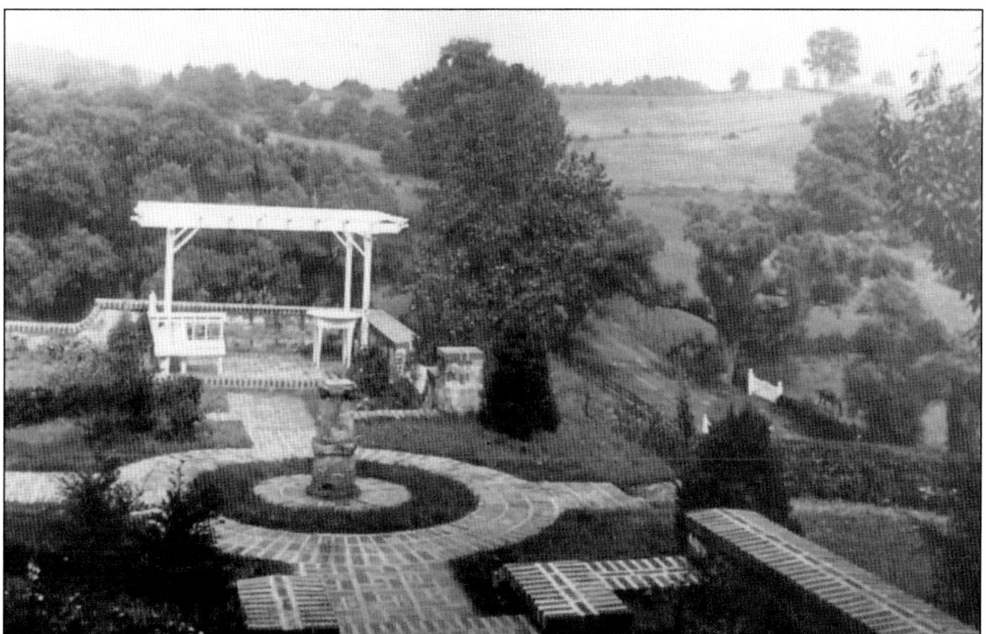

Terraced pastures are seen beyond the formal gardens at Glen Riddle Farm. After Riddle's death, the farms were sold to fund the hospital. The mansion property became a retirement home. In 1989, the residents were moved to a new retirement facility in New Jersey, and developers planned to demolish the house for a new life-care center when it was destroyed by a mysterious fire.

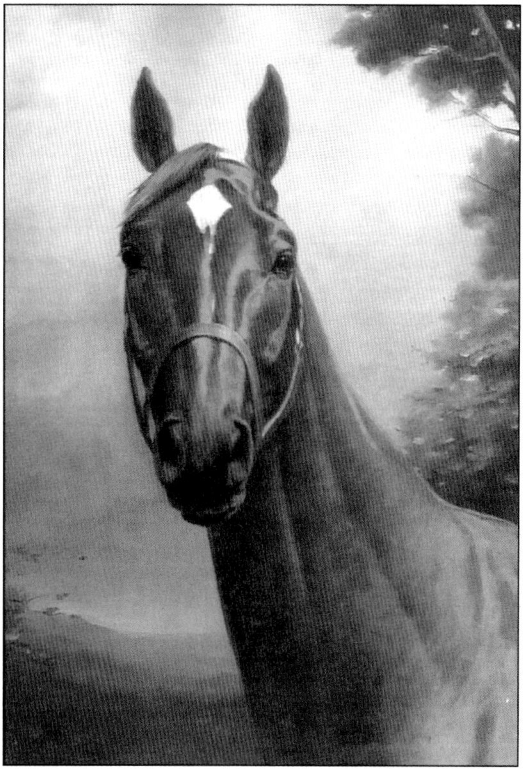

Riddle's best-known racehorse was Man O' War, pictured here in a 1920 oil portrait by equestrian artist Thomas Percy Earl. Riddle bought Man O' War from August Belmont at the yearling sale in Saratoga in 1918. Man O' War was a great racehorse as a two and three year old, but he was more important as a stallion, siring over 379 foals, 64 of which were stakes winners. (Riddle Memorial Hospital.)

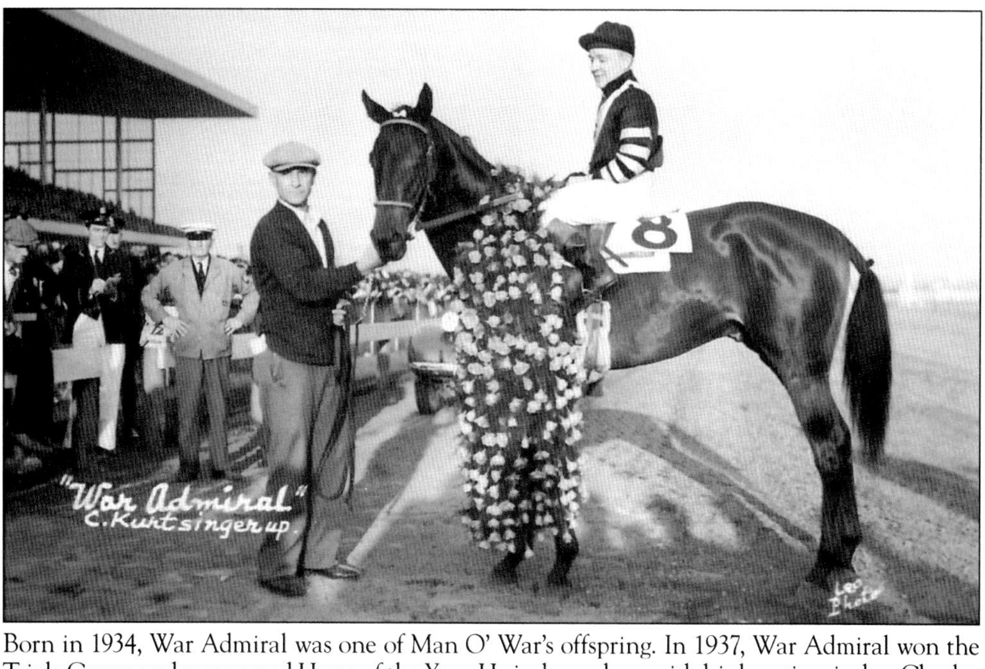

Born in 1934, War Admiral was one of Man O' War's offspring. In 1937, War Admiral won the Triple Crown and was named Horse of the Year. He is shown here with his longtime jockey Charley Kurtsinger. Few people realize that the November 1938 match race between War Admiral and Seabiscuit, popularized in the 2001 book and 2003 movie, was all in the family, as Seabiscuit was Man O' War's grandson.

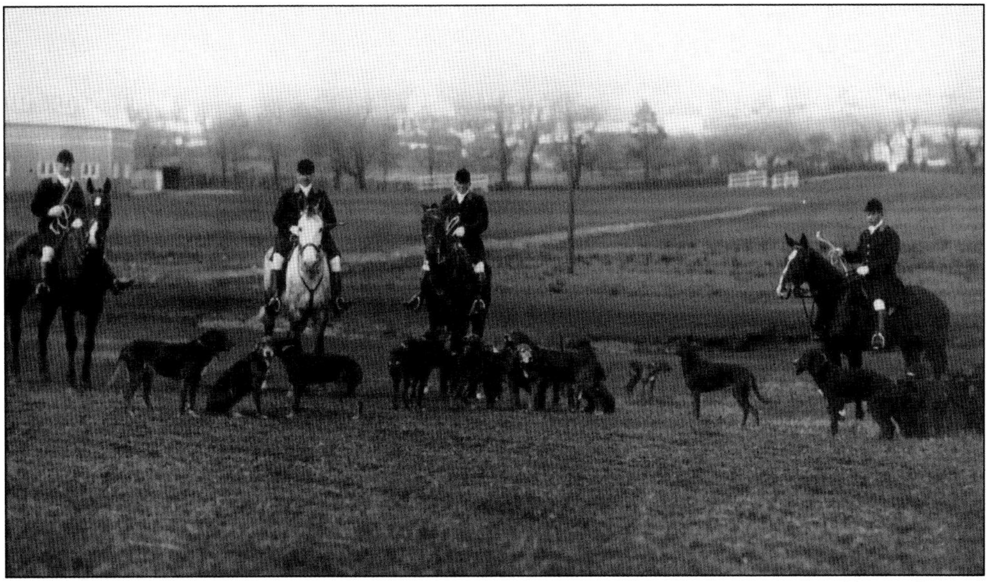

The Riddles entertained often at their home. Sam rode at the Rose Tree Hunt and hosted many hunts on his farms and hunt breakfasts at the mansion. Sam is pictured second from left on the white horse, with his prize pack of hunting hounds. He often loaned the hounds to Rose Tree Hunt to use when he was away at races or on his thoroughbred farms in Berlin, Maryland; and Lexington, Kentucky.

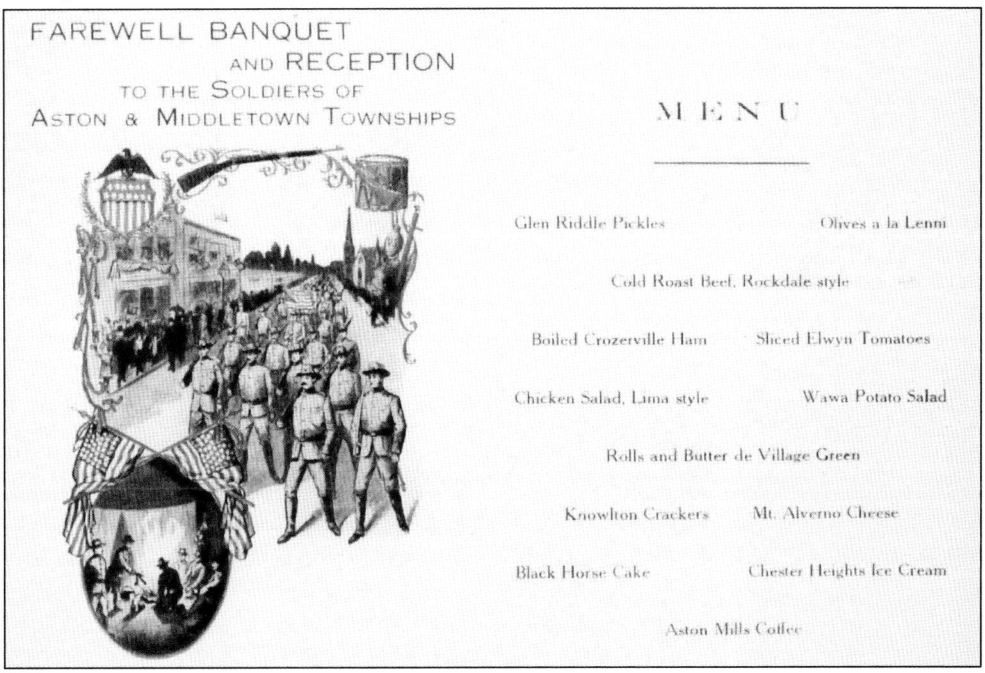

FAREWELL BANQUET
AND RECEPTION
TO THE SOLDIERS OF
ASTON & MIDDLETOWN TOWNSHIPS

MENU

Glen Riddle Pickles — Olives a la Lenni

Cold Roast Beef, Rockdale style

Boiled Crozerville Ham — Sliced Elwyn Tomatoes

Chicken Salad, Lima style — Wawa Potato Salad

Rolls and Butter de Village Green

Knowlton Crackers — Mt. Alverno Cheese

Black Horse Cake — Chester Heights Ice Cream

Aston Mills Coffee

The building in the back left of the previous photograph is the Glen Riddle Casino, a large barn where banquets were held that was owned by the Riddles. It was on the south side of Glen Riddle Road, opposite the driveway to the Riddle home, where the Turnbridge Apartments are located in 2011. This is where the Riddles held their annual farmers' breakfasts. The menu for this farewell party for World War I troops featured all "local fare."

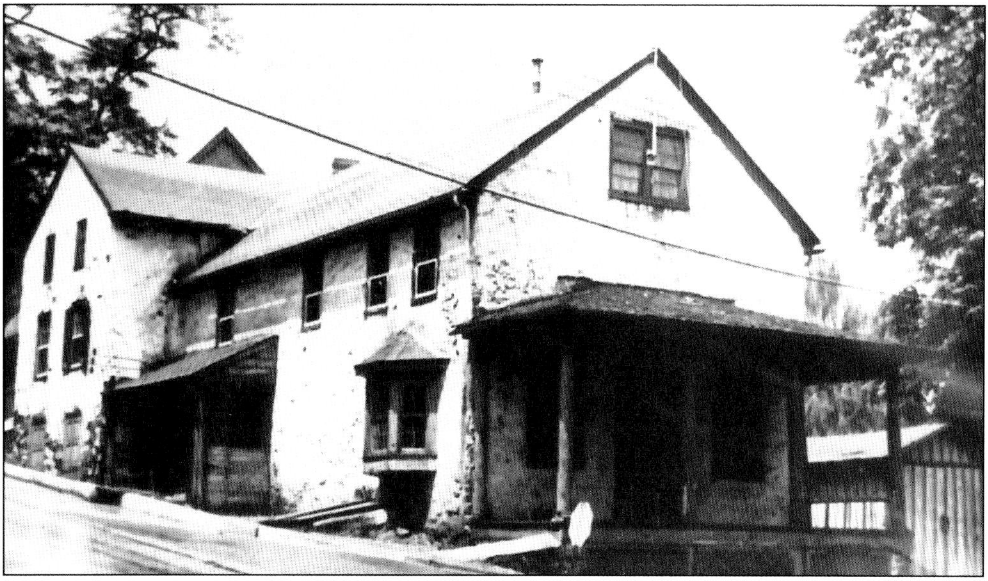

Built around 1850, these buildings stood on the northeast corner of Glen Riddle and Pennell Roads. The building in the front was a general store and housed the Glen Riddle Post Office until 1912, when it was moved to the Glen Riddle train station. The last store operator was a Mr. Maloney. The building was demolished in 1967. (Paul Dougherty/ATHS.)

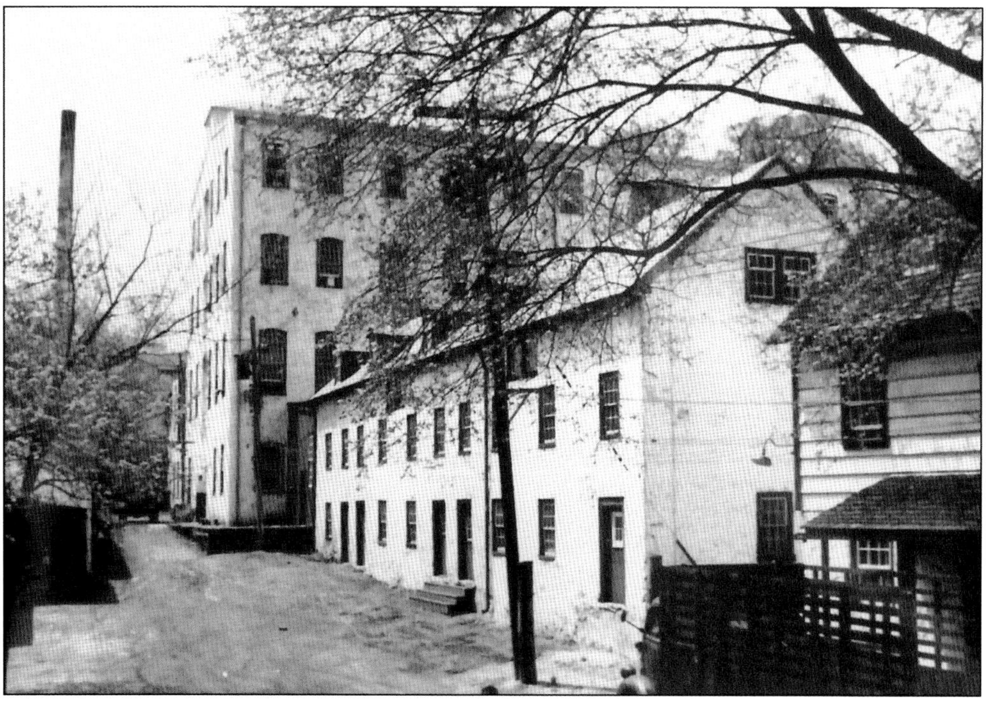

The former Riddle Mills, on the west side of Pennell Road between Parkmount Road and Chester Creek, were photographed in 1982 when they were still owned by the Sunroc Refrigeration Company. Founded in 1922 as a bottled water company, Sunroc began manufacturing water coolers in the 1930s. A federal contract issued in 1936 catapulted the company to instant success, and Sunroc became synonymous with water fountains.

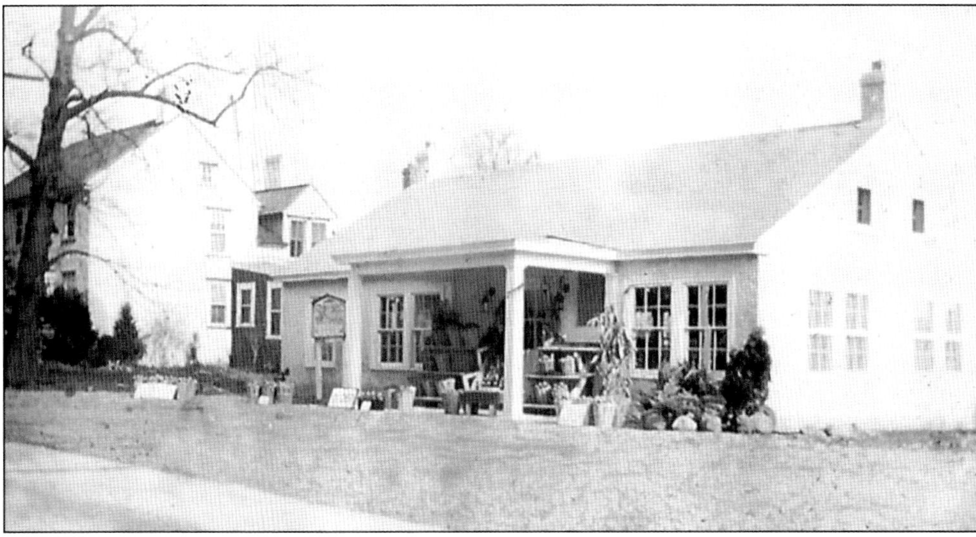

Located on the northeast corner of Pennell Road and Whirlaway Road, Wolff's Apple House celebrated 100 years of business in 2010. In 1908, Anne Wolff moved here from Bermuda with her five children and bought 24 acres of farmland. Two years later, her youngest son, Frank, at the age of 18, embarked on his dream of becoming a farmer by planting an apple orchard. He named it Sunnybrae Orchards, after a boardinghouse his mother had run back in Bermuda. Throughout the decades, the farm grew to 52 acres of apples, peaches, pears, plums, other fruits, and vegetables. Over time the fruit trees grew older and less productive, and eventually all the land around the store was sold. Today, the farm market is run by the fifth and sixth generations of the Wolff family. (Both, Wolff's Apple House.)

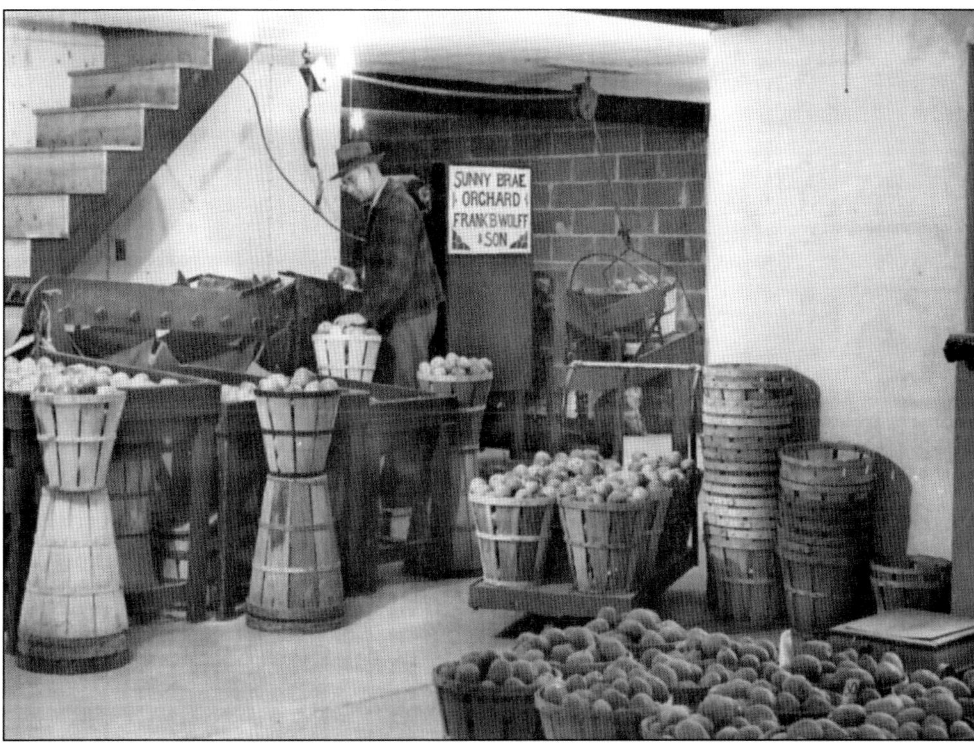

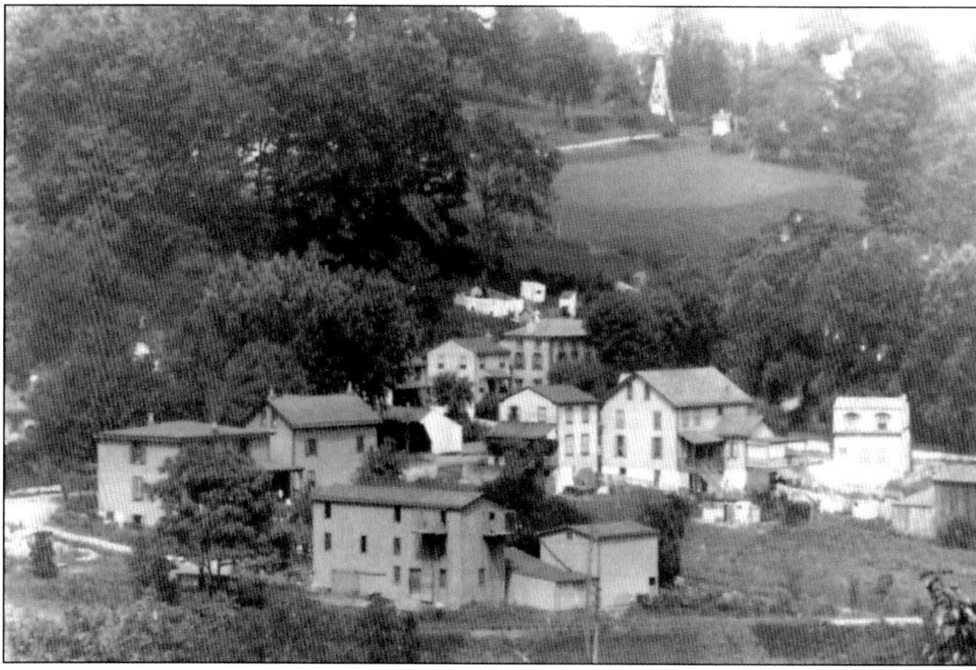

Lenni rises steeply along both banks of the East Branch of Chester Creek. The north side is in Middletown Township, the south side is in Aston Township. Beginning in the 17th century, mills lined the creek on both sides. It was called Taylortown until 1825, when it was renamed Lenni by William Martin, who owned the Lenni Mills. The Middletown side of the village is centered at the intersection of Lenni and Lundgren Roads, as shown above around 1900. Note the windmill at the top of the pasture in the upper right. Below is a 1921 view looking northwest along Lundgren Road from the railroad crossing at Parkmount Road. Into the 20th century, most residents of Lenni worked in the mills, but most had vegetable gardens, and some kept horses, cows, pigs, and chickens. (Below, DCHS.)

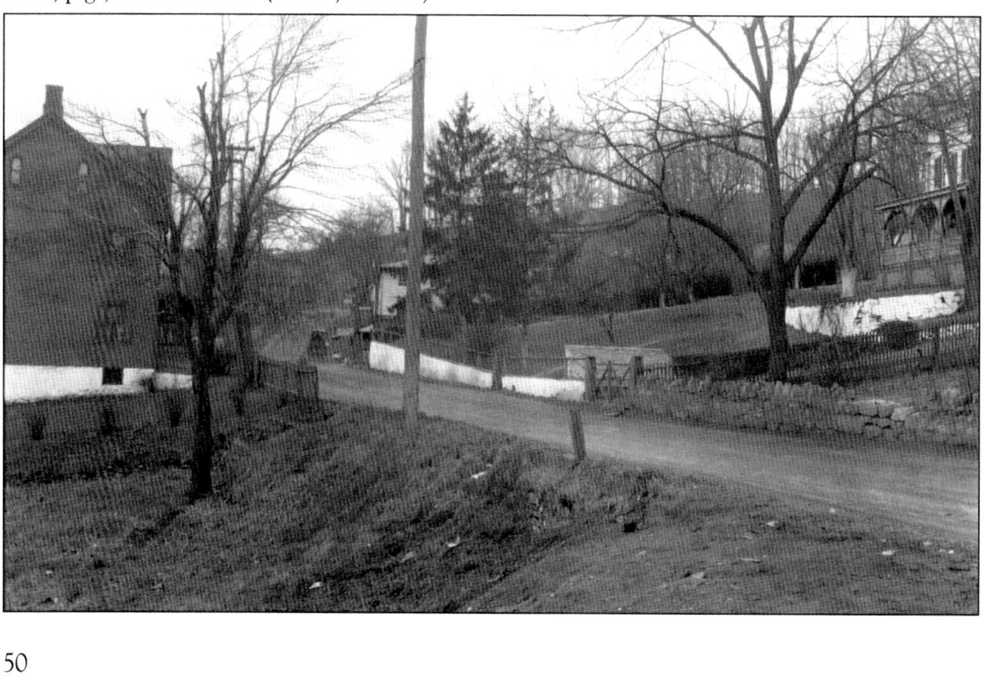

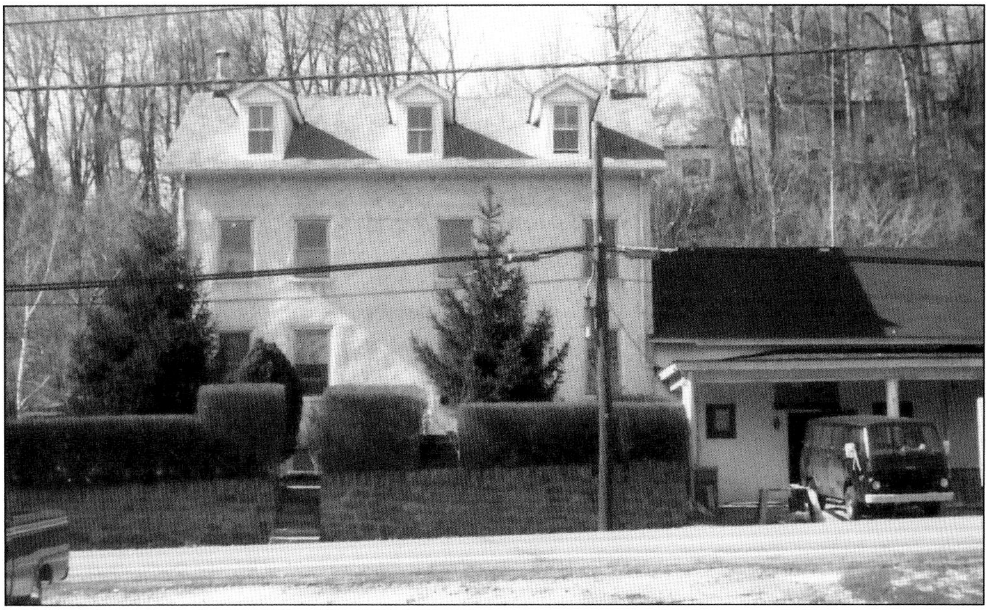

The Maplewood Hotel was on the west side of Lenni Road, a little south of Lundgren Road. A Works Progress Administration (WPA) survey of 1936 reported, "This hotel is one of the familiar landmarks of Lenni. It was erected in 1850 as a general store and residence about three hundred feet north of the Pennsylvania Railroad by a man named Steele. In 1879, a license to sell liquor was obtained by John McCartney who conducted the hostelry until 1893. From then until Prohibition several persons operated the same business here." After Prohibition, the tavern, seen above in 1979, was reopened and operated until the late 1970s by Bob and Sally McCue, who lived above the bar. As of 2011, the building has been restored to its 1850s appearance and is now a residence with a barbershop on the lower level. (Below, Mary Anne Eves.)

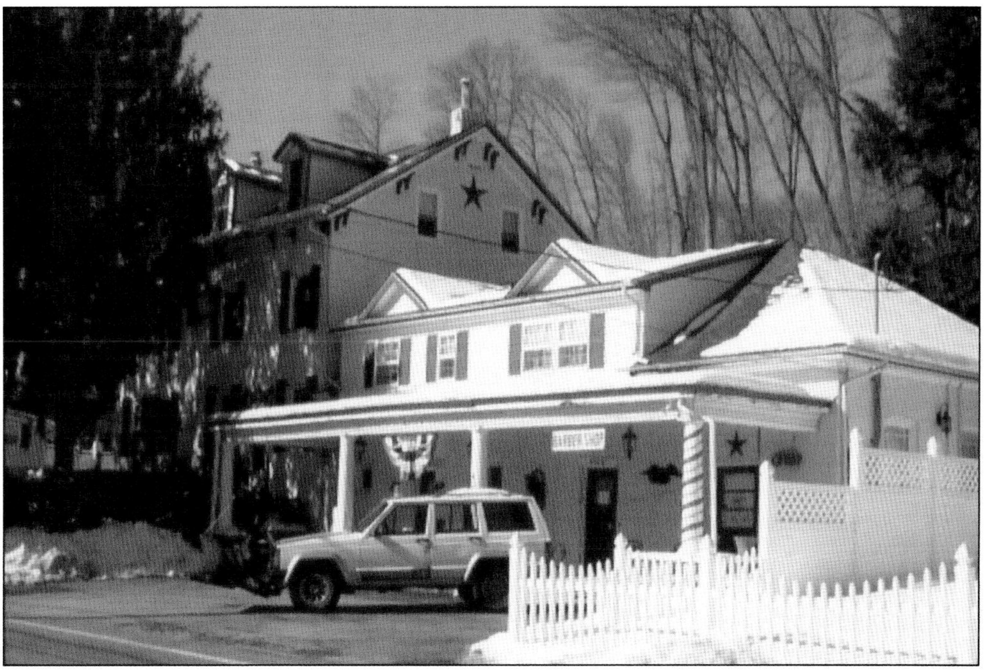

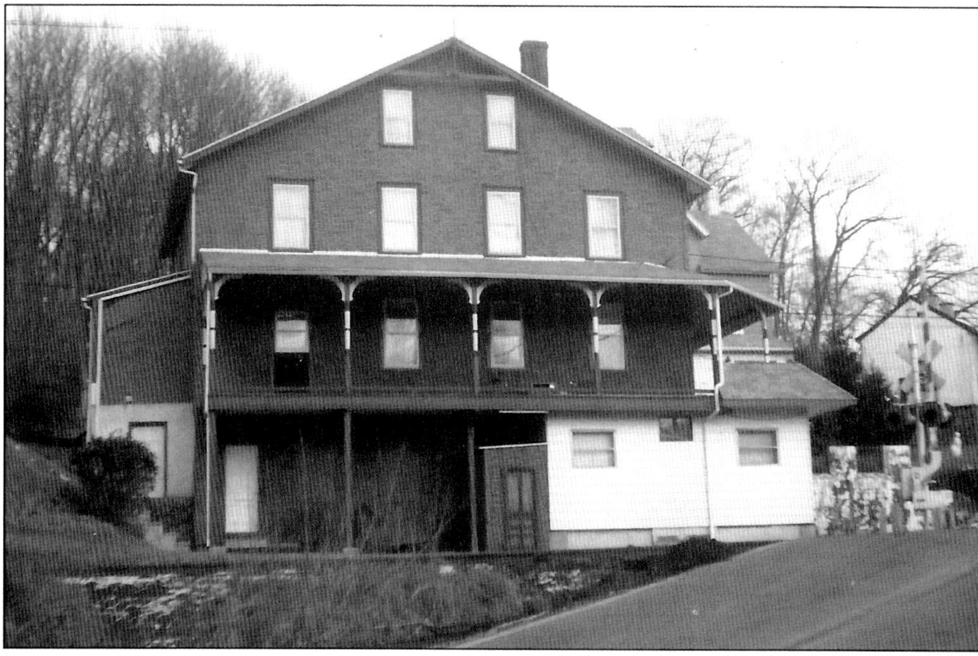

This is a 1982 view of the former Witten's Store, now a residence on the west side of Lenni Road at Station Avenue. A post office was established in the railroad station, which was just to the left of this building, in 1875. In 1921, the post office was moved to this building. The current Lenni Post Office was built in 1955, a few hundred yards north on Lenni Road.

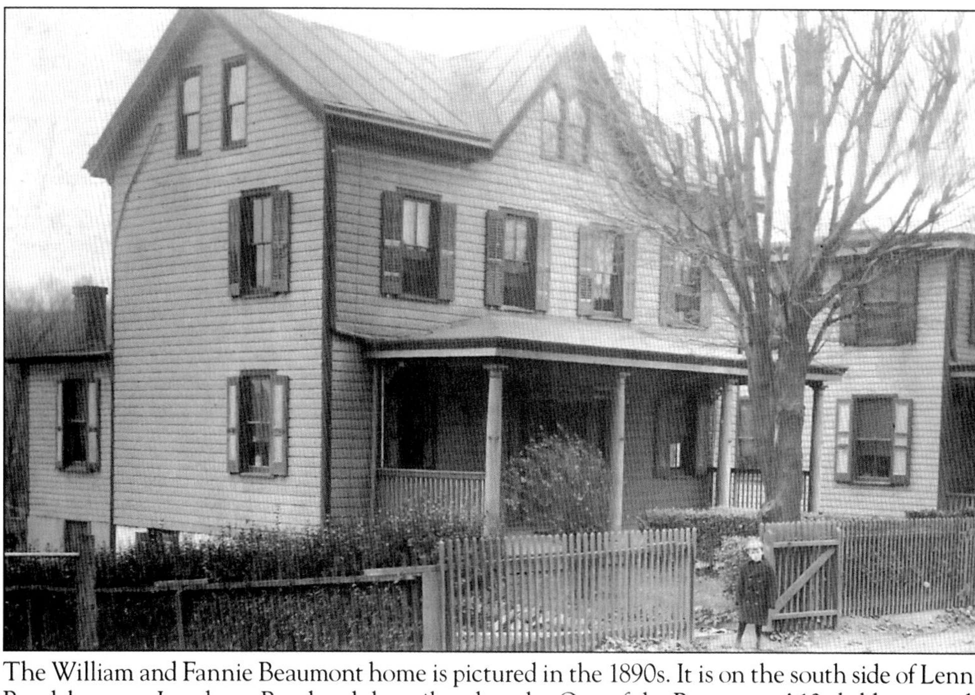

The William and Fannie Beaumont home is pictured in the 1890s. It is on the south side of Lenni Road, between Lundgren Road and the railroad tracks. One of the Beaumonts' 10 children stands by the fence. Unfortunately, William Beaumont was killed by a train as he walked on the railroad tracks from Rockdale to Lenni in 1911. (J. Karl Thomas.)

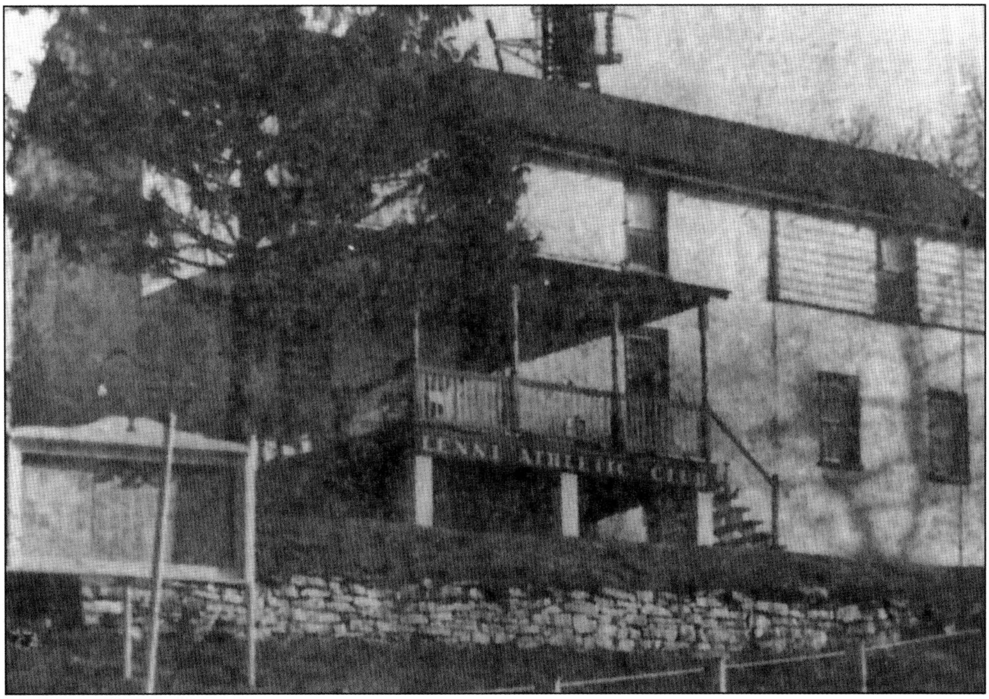

The clubhouse of the Lenni Athletic Club is perched on a hill on the north side of Lundgren Road, next to the railroad bridge. The club was chartered in 1937, the year they won the now defunct Delco Valley Baseball League. They were formed from the previous Lenni Athletic Association, which was organized in the mid-1920s. Today, the club is mainly social. (DCHS.)

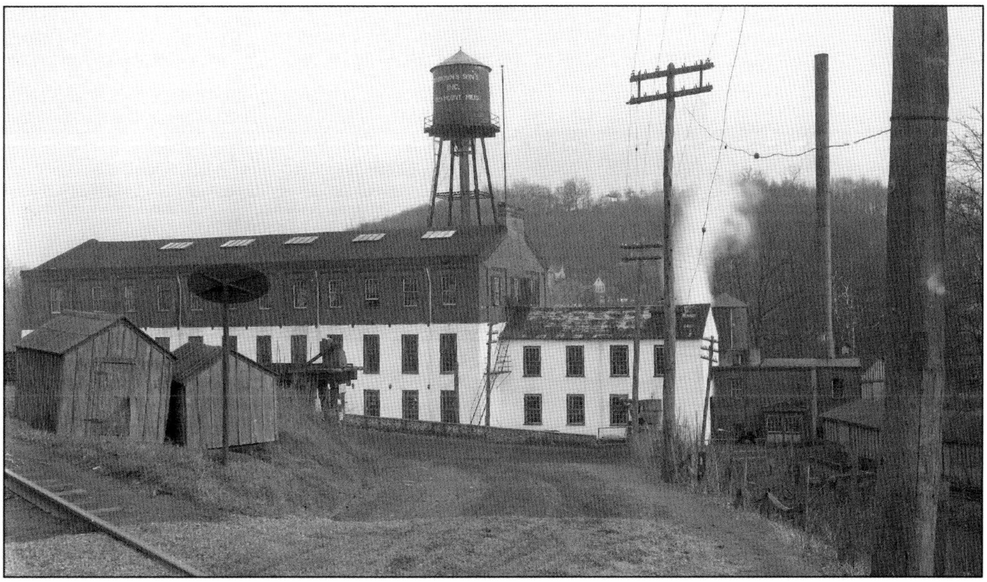

This view of the Parkmount Mills, located at the intersection of Lundgren and Parkmount Roads, is from the 1900s. The first Parkmount Mills were built in 1829 by Peter Hill for Samuel Riddle, the father of the horseman. The buildings burned in 1863 and again in 1887. Fires in textile mills were common in the 19th century. The buildings above were rebuilt on the site in 1888 and are still in use in 2011 housing a variety of businesses. (DCHS.)

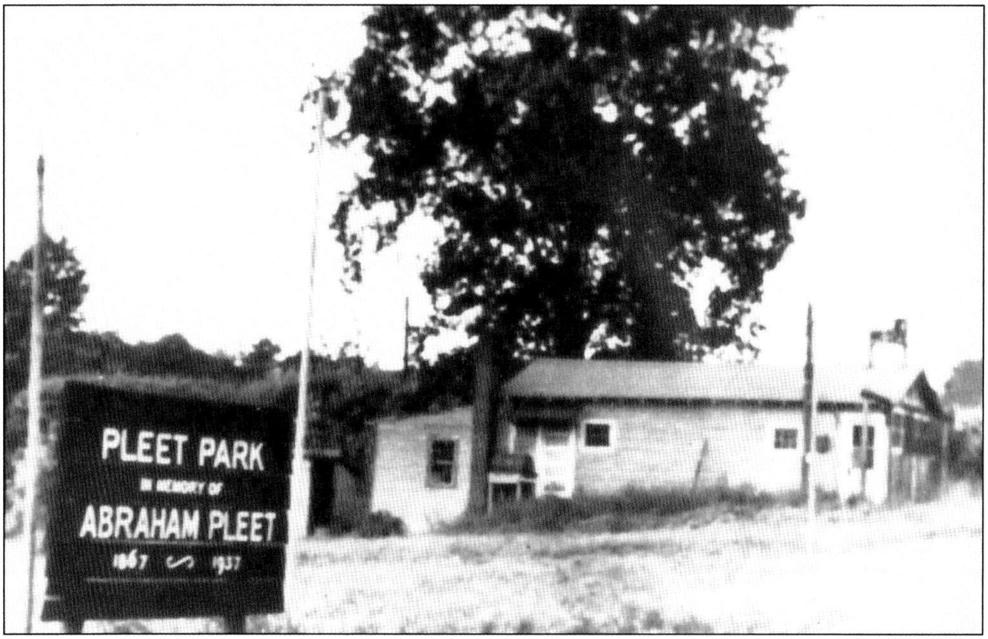

The all-volunteer Lenni Heights Fire Company was organized in 1923 by the Lenni Community Association and chartered the following year. Prior to then, the closest fire company was in Media, five miles to the northeast. Mill owners and residents were asked for contributions toward the purchase of equipment. Fire was always a danger in mills, especially textile mills. The c. 1940 photograph above shows the first firehouse on Elm Avenue, located just off Lenni Road next to Pleet Park. Abraham Pleet was the owner of the Yorkshire Worsted Mills on the Aston side of Chester Creek. In 1949, a new firehouse was built in the same location with the main garage entrance moved to Lenni Road. Over time, the 1949 building has been enlarged, and new equipment has been purchased, including a marine unit for rescues when Chester Creek floods.

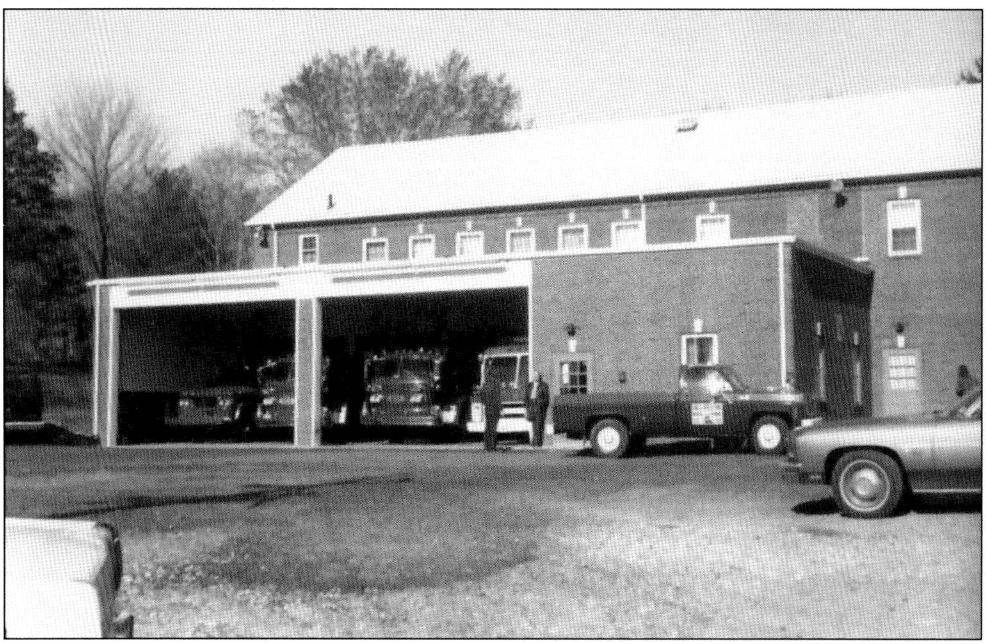

Five

Roads, Bridges, and Rails

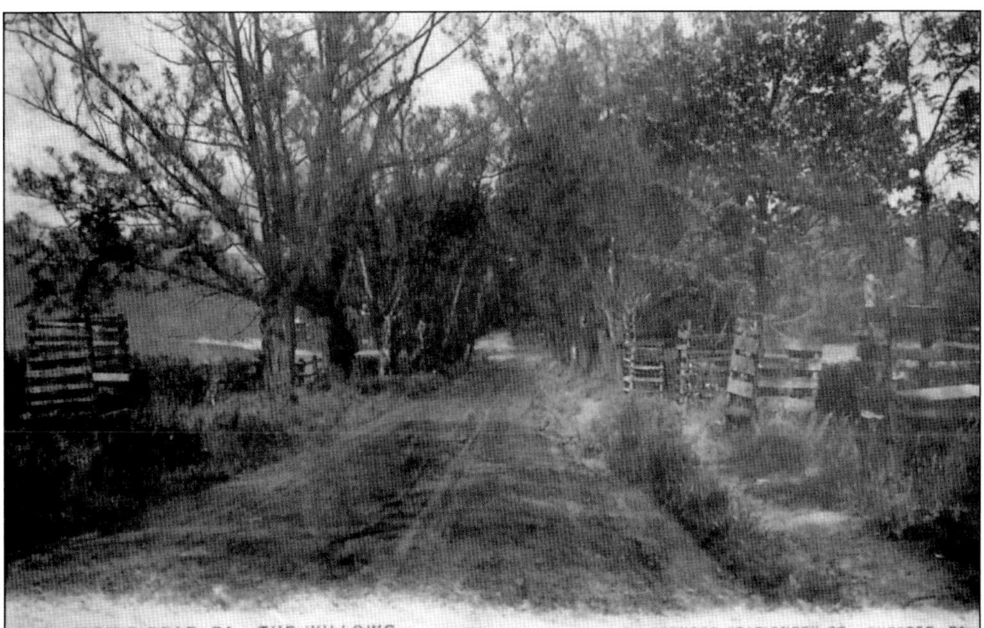

In the early 20th century, when area residents said they were "going through the willows," they meant the part of Glen Riddle Road between Lenni Road and the entrance to Glen Riddle Farm. In the late 19th century, Samuel D. Riddle planted an alley of willow trees along both sides of the road. This view is from about 1910. (DCHS.)

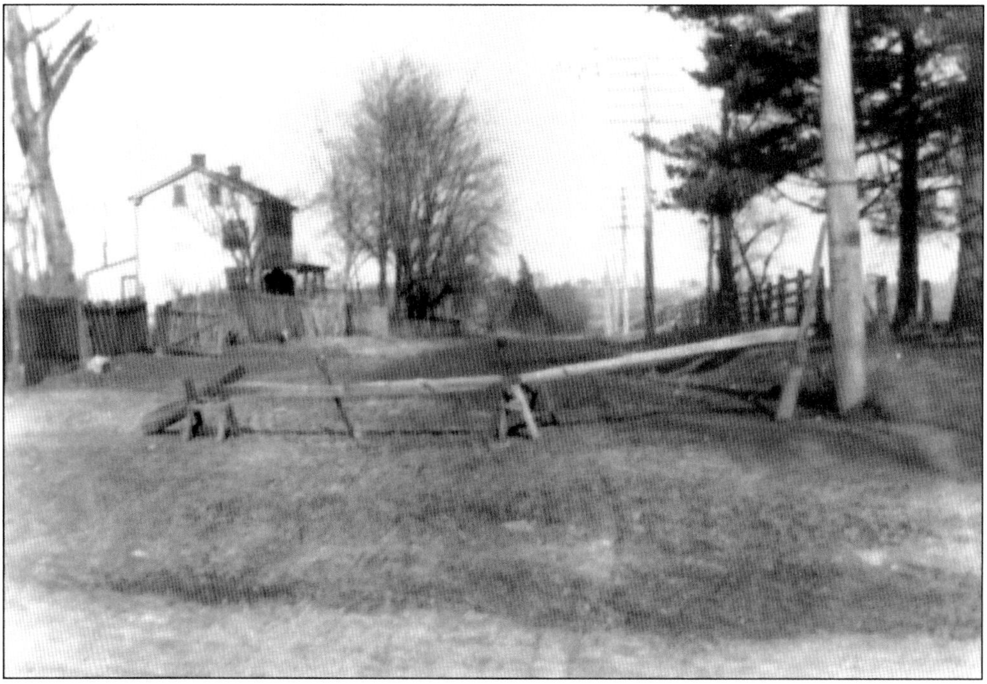

This photograph was taken in 1912, just before Baltimore Pike was paved. It was shot looking east on Baltimore Pike from Pennell Road. The house at left is the present site of Weathers Motors. As a youngster, Lawrence "Lar" Weathers was paid 15¢ per month to hang a lantern on the barricade when the dirt road was in poor condition or under repair.

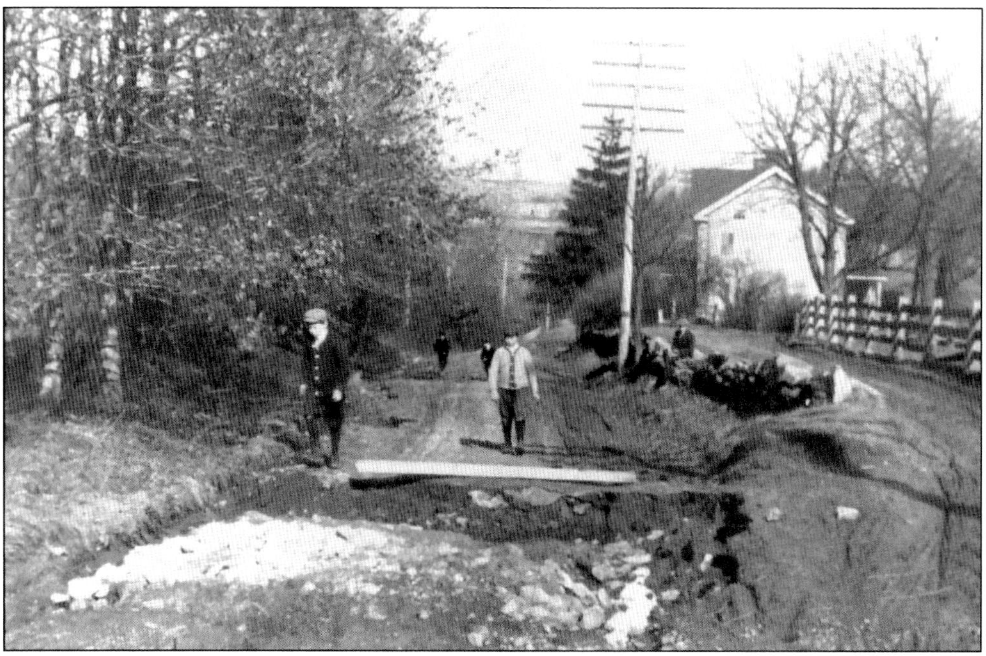

This 1912 photograph was taken looking east near where Oriole Avenue would be laid out. The Hibberd farmhouse, now the site of Riddle Hospital, is behind the boys on the right. A trapshooting club was off to the left. Before paving, roadwork was a continuous job of filling in the ruts.

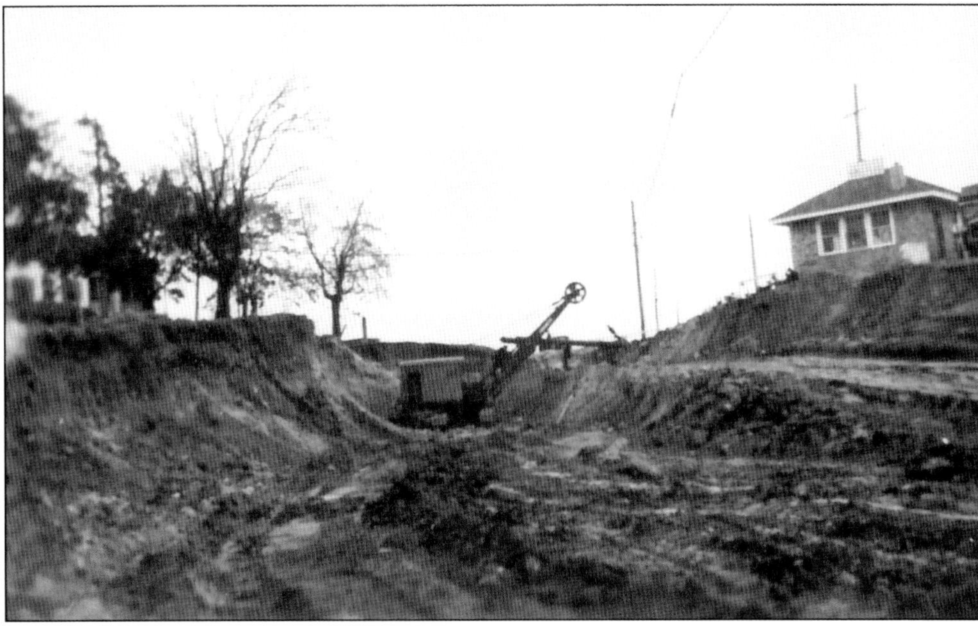

In 1938, Baltimore Pike was lowered at the intersection of Middletown Road for the construction of the cloverleaf interchange, the second of its kind in Pennsylvania. The contract to demolish the Black Horse Inn, at left above and below, was issued in April 1939. On September 1, 1939, the new roadway was opened with great fanfare. A parade of dignitaries, police cars, and fire trucks started in Media and proceeded to the railroad bridge in Wawa. The participants then backtracked to Black Horse to dedicate the new cloverleaf bridge that carries Middletown Road over Baltimore Pike. Following speeches, the new bridge was officially opened with a ribbon cutting by six-year-old Nancy Weathers of Lima, daughter of Lawrence and Rose Weathers and granddaughter of James J. Skelly, the main contractor for the paving project. The Elwyn School Band provided music at the ceremony. (Both, DCHS.)

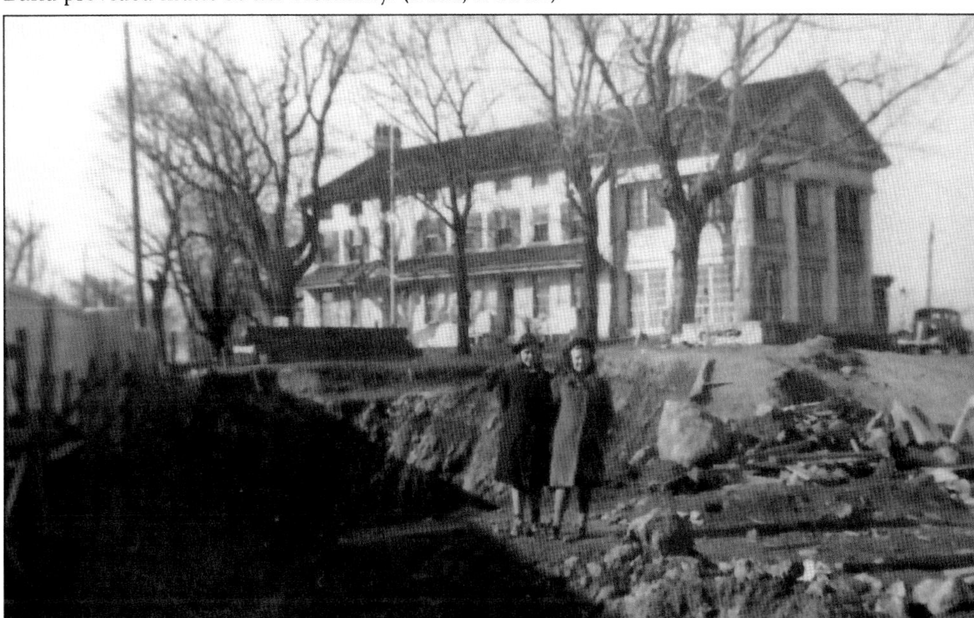

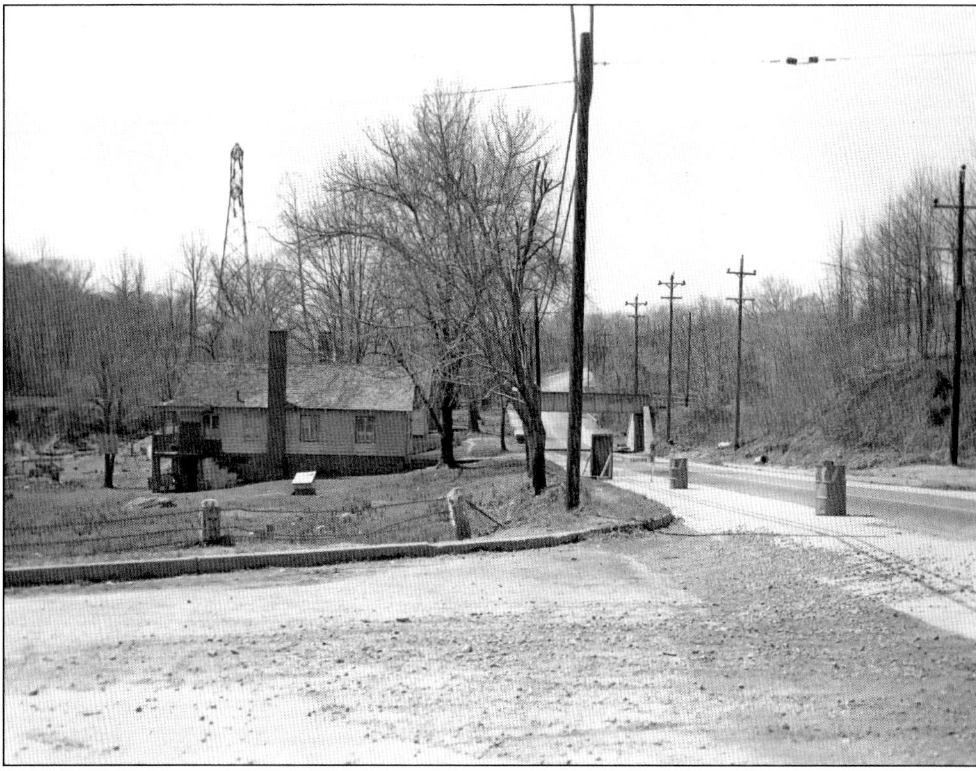

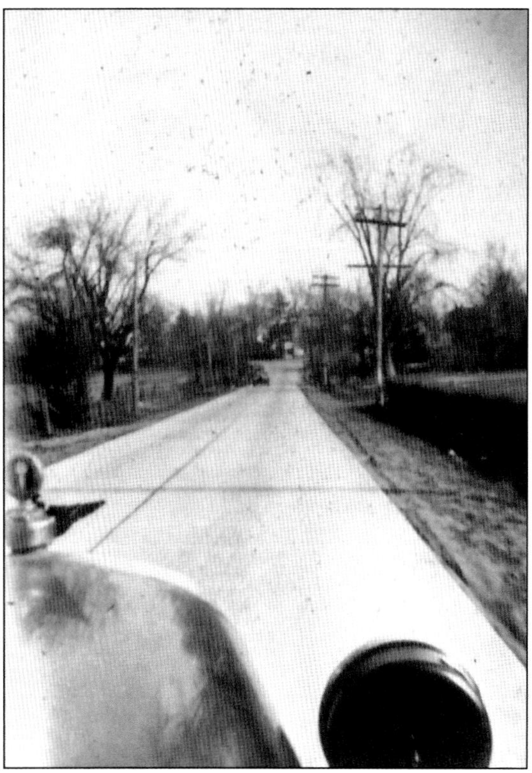

This photograph looks south on Baltimore Pike at Valley Road about 1962. The bridge carries the railroad over Baltimore Pike. The buildings on the left were tenant houses for Wawa Dairy Farm workers and staff. Among the residents was the driver for Miss Dorothea Wood, the youngest daughter of George Wood, founder of Wawa Dairy Farm. Miss Dorothea, who never married, lived just beyond the railroad bridge on Forge Hill Farm. (Hagley.)

This view was taken around 1920 from an automobile driving southeast on Middletown Road toward the intersection of Pennell and Barren Roads. The Lima Store is ahead in the distance, where Middletown Road curves to the left. The Lima School House is just beyond the picture to the right, between the two telephone poles. On the hood ornament of the car is a thermostat to make sure the radiator is not overheating.

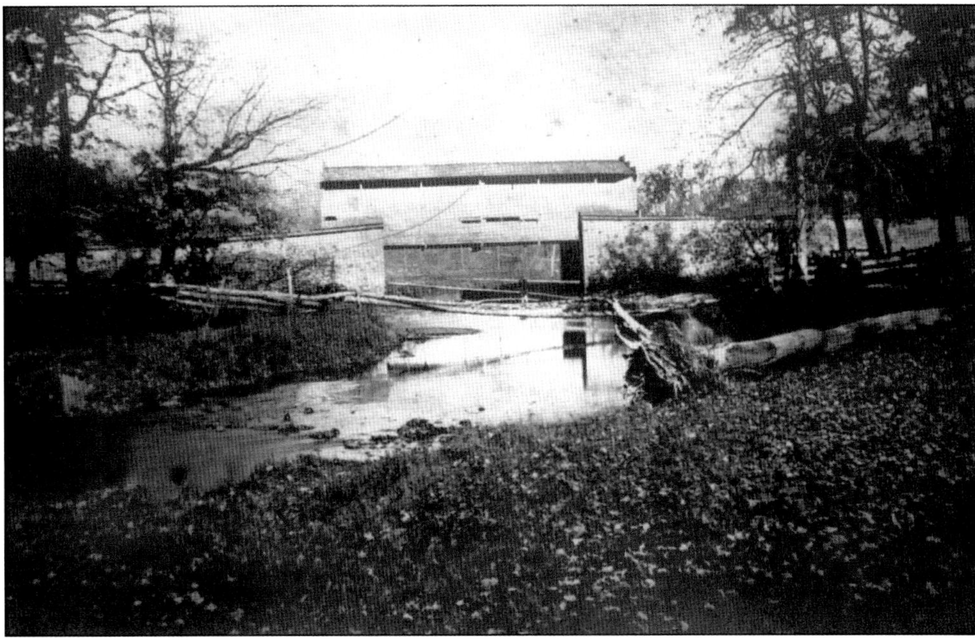

The 1880s photograph above includes the covered bridge that carried Baltimore Pike over Ridley Creek. It was replaced with a concrete bridge in 1915. Below is Palmer's Dam on the west side of Ridley Creek; the covered bridge is visible on the left edge. The dam was created to hold water for the mills on the west bank of the creek south of the bridge. A gristmill was built there in 1701. By 1775, Isaac Levis was operating a paper mill there. His paper was of high quality and in demand by printers in Philadelphia. Benjamin Franklin stayed at the Pineapple Tavern when he came to buy paper from the Levis Mills. The mills were destroyed in the great flood of 1843 and never rebuilt. Palmer's Dam was used to cut ice into the 20th century. In 1893, the Palmers charged 35¢ per week to deliver five pounds of ice each day. (Keith Lockhart.)

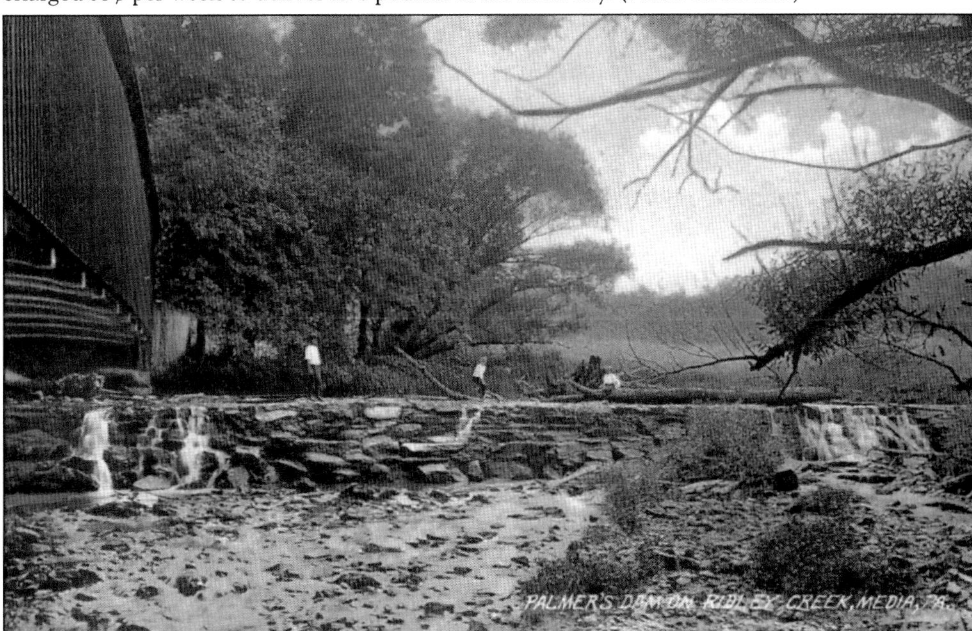

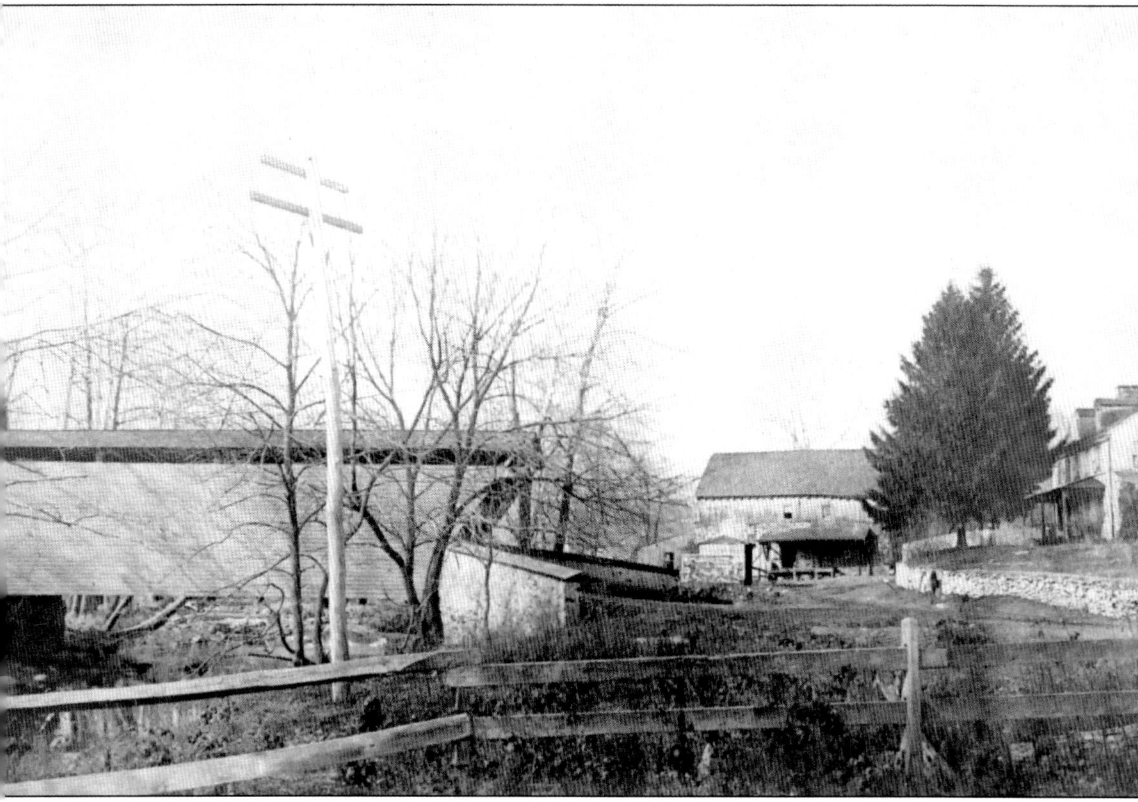

The Long Bridge crosses Ridley Creek where Barren Road meets Bishop Hollow Road. The mill town of Sycamore Mills grew here at the intersection of three different townships—Middletown, Edgemont, and Upper Providence. This c. 1900 photograph was taken on the Upper Providence side, looking north. The mill owner's house is to the right of the tree, and the gristmill is to the left. The mills were all on the Upper Providence side and the workers' cottages were in Middletown and Edgemont. In 1718, when the Edge family built the first mill here, a gristmill, the area was called Providence Mills. Over the next 150 years, a sawmill, a slitting mill, a rolling mill, a nail factory, a blacksmith, and a wheelwright shop were added to the complex. New owners in 1868 changed the name to Sycamore Mills. The first bridge was built in 1763 about 100 feet south of the present concrete bridge that was built in 1927. (Keith Lockhart.)

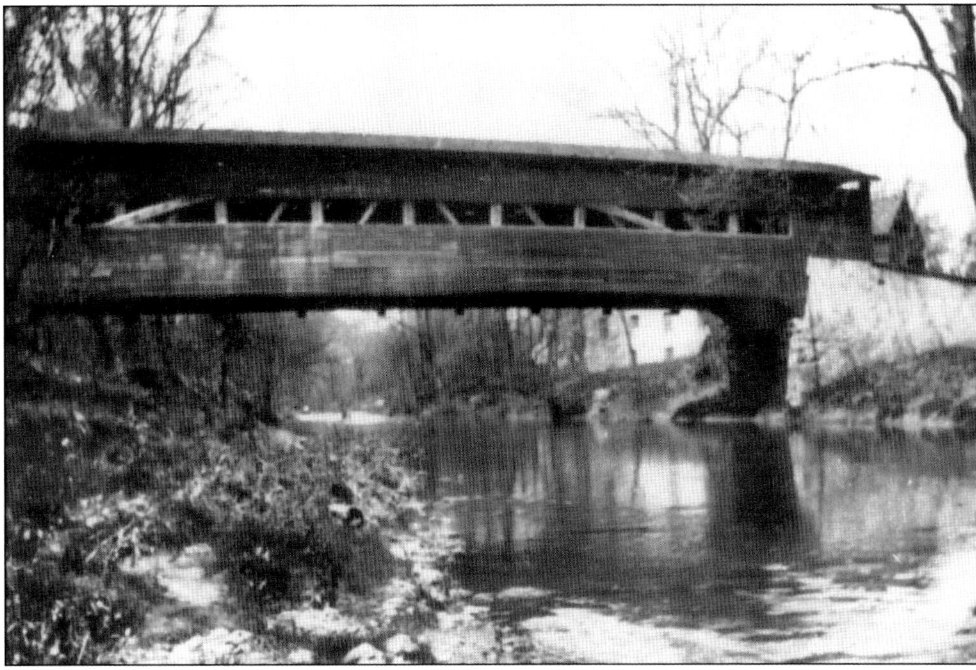

This is the bridge over Chester Creek at Dutton Mill Road just before it was replaced with a concrete bridge in 1923. The beautiful Carpenter Gothic house, visible though the bridge in the 1918 photograph below, is still there and was recently beautifully restored to all its Victorian glory. Dutton's Mill was to the left of the bridge along the west bank of the creek, just within the Middletown Township line. In 1687, Thomas Coburn built a gristmill here. A stone mill replaced Coburn's log structure in 1750. In 1775, Nicholas Fairlamb bought the mill. Later a boulting mill (for sifting flour) and a sawmill were added. All the mills were washed away in the flood of 1843, but a new mill was built in 1844. In 1880, the Dutton family owned and operated the mill. (Below, Keith Lockhart.)

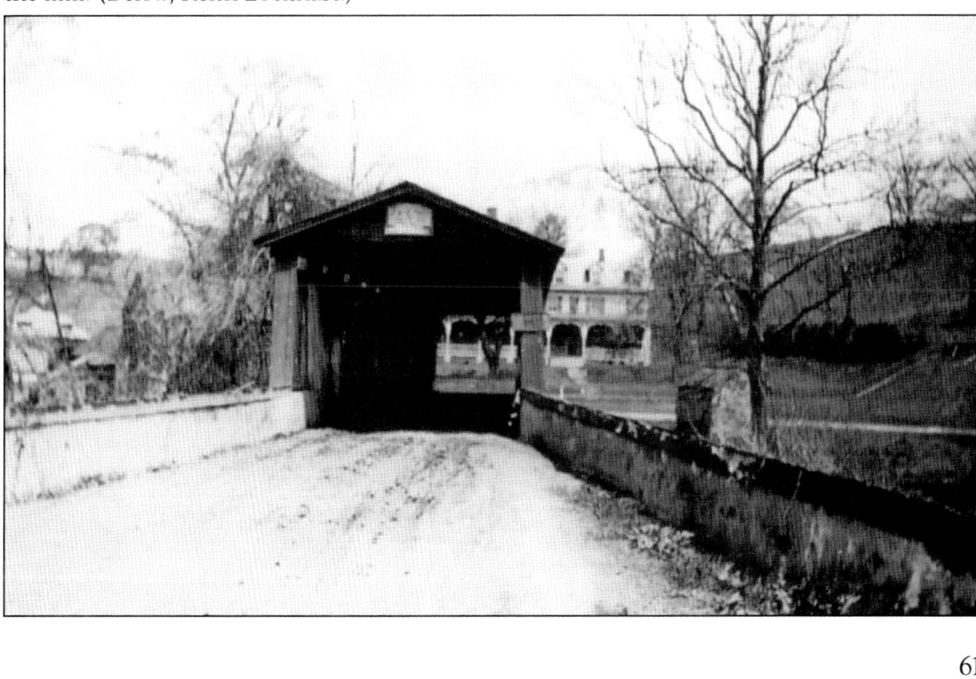

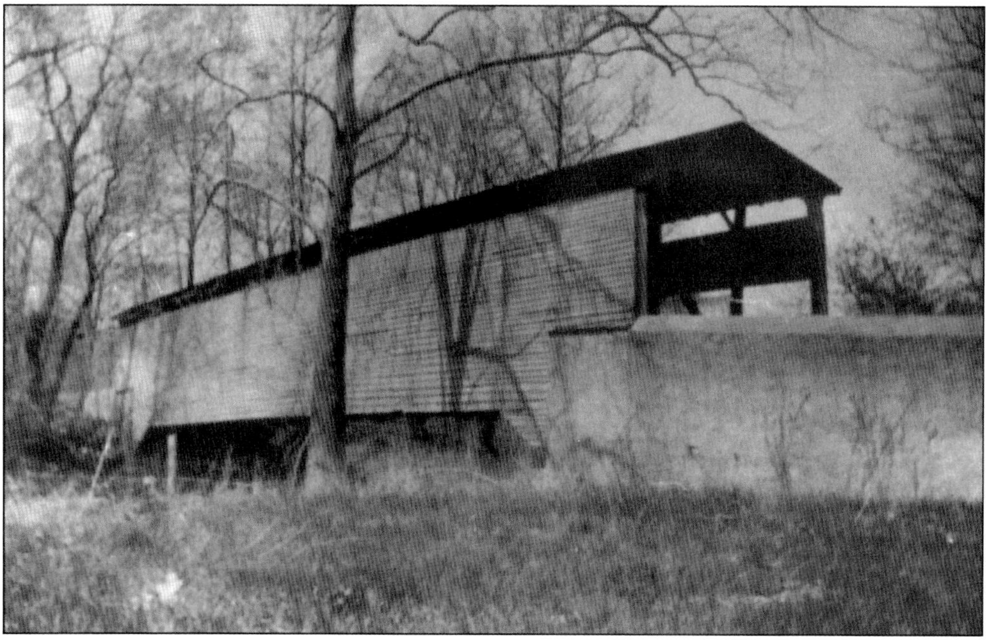

Pictured above is the bridge across Chester Creek at Mount Alverno Road around 1920. It was replaced with a concrete bridge in 1925. The Colonial Quakers had a saying that one should not cross a creek to "marry, market, or go to meeting." Early in the 18th century, before a bridge was built here, this area was known as Presbyterian Ford. The Presbyterians who worked at the mills in Aston Township crossed here to go to Middletown Presbyterian Church near Elwyn. Founded in 1729, it was the first Presbyterian congregation in Delaware County. The photograph below shows a ford still on Chester Creek in the late 19th century. Notice the wagon-wheel ruts in the dirt road. It was unusual for fords to have pedestrian footbridges. This fellow was lucky: most people had to get their feet wet. (Below, DCHS.)

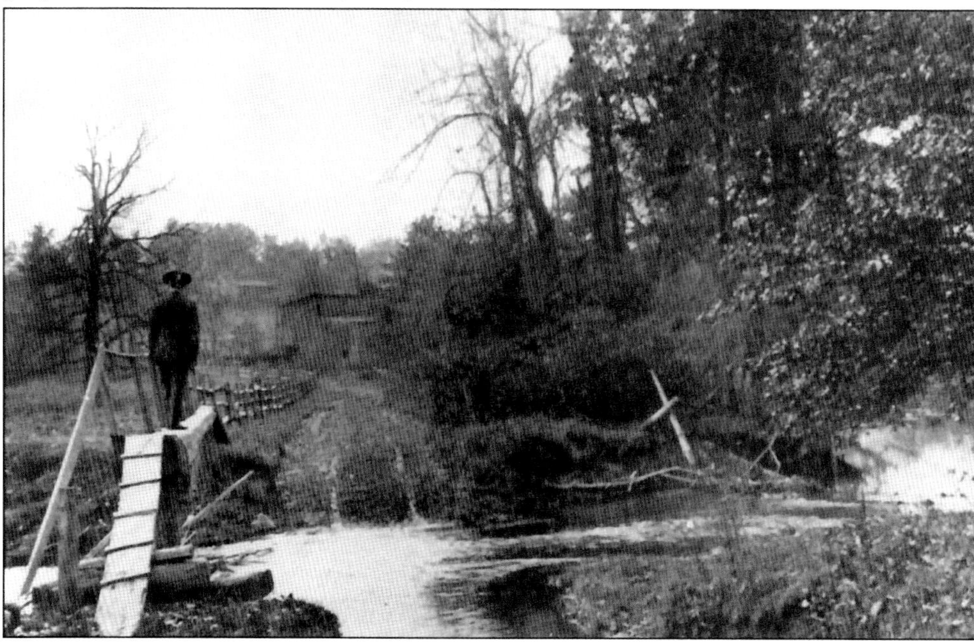

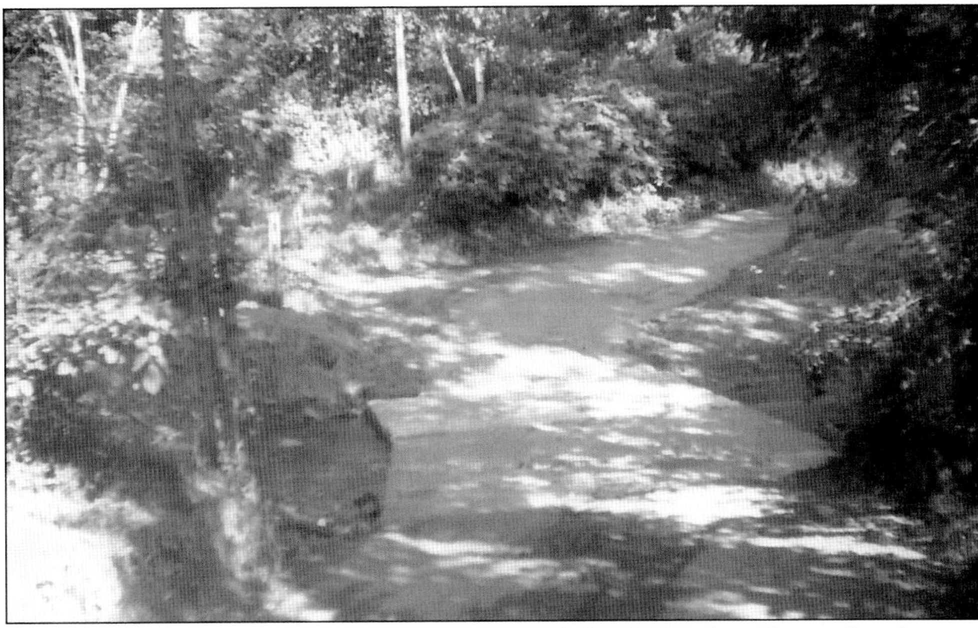

Until the late 1970s, there was still a ford on Howarth Road (above) at Chrome Run between Glen Riddle and Mount Alverno Roads. It was necessary to walk or drive through a shallow run of water unless it was very dry. The stream is now channeled into pipes under the roadbed, but when the water is high, it still runs over the road. Chrome Run gets its name from a chrome mine that was opened on Jesse Hibberd's farm in about 1856 and closed in 1876. It is now on the grounds of Williamson School. Below, in 1979, Alexander Wilson shows the remains of the chrome mine. About 500 feet of ditch was visible then, but the chrome pits had been filled in. Other minerals mined in Middletown in the 19th century include iron ore, serpentine, mica, amethyst, and brick clay.

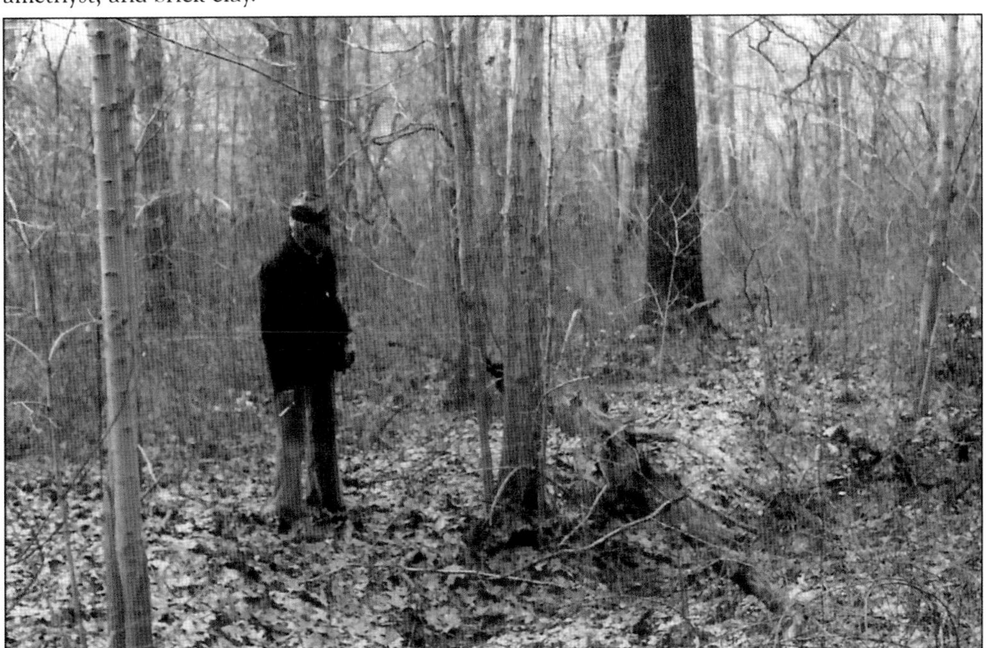

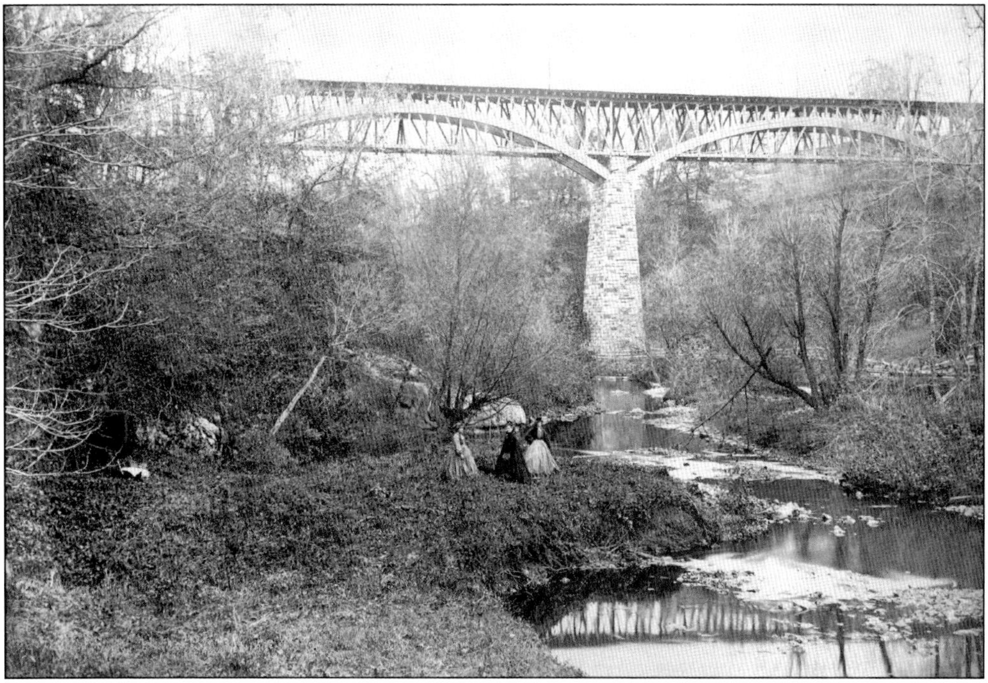

The West Chester and Philadelphia Railroad was chartered in 1848. Construction began in Philadelphia in 1852 and reached Kellyville (Gladstone) in November 1853 and Media in November 1854. In July 1855, while building the high bridge over Ridley Creek, five workmen fell 110 feet to the creek when part of the bridge gave way; three of the men died. The high cost of so much bridge construction across streams and deep cuts to maintain grade among the many hills and valleys caused financial difficulties. Work was suspended until 1856, when the line opened to Grubb's Bridge (Wawa). The remaining section to West Chester was completed in November 1858. The photograph above was taken on the east bank of Ridley Creek in 1868. The photograph below, from the other side of the creek in 1891, shows the second bridge, which was built in the 1880s. (Below, Keith Lockhart.)

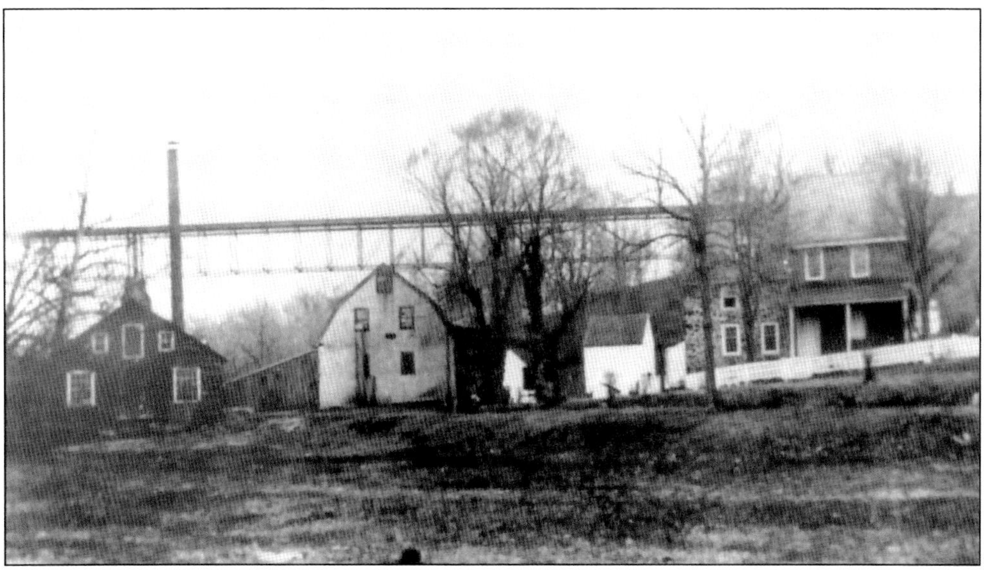

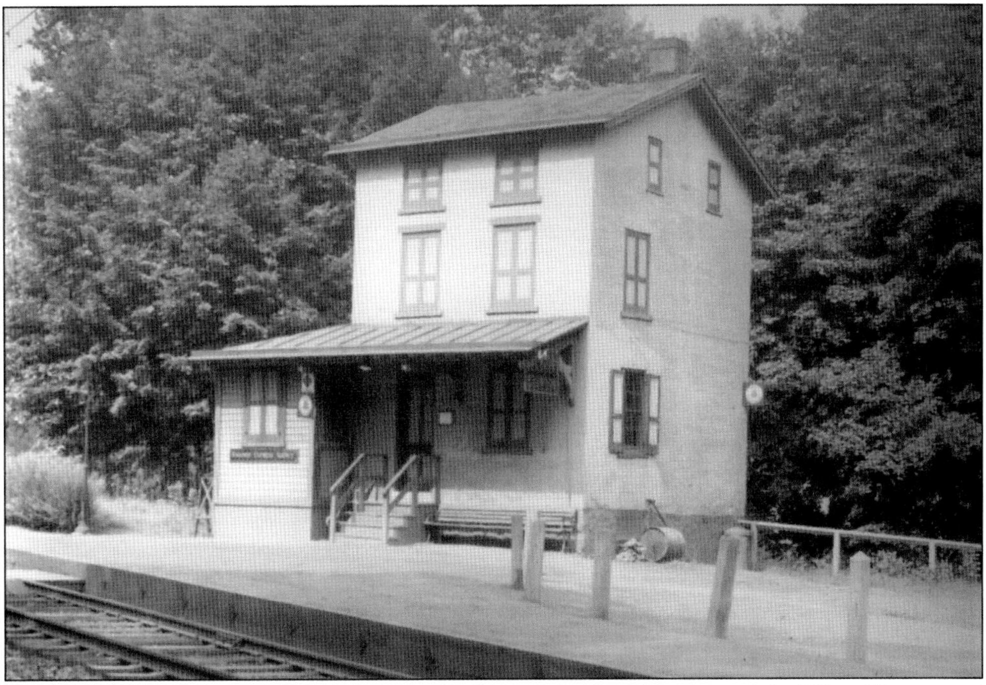

In 1880, the Philadelphia, Wilmington and Baltimore Railroad purchased the West Chester and Philadelphia Railroad and in 1881 consolidated it into the Philadelphia and Baltimore Central Railroad. All these lines were controlled by the Pennsylvania Railroad. Prior to this sale, the first stop in Middletown had been called Greenwood. There was no station building there until 1880, when the stop was renamed Elwyn (above). The path of the railroad ran due west across Middletown Township to Lenni and then turned northwest running along Chester Creek on its way to West Chester. The builders of the line knew that the mill owners and farmers along the creek were anxious to receive raw materials and to ship their products by rail. The train below is running east toward Elwyn Station, past the Hiram Schofield farmhouse on the future site of Williamson School. (Both, Keith Lockhart.)

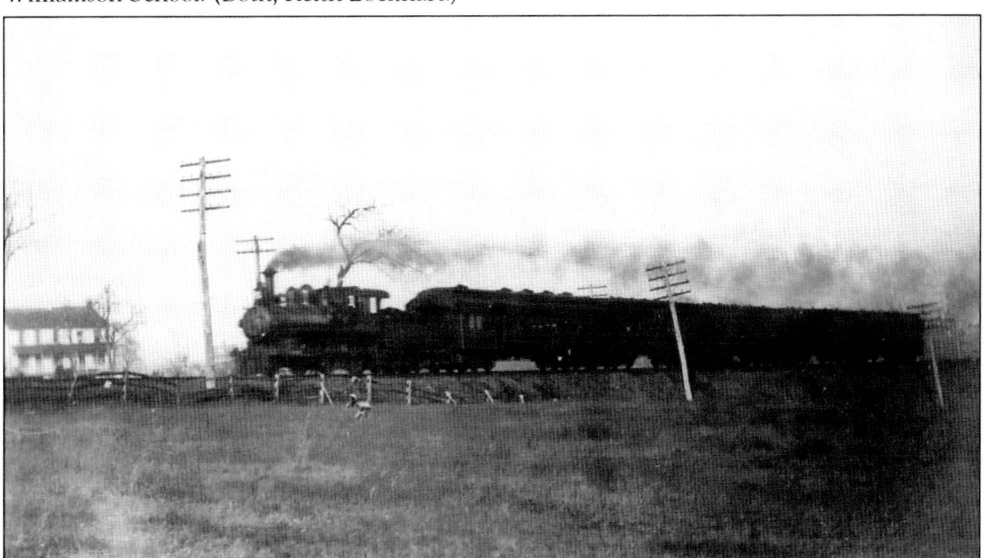

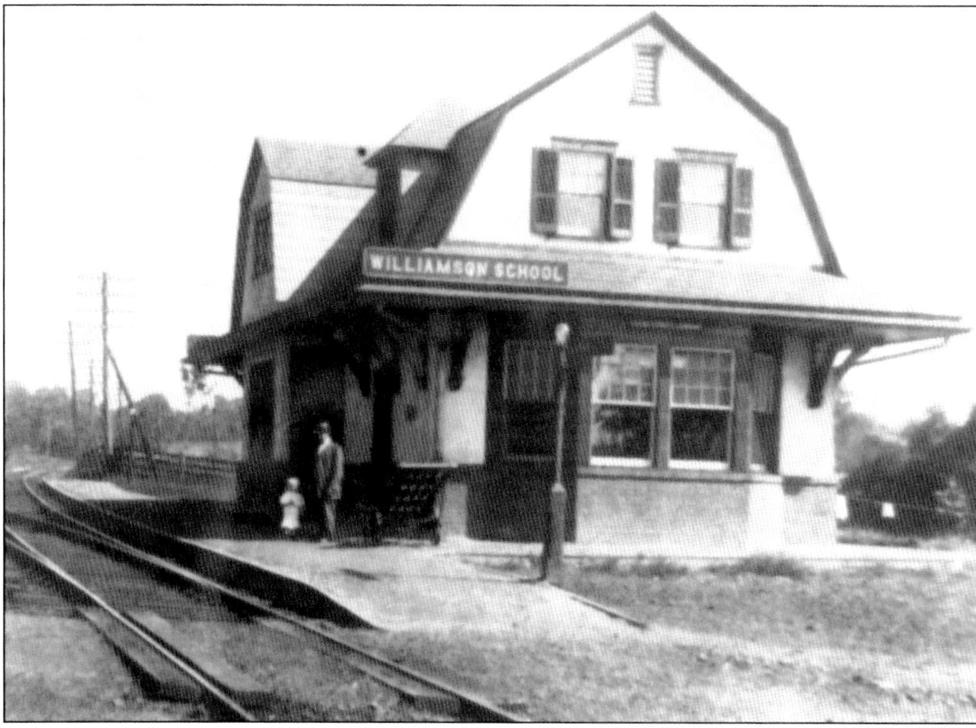

From the 1950s to the 1980s, rail service in America declined. Regular service was discontinued from Elwyn to West Chester in 1986. The Williamson School Station (above) was not on the original line; the stop was added in 1891 when the school opened. Clara Naglee and her father, the first and only ticket agent at the Williamson Station, are seen here in 1909. The tracks of the spur curving to the left were used to take coal to the powerhouse at Williamson School. The Glen Riddle Station (below) was in a grade cut north of Glen Riddle Road and east of Pennell Road on the south side of the tracks. This photograph from around 1910 looks west. The bridge carries Pennell Road over the tracks. The Glen Riddle Station building burned down in 1983.

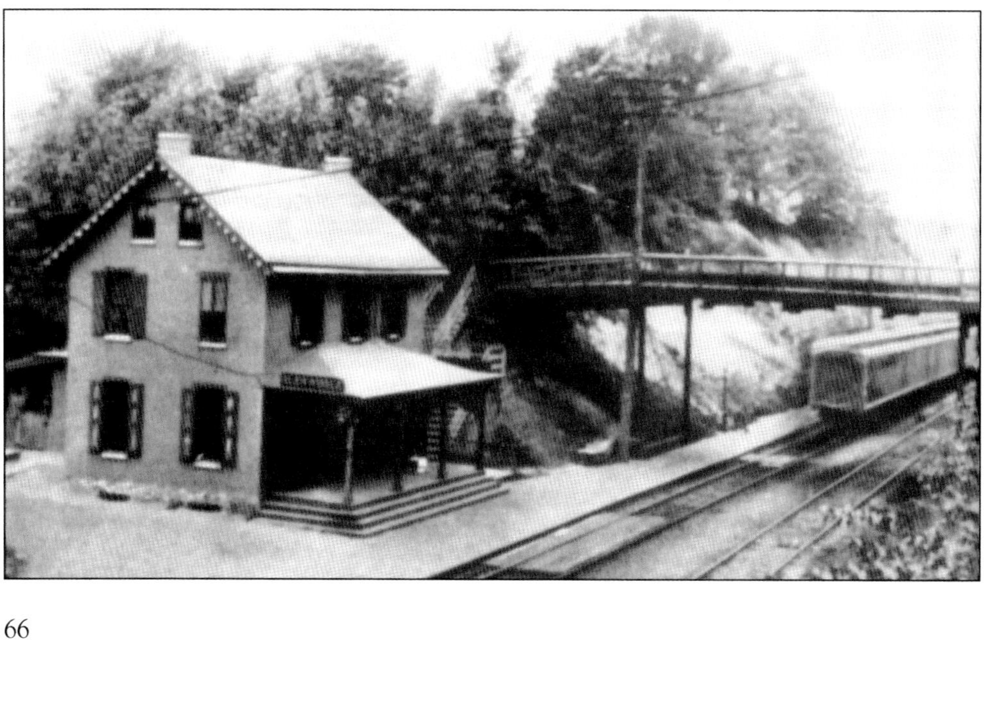

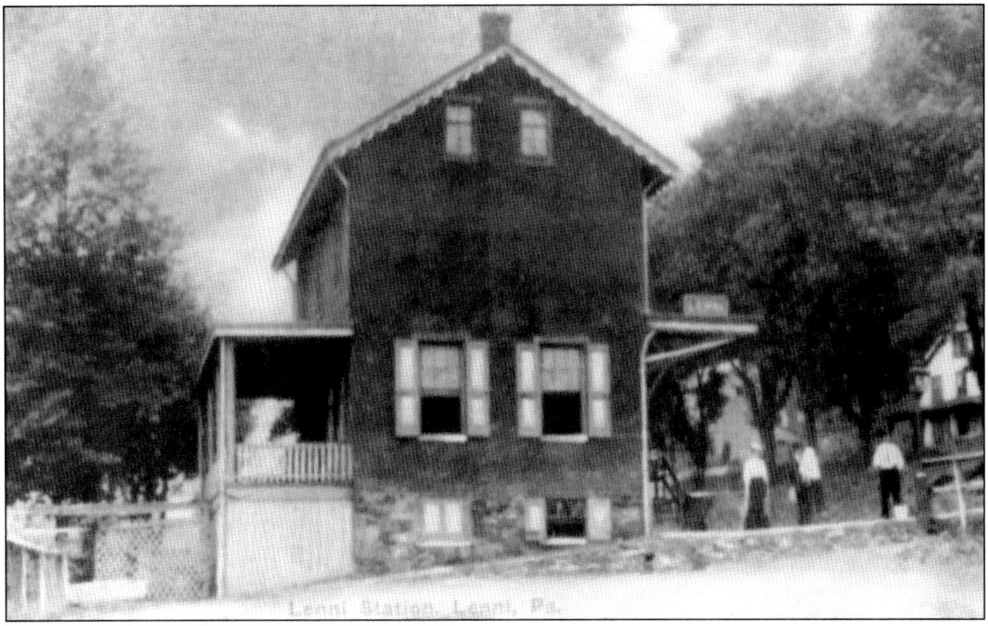

Both Lenni Station, above about 1910, and Wawa Station, below about 1890, were the locations of spur lines. Beginning in 1869, the Chester Creek Branch railroad ran from Chester to Lenni with two additional stations in Middletown—Presbyterian Ford/Mount Alverno and Knowlton Station. In 1972, the Chester Creek Branch sustained severe damage from flooding associated with Hurricane Agnes and was never rebuilt. The Philadelphia and Baltimore Central Railroad's Octoraro Branch (the tracks curving to the left in the photograph below) ran from Wawa to Octoraro Junction, Maryland. The line started construction in 1855 in Concordville, opening from Wawa to Chadds Ford in 1859. It reached Oxford, Pennsylvania, in 1860, Rising Sun, Maryland, in 1865, and Octoraro Junction in 1868. The Pennsylvania Railroad abandoned the Octoraro Branch south of Colora, Maryland, in 1961. In 1972, Hurricane Agnes's floods made the line unusable north of the Brandywine Creek.

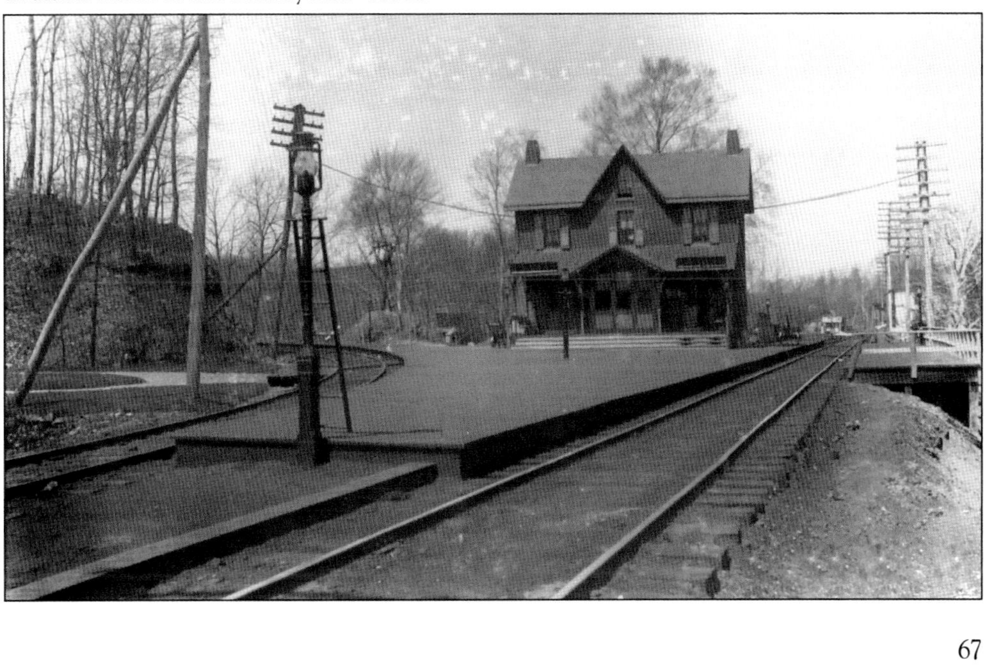

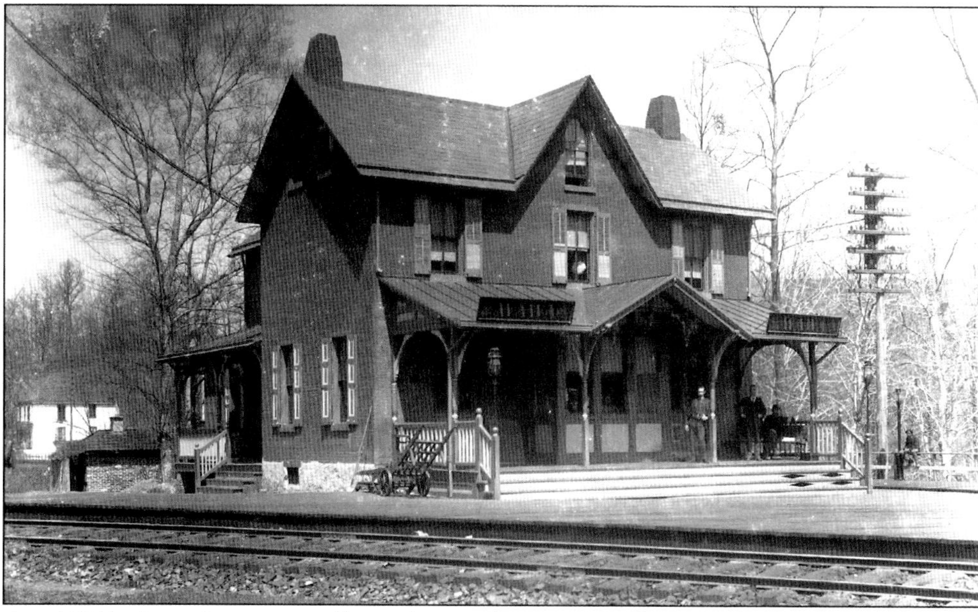

As of 2011, the only station still standing is the one at Williamson, but plans are to return Southeastern Pennsylvania Transportation Authority (SEPTA) Regional Rail service across Middletown in the near future with the construction of a new station and 600-space parking garage at Wawa. The current single track will become a double track. Track bed stabilization and reconstruction are currently underway, including the replacement of three bridges and the rehabilitation of a fourth.

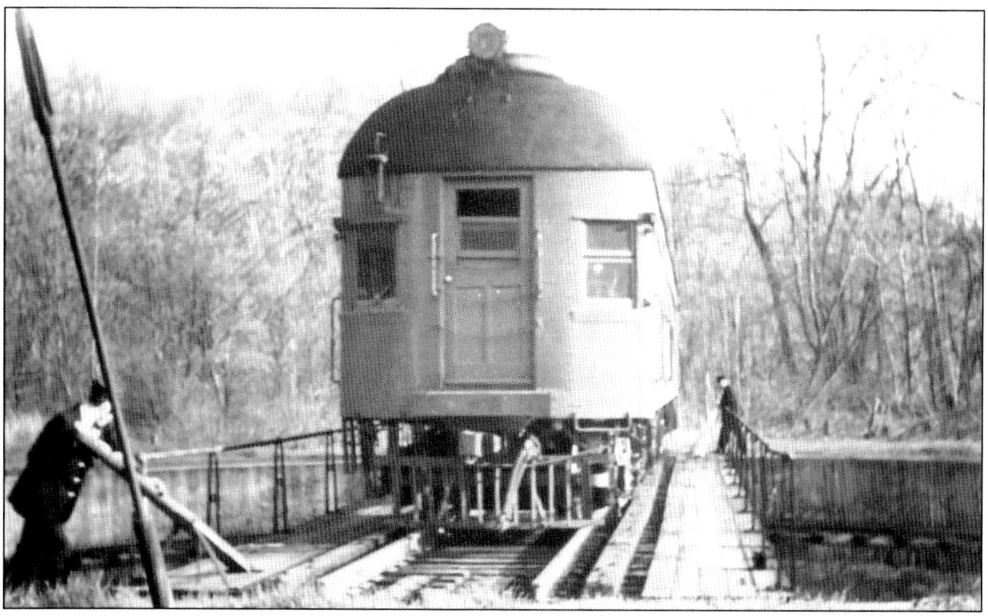

Self-propelled gas-electric rail cars like this one were commonly called "Doodle Bugs." By the 1920s, the gas-electric car had become one of the main providers of branch-line rail service, replacing steam-driven locomotives on short stretches. This one ran on the Octoraro Branch, making two roundtrips a day from Wawa to Oxford six days a week. The motormen are turning the car around on the manual turntable at Wawa.

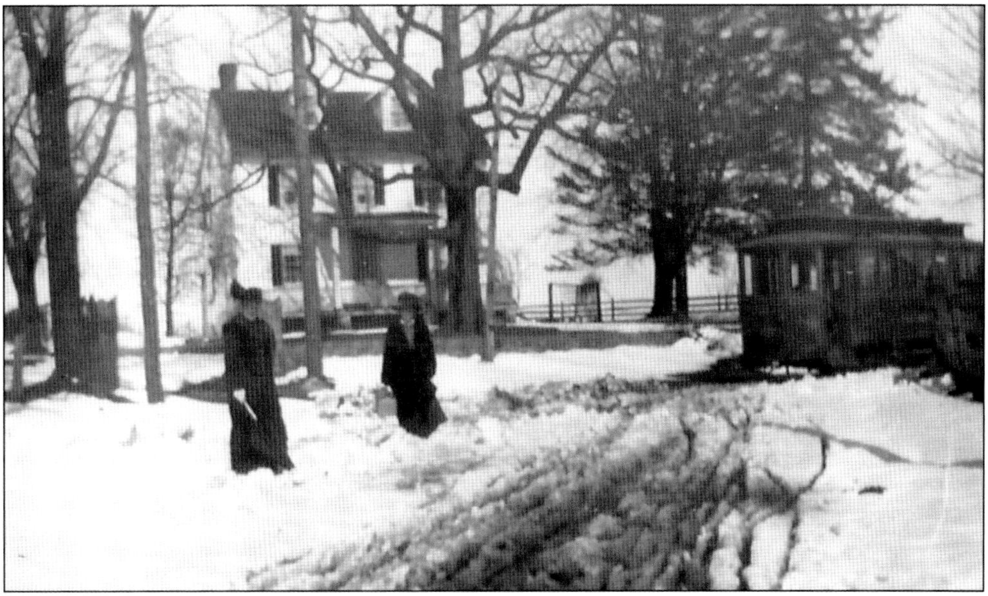

Two trolley lines ran through Middletown. The "Glen Riddle" trolley was organized in 1893 as the Media, Middletown, Aston, and Chester Electric Railway Company. It crossed Ridley Creek on a trestle by Baltimore Pike, ran southwest on Elwyn Road, and turned northwest onto Middletown Road to Pennell Road, where it turned and ran south to the top of the hill at Glen Riddle Station. In April 1901, the line was reorganized as the Media, Glen Riddle, and Rockdale Electric Street Railway Company and reopened in 1903. In 1910, it was known as the Delaware County Division of the Southern Pennsylvania Traction Company. The line was abandoned in August 1930. The trolley above is on Middletown Road at Rose Tree Road. Below, the trolley is on south Pennell Road by the Ivison house. (Both, MHAC.)

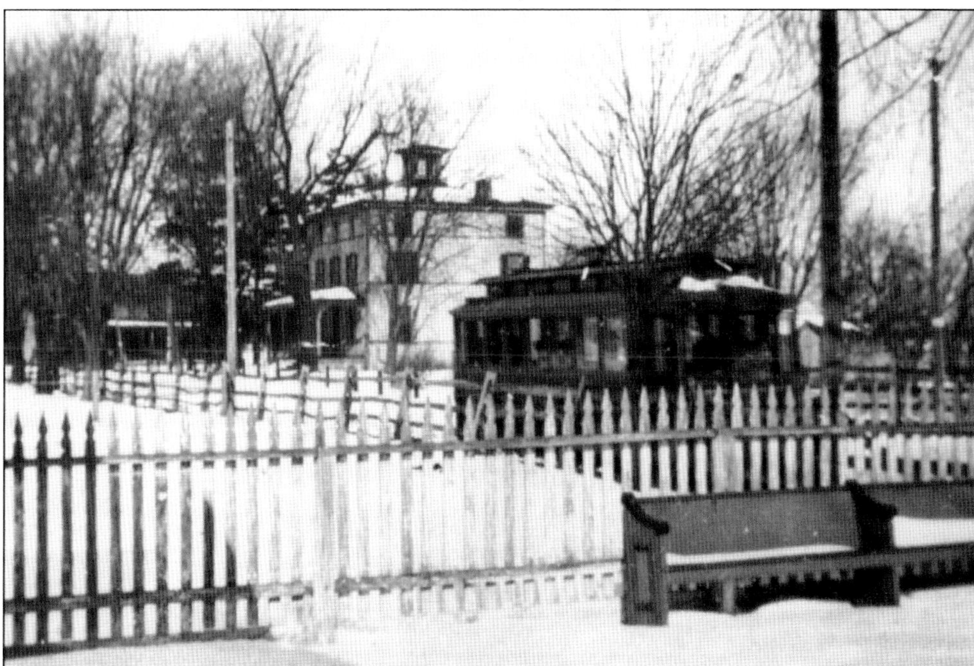

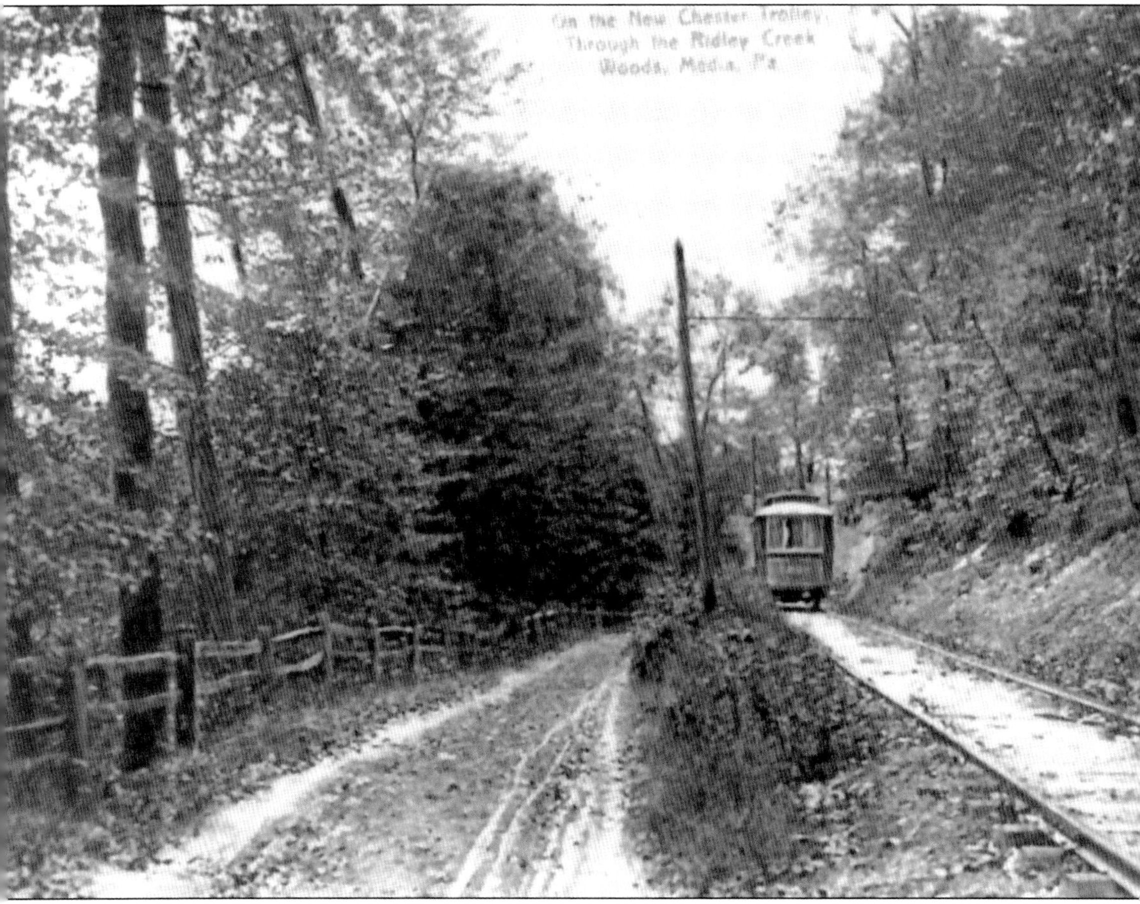

The second trolley line in Middletown was the Philadelphia Rapid Transit Company's Route 77. It ran out Middletown Road from Chester, turned northeast on Bortondale Road, then northwest on Ridley Creek Road and north on Orange Street into Media. The first half of the line opened in January 1901 from Chester to Wells' Corner, which was at the intersection of Old Middletown and Bortondale Roads. Bortondale Road would not become a public thoroughfare until after 1910. The trolley leased the right-of-way from Samuel Wells, whose farm ran northeast as far as Ridley Creek. The second half of the line was opened from Wells' Corner to Media in April 1905. The photograph above was taken at the Middletown end of the bridge crossing Ridley Creek at the end of Orange Street. Residents living on this line who needed a prescription filled could give their money to the motormen. They would have it filled at the Ellis Drug Store, at the end of the line, and bring it back on the return from Media. (MHAC.)

Six

Founding Families

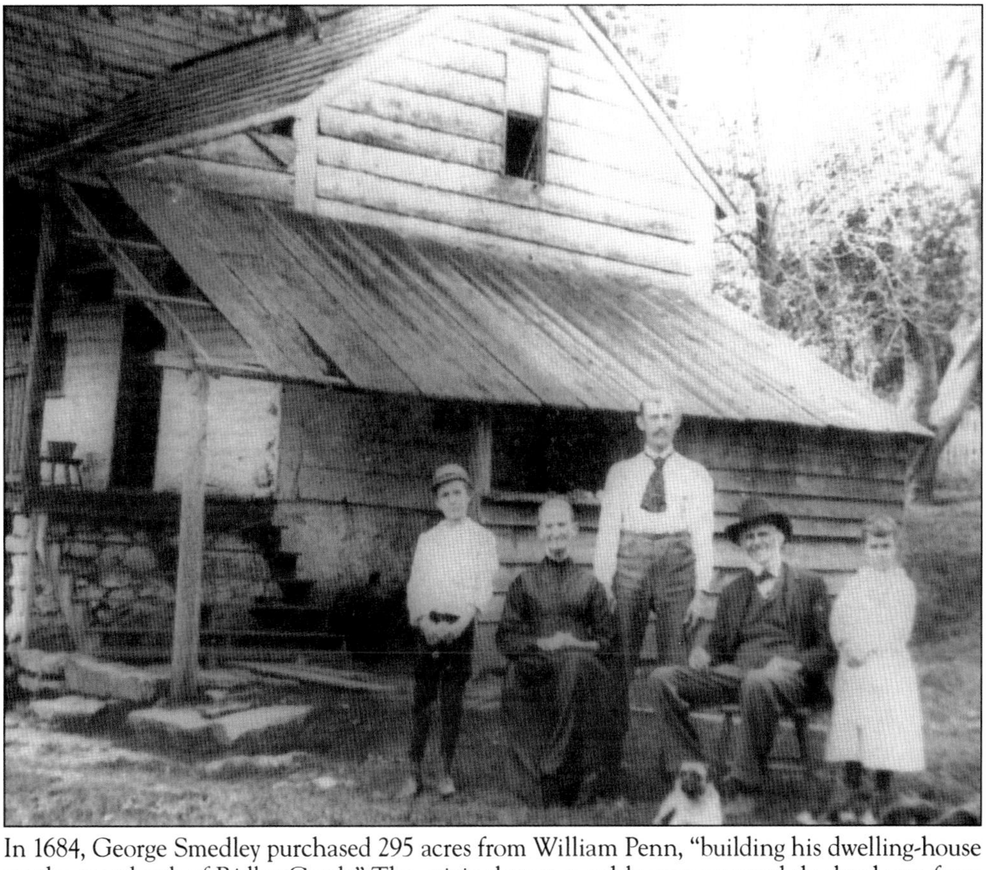

In 1684, George Smedley purchased 295 acres from William Penn, "building his dwelling-house on the west bank of Ridley Creek." The original tract roughly encompassed the land east from Ridley Creek, north from Baltimore Pike, and south from Dismal Run to the western point where Dismal Run meets Middletown Road. This is the John Smedley family in 1895 on their Painter Road farm.

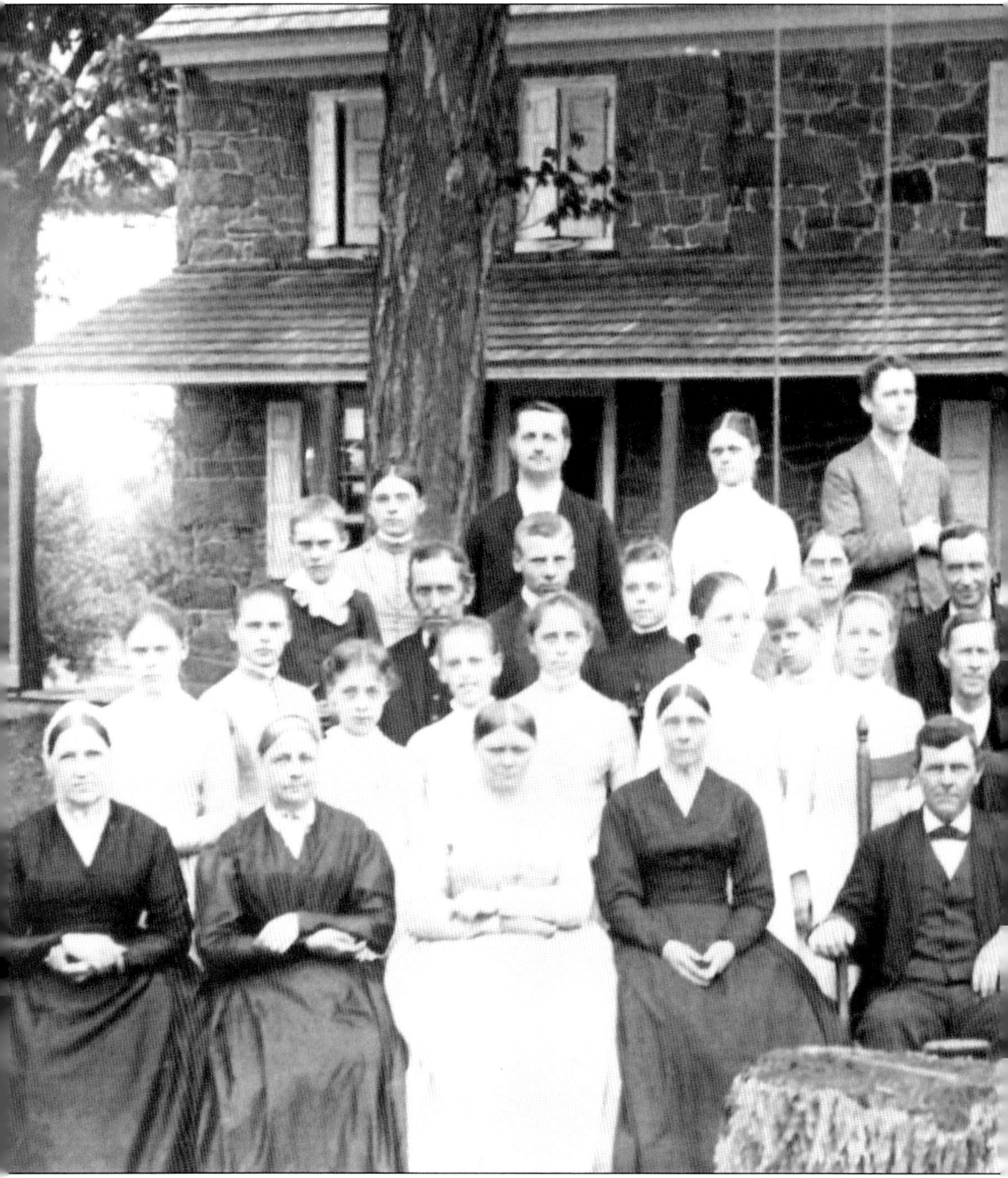

Descendants of George Smedley gather in 1888 at the William Smedley Homestead, Penncrest Farm, on Rose Tree Road at Middletown Road. The house still stands and is occupied by members of the Smedley family. Pictured here are, from left to right, (first row, seated) Philena Y. Smedley, Deborah C. Smedley, Deborah S. Allen, Rebecca Smedley, Edward G. Smedley, Elizabeth Sharpless Smedley, Ellis Smedley, Sarah Hinkson Smedley, Mary Lang Smedley, and Ruth Lite Smedley; (second row) Lydia G. Allen, Mary S. Allen, Deborah Smedley, Elizabeth Allen, Caroline R. Allen, Emily C. Smedley, Mabel C. Webster, Susanna Smedley, Jacob Smedley, Elizabeth T. Yarnall,

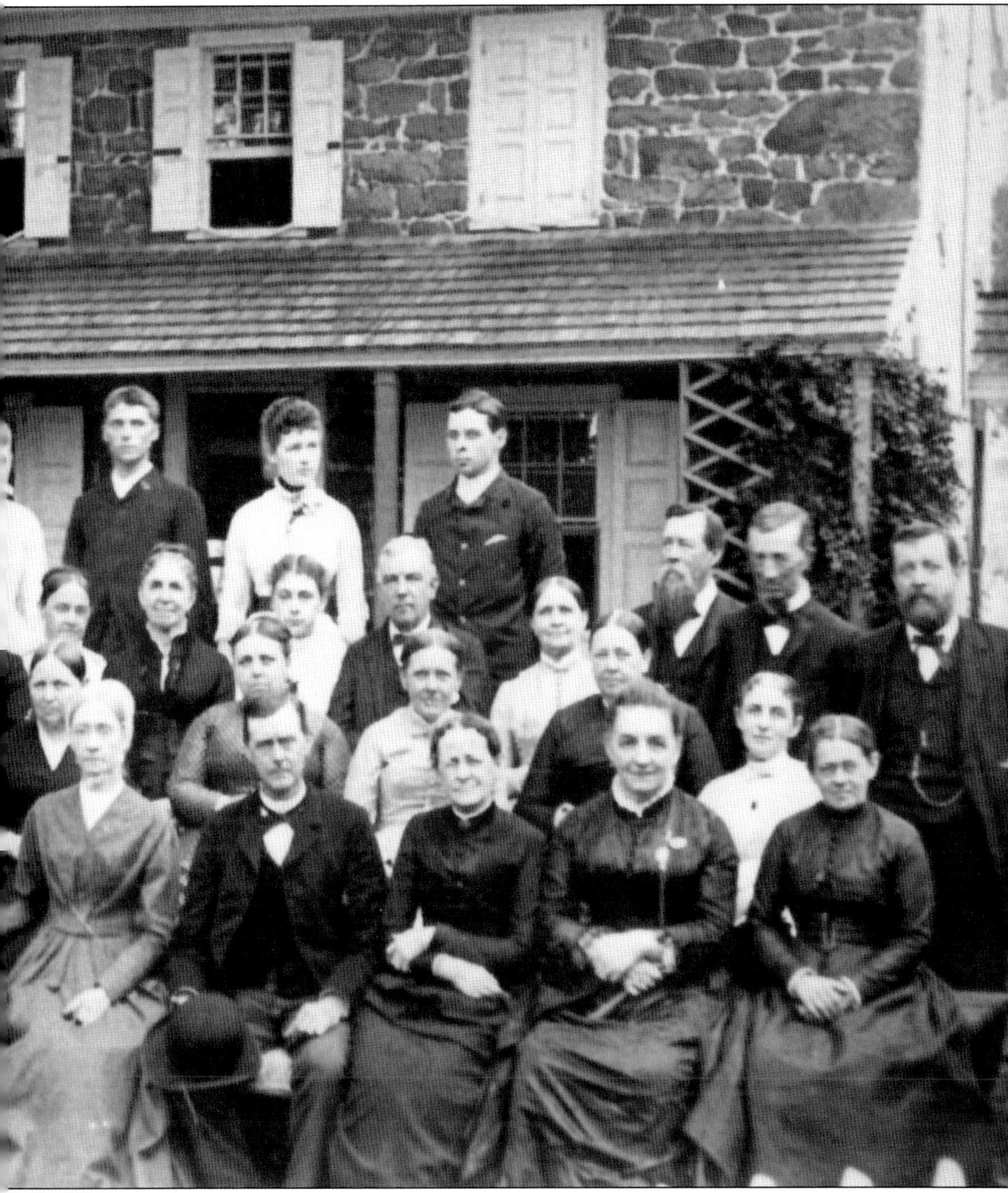

Hannah P. Smedley, Sarah Allen Smedley, Lydia S Webster, and Emma Cope; (third row) Clement E. Allen, George B. Allen, Edward Smedley, Emma Smedley, Jane Garrett Smedley, William P. Smedley, George L. Smedley, Jane H. Smedley, Josephine Cadmus, Edith Smedley, William T. Kirk, Deborah S. Kirk, Samuel L. Smedley, John H. Webster, and Bennett L. Smedley; (fourth row) Lydia H. South, Edward L. South, Harriet Smedley, Walter Smedley, Edith F. Smedley, Horace W. Smedley, Josephine L. Smedley, and Roland Smedley.

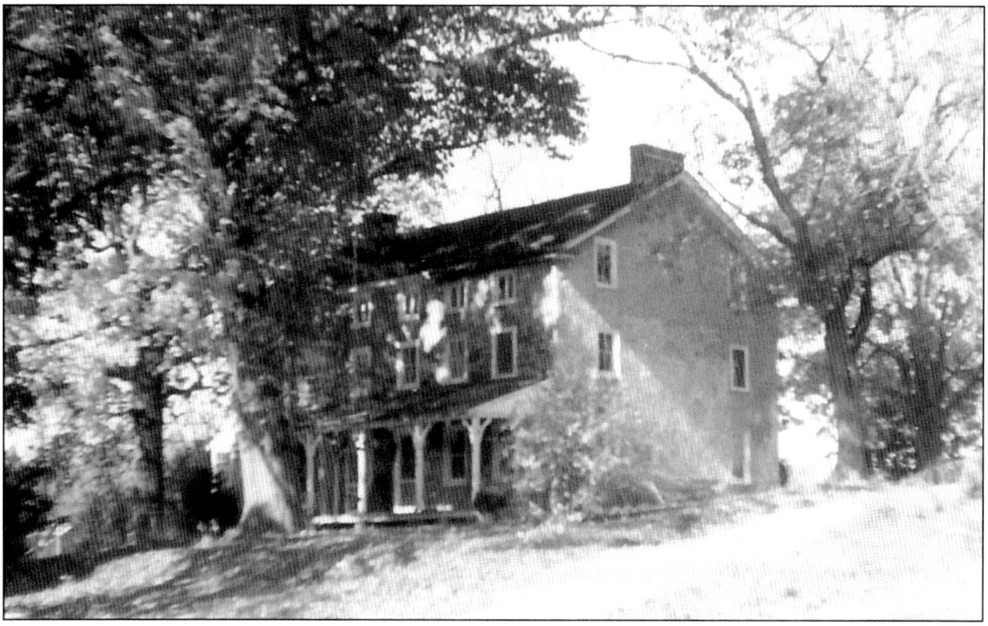

In the 18th century, this stone farmhouse north of Baltimore Pike behind the Wawa Dairy Farm plant was a single 14-by-20-foot room. It was enlarged by Abraham Pennell in 1799. He inherited the land from his father, William, who operated mills on Chester Creek. William purchased the 417-acre "Grubb tract" from Henry Grubb in 1753. Successive generations of Pennells inherited the land and made many changes and additions to the house in the 19th century, including adding a third floor, a two-story bay window, and a porch with Victorian scrollwork. In 1900, George Wood bought the house and surrounding land from the Pennell family as part of Wawa Dairy Farm. In 1980, Wawa Inc. restored the dwelling to its pre-1830 appearance to use as offices. Seen above is the front in 1890; below is the rear in 1865. (Below, Keith Lockhart.)

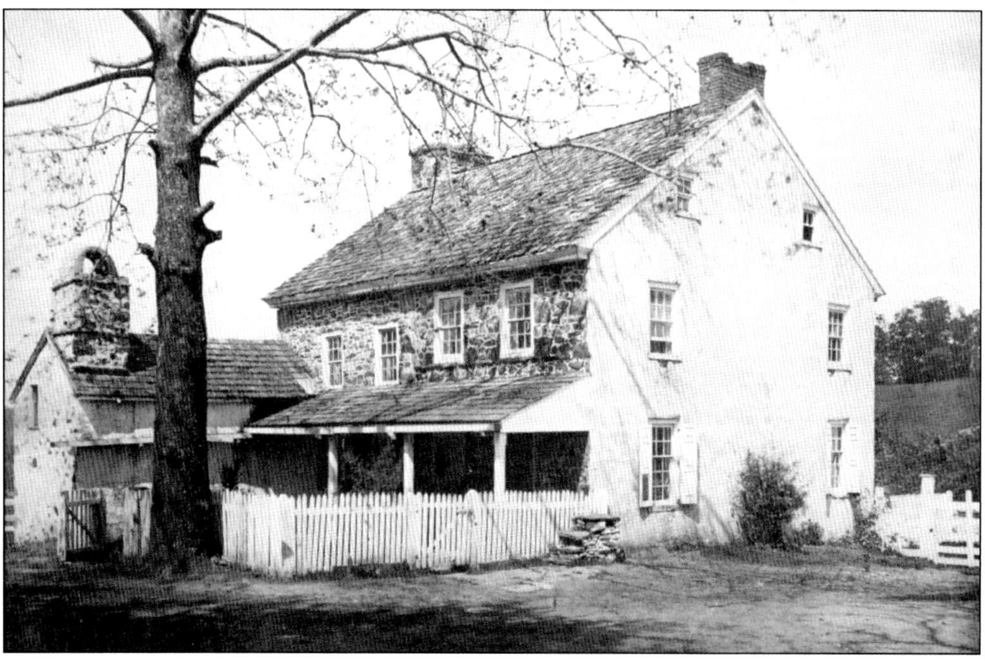

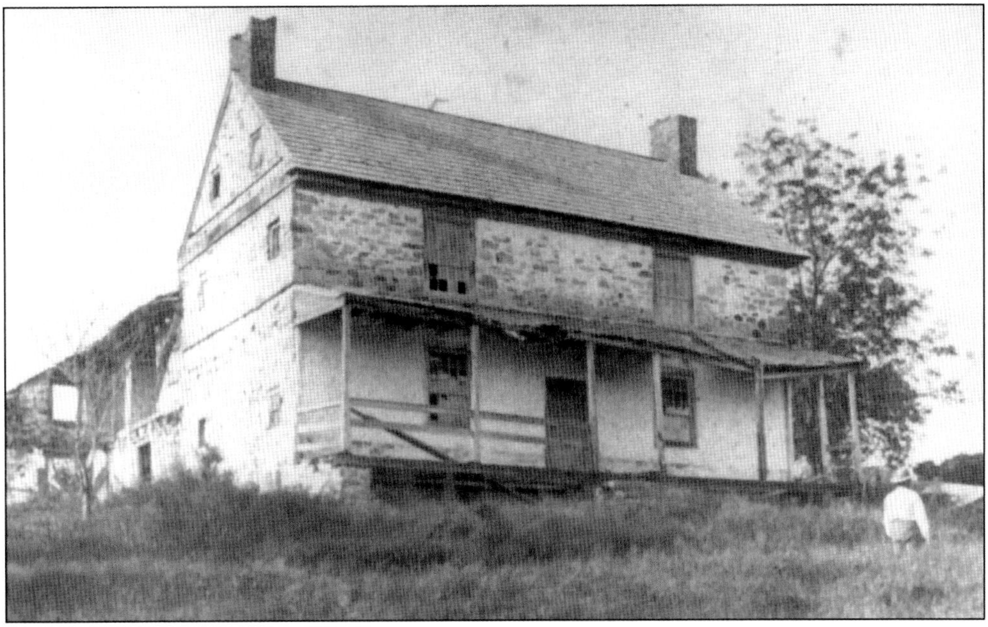

The William Pennell house, pictured above about 1865, was built around 1750 on the north side of Glen Riddle Road east of Palmer's Lane. It continues as a private residence. William owned a large tract east of the road to Pennell's Mill, now Pennell Road, and the road to Pennell's Forge, now Glen Riddle Road. In 1766, he was taxed on a sawmill and gristmill. In the 1760s, Pennell paid the highest amount of tax in the township. At his death in 1783, he owned 735 acres in Middletown. The house below, photographed in 1981, was also a longtime Pennell family residence. It stands on the south side of Baltimore Pike on land once owned by the Franklin Mint and has been vacant since 2005.

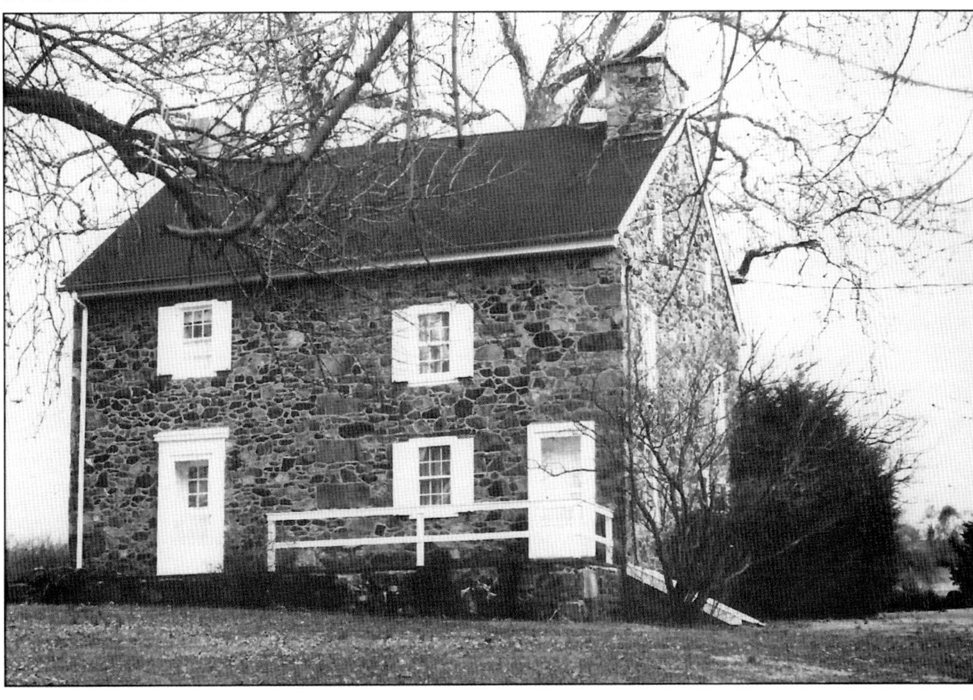

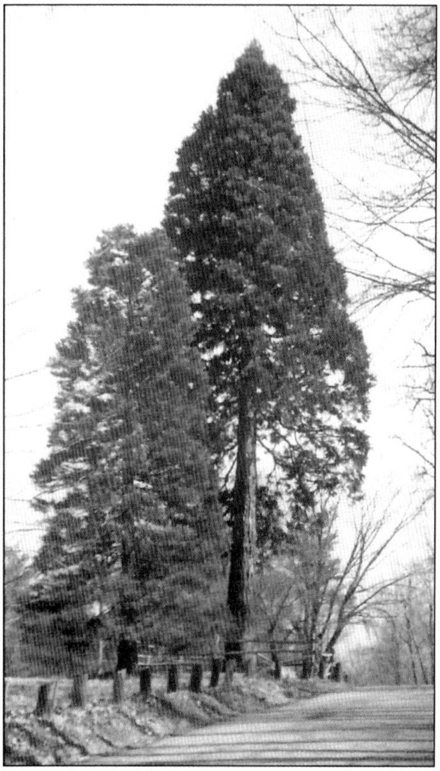

Thomas Minshall I of Lathford, Cheshire, England, received a grant of 625 acres from William Penn in 1681 that contained the site now occupied by the John J. Tyler Arboretum. Between 1681 and 1944, the property was home to eight generations of the same Minshall/Painter/Tyler family. In 1944, Laura Tyler, a direct descendant of Thomas Minshall, bequeathed the property as an arboretum, named in honor of her husband, John. Brothers Minshall Painter (1801–1873, bottom left) and Jacob Painter (1814–1876, bottom right), the creators of the arboretum, were members of the sixth generation to live on the land. In 1825, the brothers set aside some of their land to begin the systematic planting of more than 1,000 varieties of trees and shrubs. More than 20 of the original Painter plants still survive, including the giant sequoia, the majestic symbol of Tyler Arboretum. (Below, Tyler Arboretum.)

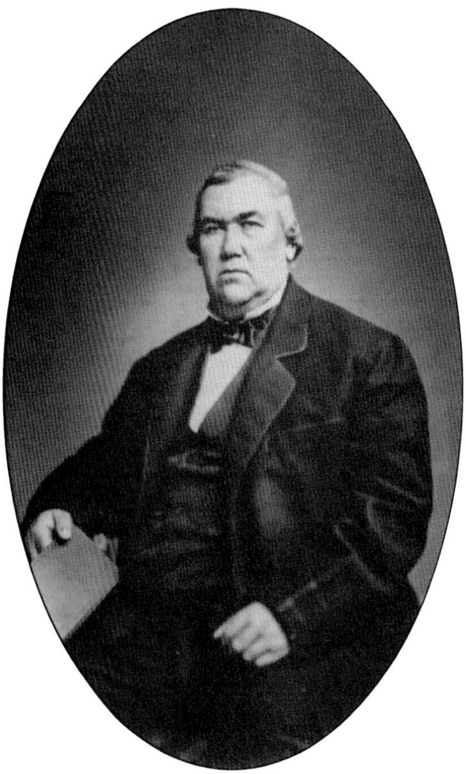

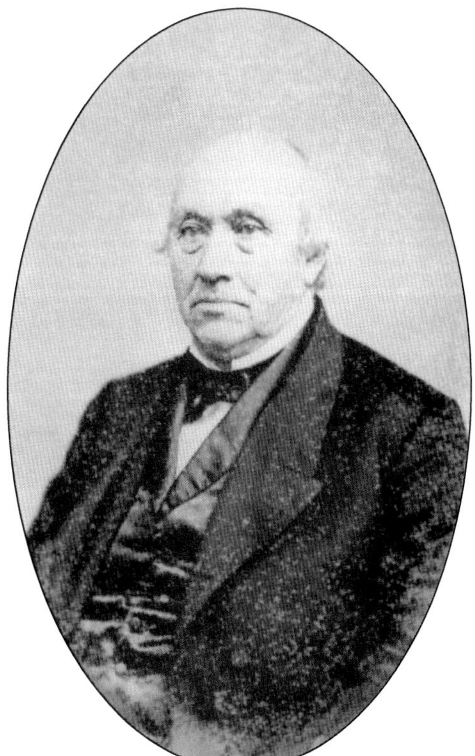

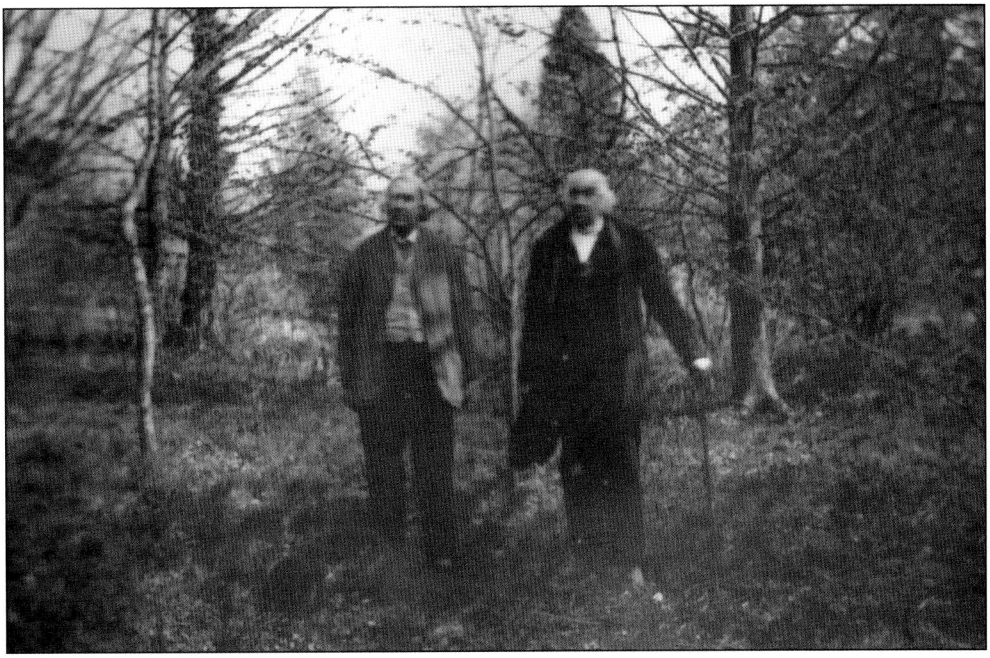

Minshall (left) and Jacob (right), are pictured above among their trees. They inherited 500 acres from their parents, Enos and Hannah Minshall Painter, and added 150 acres in their lifetimes. Enos and Hannah raised seven children in Lachford Hall, pictured below from an 1875 atlas. Thomas Minshall II built the first part of Lachford Hall in 1738. Successive generations continued to make additions. Minshall and Jacob improved the farm with a number of springhouses, smokehouses, and other structures, including the Painter Library in 1863, seen below to the left of Lachford Hall. The brothers added a number of fruit trees to their grandfather's orchard, including an orange tree that they kept in their greenhouse, built in 1849, seen on the left side of Lachford Hall. They expanded their plantings to include important specimen trees, creating the original Painter Arboretum. (Both, Tyler Arboretum.)

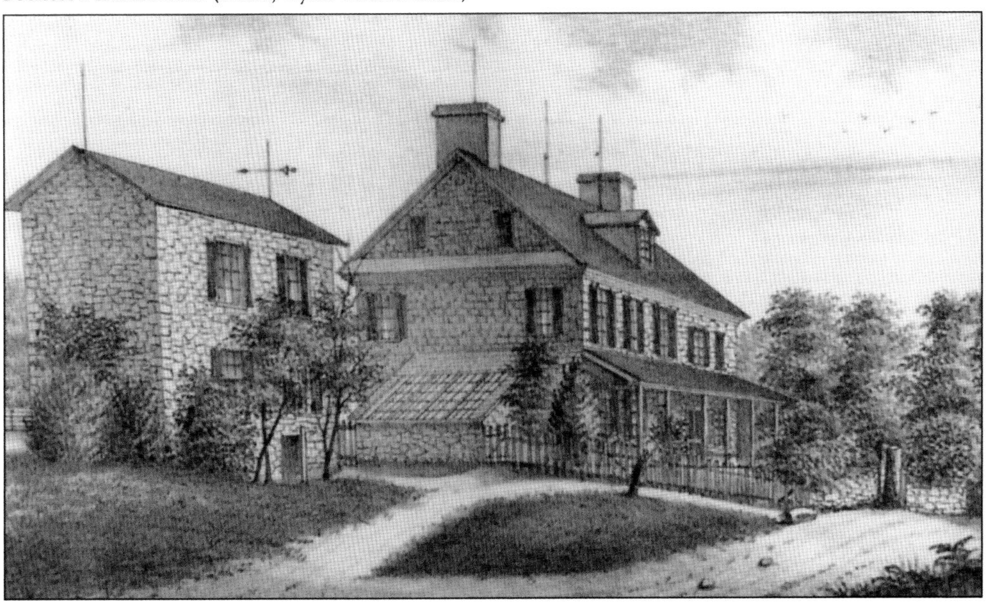

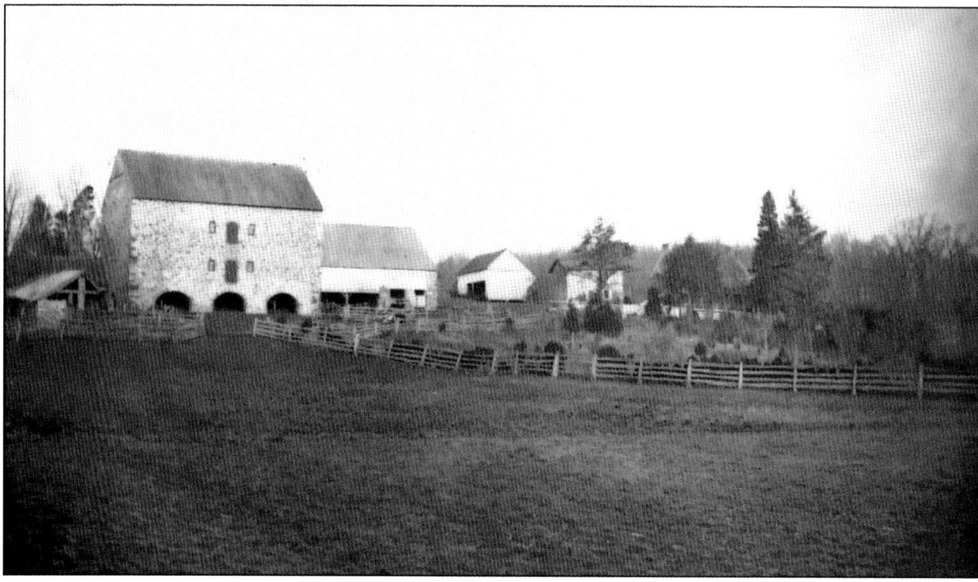

The photograph above was taken about 1870. Ann Painter, the youngest child of Hannah and Enos, married William Tyler in 1847. Ann inherited the family farms from her brothers in 1876 but took no active role in running the farms. The Tylers lived in Philadelphia and used Lachford Hall as a summer home. John J. Tyler, son of Ann and William, took control of the farms for his mother. About 1877, John began renovating Lachford Hall with many Victorian additions, as seen below. In 1881, he married his cousin Laura Hoopes. Laura was a great-granddaughter of Hannah and Enos, through their daughter Sarah Painter Barnard. John and Laura had no children, and when Laura died in 1944, a family tradition of eight generations ended. (Above, Tyler Arboretum; below, DCHS.)

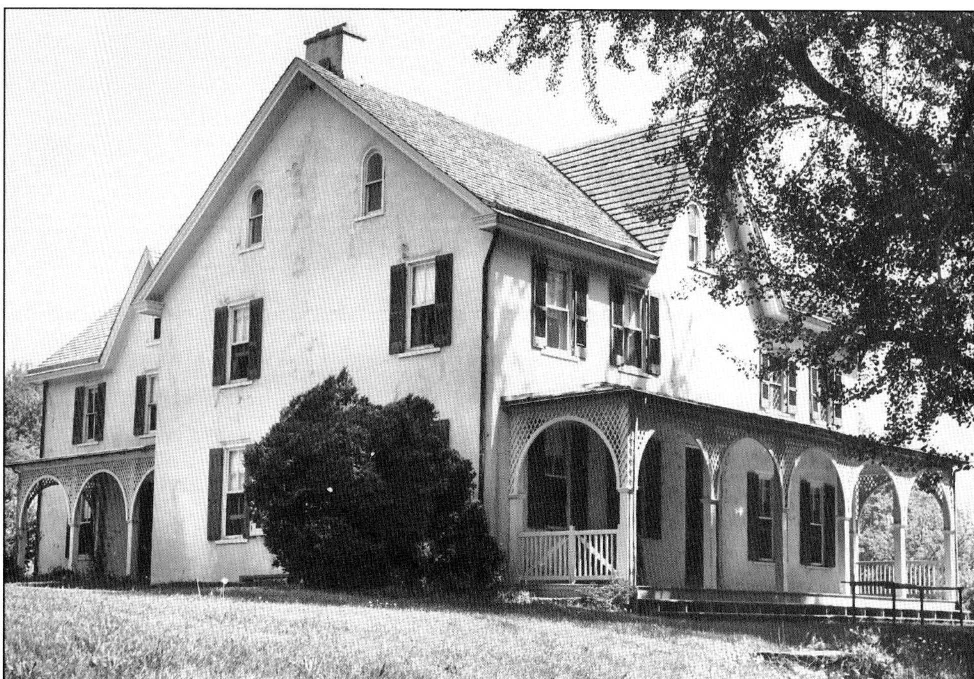

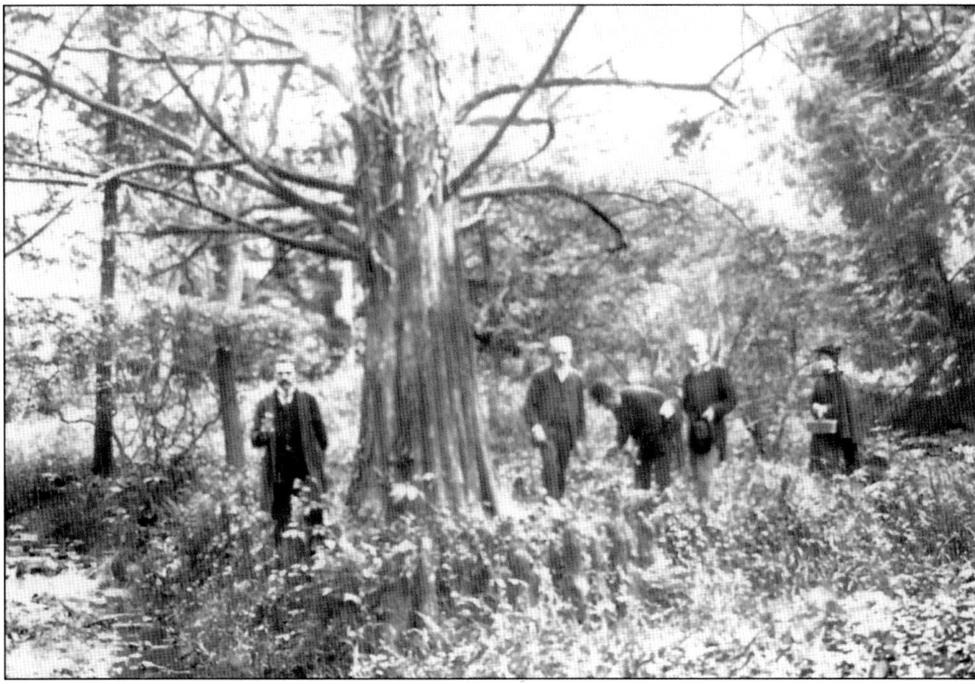

The note on the back of this photograph reads, "Cypress Tree near Rocky Run in Tyler Arboretum visited by the Middletown Geographical Society, May 1903." Minshall and Jacob were founding members of the Delaware County Institute of Science (DCIS) in 1833. The present DCIS building was erected in 1867, one block south of the Delaware County Courthouse in Media, on land donated by Minshall. (DCHS.)

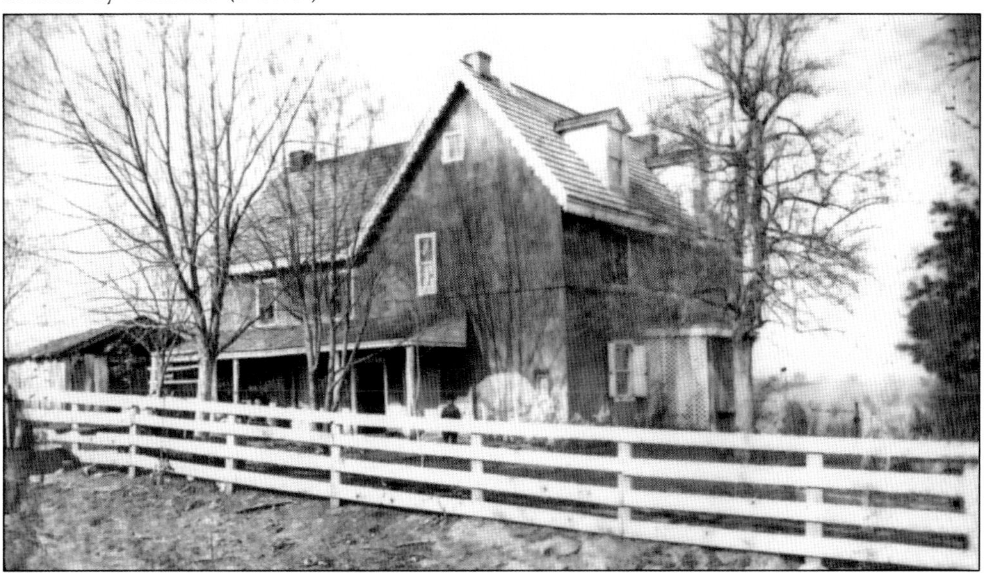

Jacob Minshall I, the son of Thomas I, married Sarah Owen in 1707 and was given 500 acres of his father's land in Middletown. Around 1710, he built the first stone house, called Round Top, on the property. In this house, Thomas I and Margaret lived out the remaining years of their lives. Round Top and the land surrounding it were deeded to Ridley Creek State Park in the late 1970s. (Tyler Arboretum.)

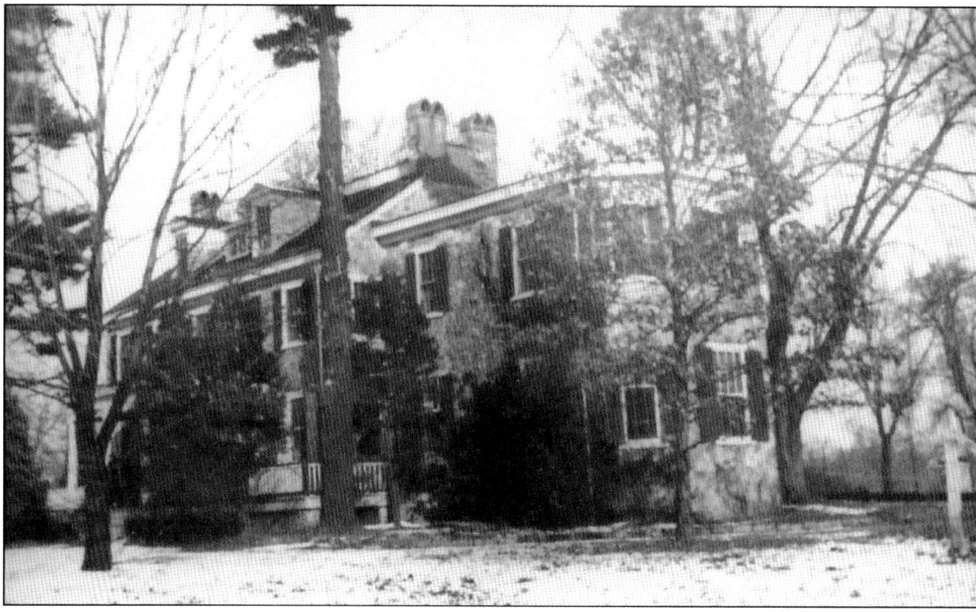

Maple Linden, seen above in the early 20th century when it was the home of Frederick T. Pusey, is located on the east side of Middletown Road on the grounds of Lima Estates. The original part of the house, left of the chimneys, was built in 1835. In 1888, Frederick's father, Joshua H. Pusey, purchased the property and named it Maple Linden Farm. It was here, in 1889, that Joshua invented and patented the paper matchbook. The photograph below was taken in 1978 when the original developers of Lima Estates were using it as offices. In order to waive the zoning standards and be allowed to build Lima Estates to three stories, the developers made an agreement to retain and restore Maple Linden. They were never held accountable to that agreement and eventually abandoned the house. It is now in ruins and not economically feasible for the current owners to restore.

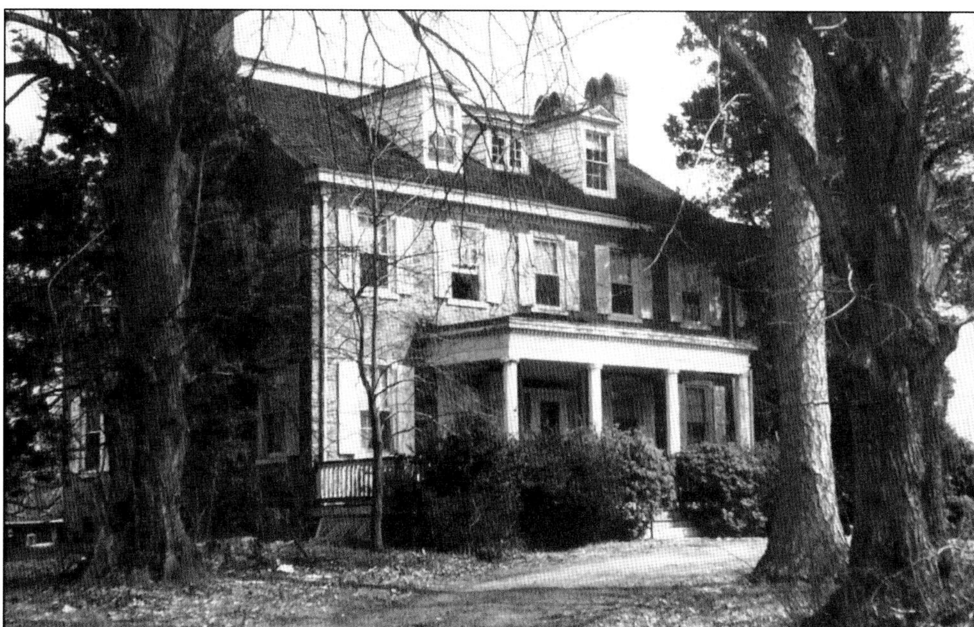

Joshua H. Pusey was a patent attorney in Philadelphia. He is seen below in his office on Walnut Street with his son Walter C. Pusey. Pusey commuted to Philadelphia by train and liked to smoke cigars. Legend has it that he did not like the bulkiness of his silver match case, which most gentlemen carried to hold their wooden match sticks. He took a narrow piece of cardboard and cut strips on one end. He dipped the strips into a mix of chemicals that when dried would be combustible when struck on flinty surfaces. He folded the end with the strips against the middle of the cardboard, added a striking surface below the strips, then folded the other end over the strips, and the paper matchbook was born. Pusey received patent No. 483,166 on September 27, 1892. He sold the patent to a match manufacturer in 1895.

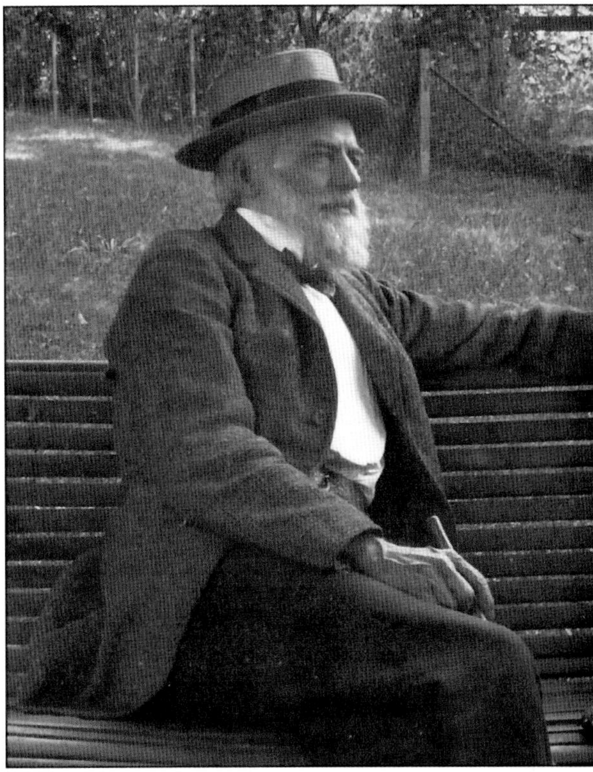

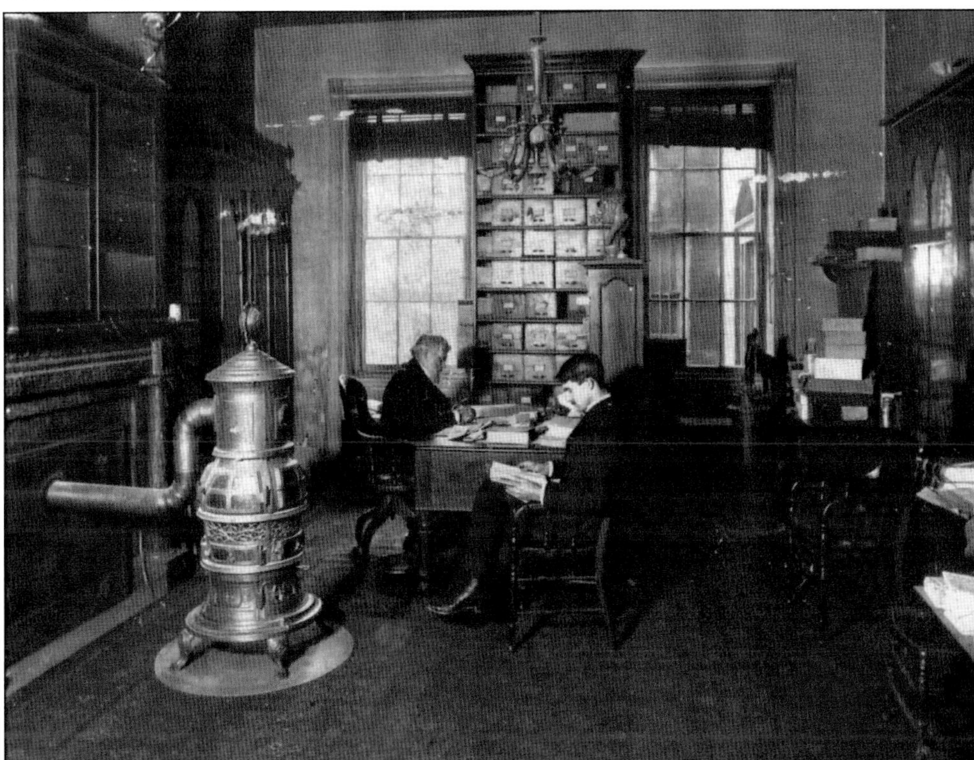

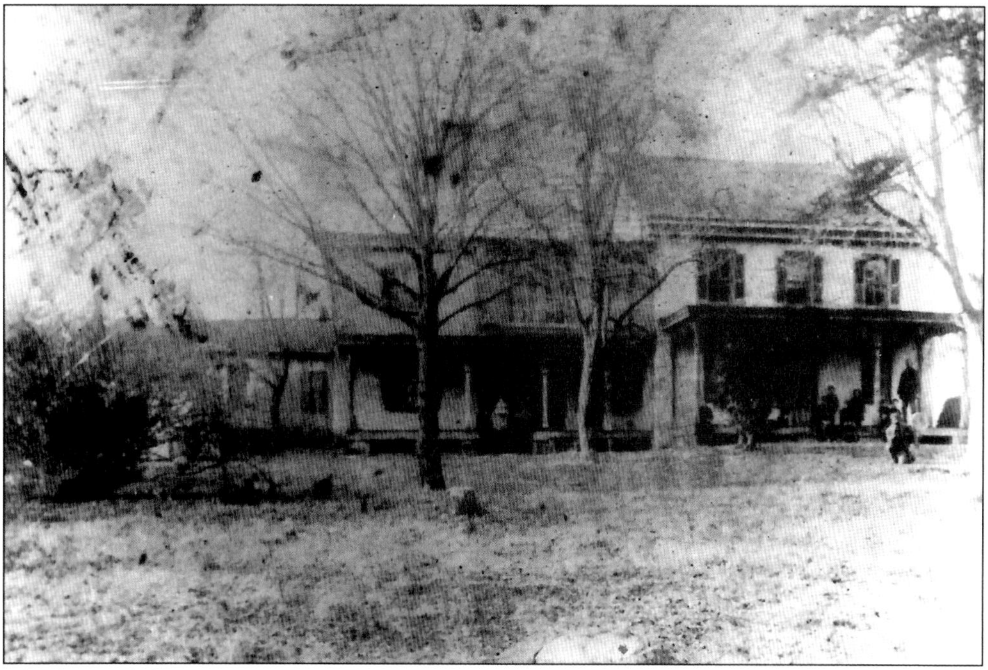

The front of the Peter W. Pratt farmhouse is pictured about 1900, when it was owned by the Crooks family. Below, from an 1875 atlas, is an engraving of the rear of the farmhouse. The house was on the southwest corner of Middletown Road and Yearsley Mill Road. Peter and his brother William were the sons of Thomas Pratt (1818–1882). The Pratts owned three large farms on both sides of Middletown Road, from approximately Old Forge Road to East Forge Road. From there, they manufactured large quantities of ice cream, which they shipped by cart to Chester and then by boat to Philadelphia. (Below, DCHS.)

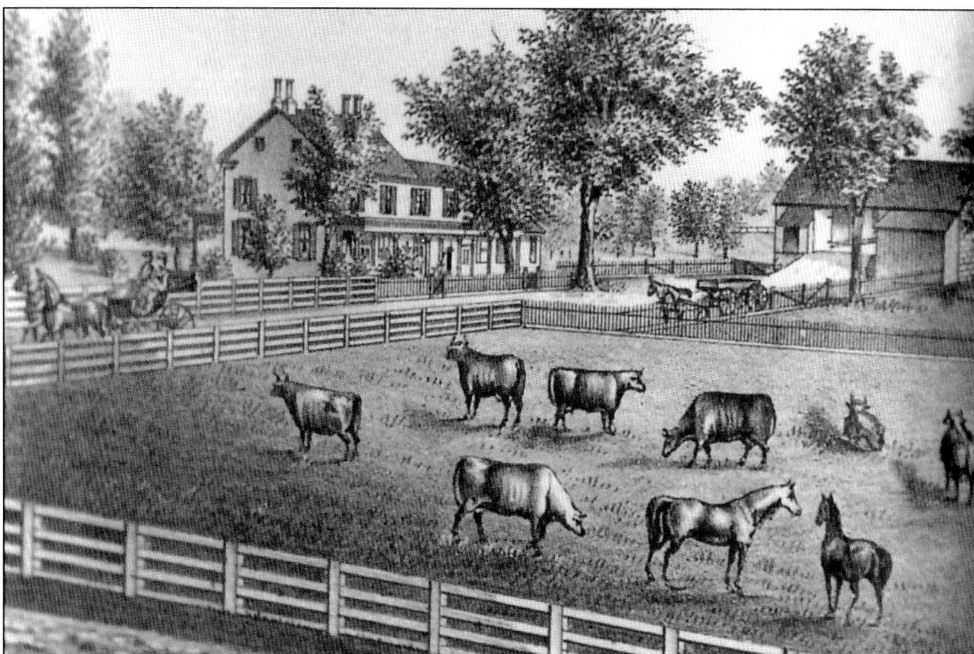

Seven

Churches and Cemeteries

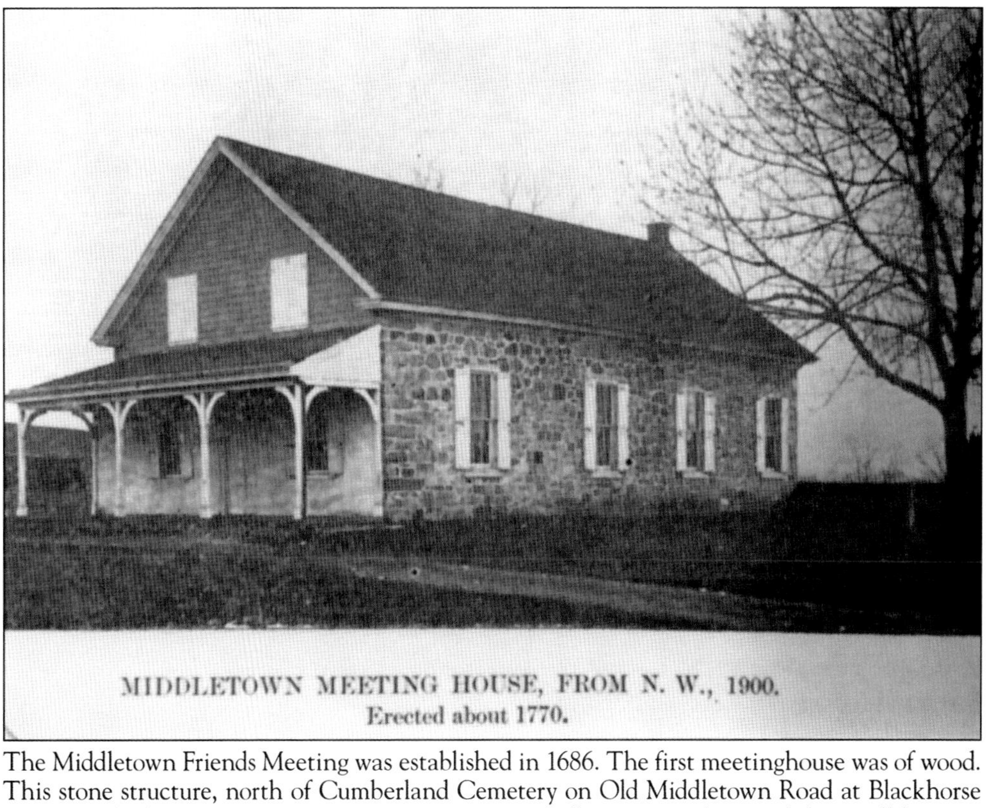

The Middletown Friends Meeting was established in 1686. The first meetinghouse was of wood. This stone structure, north of Cumberland Cemetery on Old Middletown Road at Blackhorse Lane, was built in 1770. From 1763 to 1773, a stone wall was erected around the small burying ground. A schoolhouse was built in 1783. The meetinghouse is currently used by the Middletown Progressive Meeting.

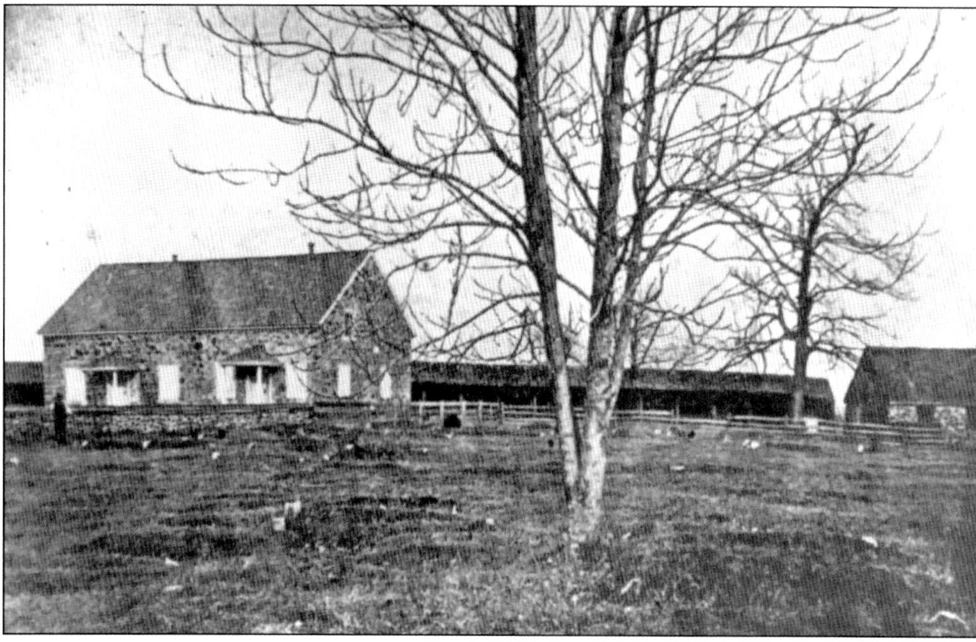

In 1827, there was a serious theological split among the Friends in the Philadelphia Yearly Meeting; it was precipitated by the preaching of Bucks County Quaker Elias Hicks. Hicks's followers were called Hicksites, and the other sect was the Orthodox Friends. The Middletown Orthodox Friends first met in the home of James Emlen beginning in 1828. In 1835, the meetinghouse was built south of Cumberland Cemetery on the east side of Middletown Road on land donated by Joseph Pennell. The Hicksites retained the original 1770 meetinghouse. In the 1870 photograph above, the Orthodox meetinghouse is on the left, the carriage shed is in the middle, and the schoolhouse is on the right. The meetinghouse is seen below in the 1930s. It is still in use by the Middletown Friends Meeting. (Below, Richard D Pusey.)

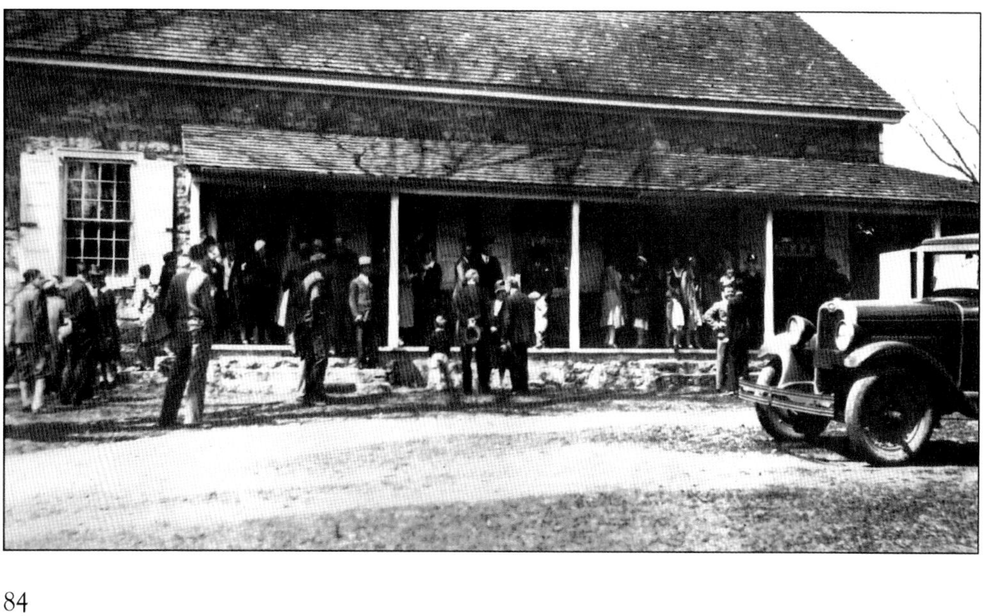

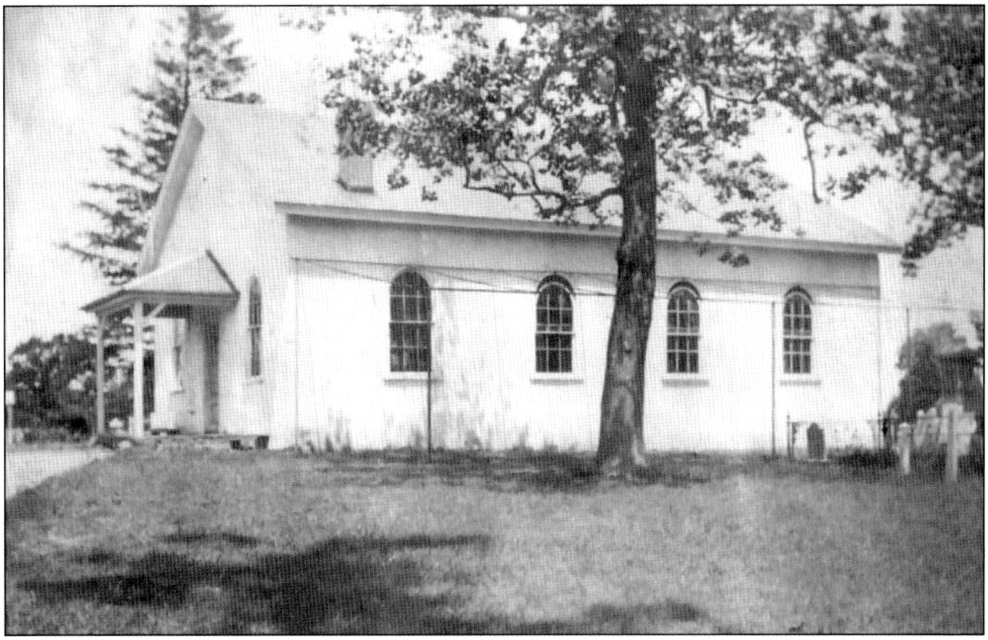

The Middletown Presbyterian Church was founded in 1729, the first of that faith in Delaware County. The congregation built a log church on the site of the current church on the northwest corner of Old Middletown Road and Indian Lane in Elwyn. A stone church was built in 1766. A fire destroyed the interior of the stone church in 1879, and it was rebuilt in a Victorian ecclesiastical style. Until that time, there was a high pulpit and box pews, and the entrance was probably on the south side, facing present Old Middletown Road. In 1923, a new sanctuary was built (below). The original church was then used for Sunday school. (Above, DCHS; below, Barbara Anderson.)

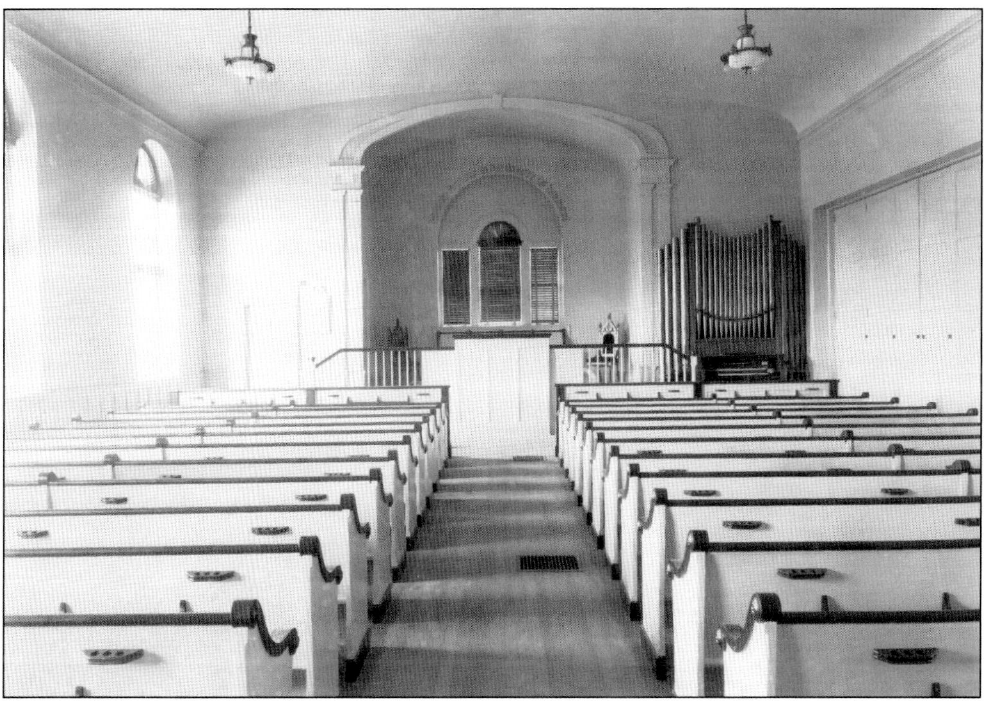

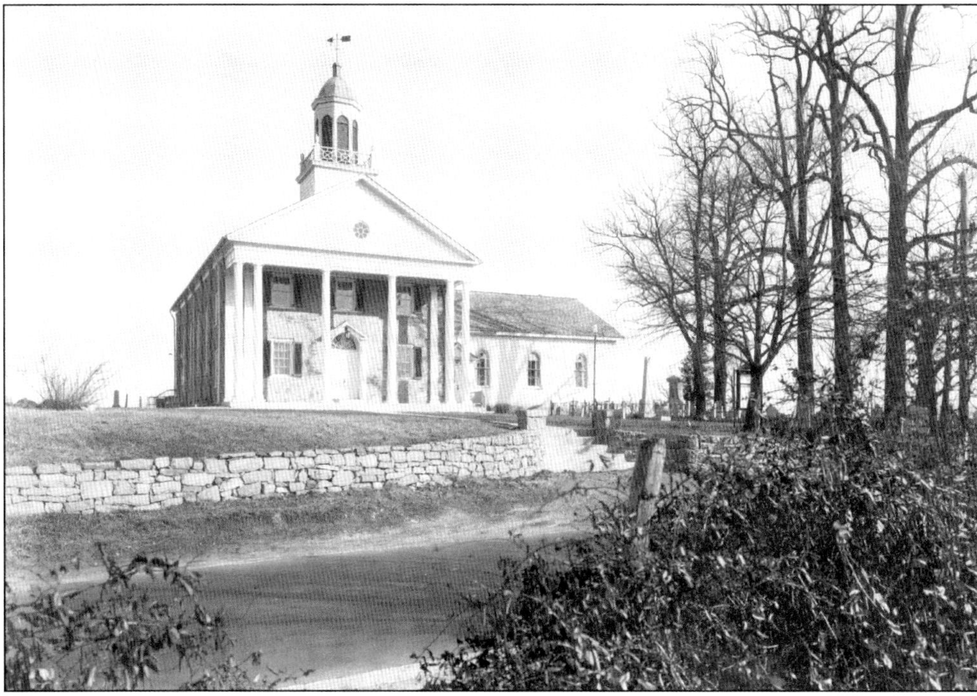

The 1923 sanctuary is seen above in 1928, with the first church as a wing on the right. In the 1950s, a new Sunday school wing was added on the other side of the original church. Below is a view of the campus from 1966. That year, the sanctuary was doubled in size, and the tower and administration wing, at left below, were added. Behind the church, along Church Road, is the burial ground. The oldest graves are those of James Cooper and Martha Dickey, who both died in 1731. Also buried here are the remains of several pastors of the church and Samuel D. and Elizabeth Riddle. (Above, Barbara Anderson.)

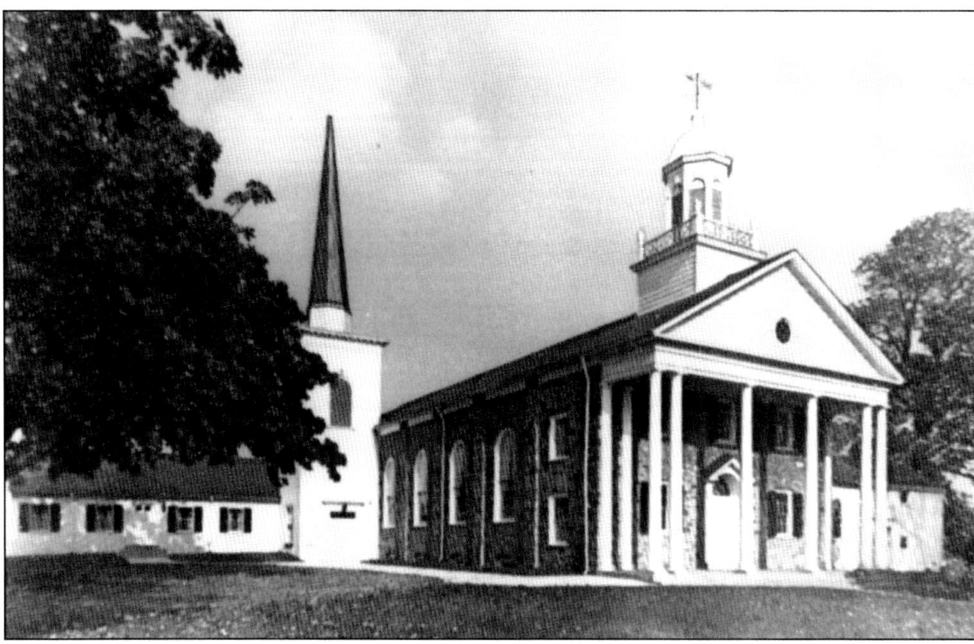

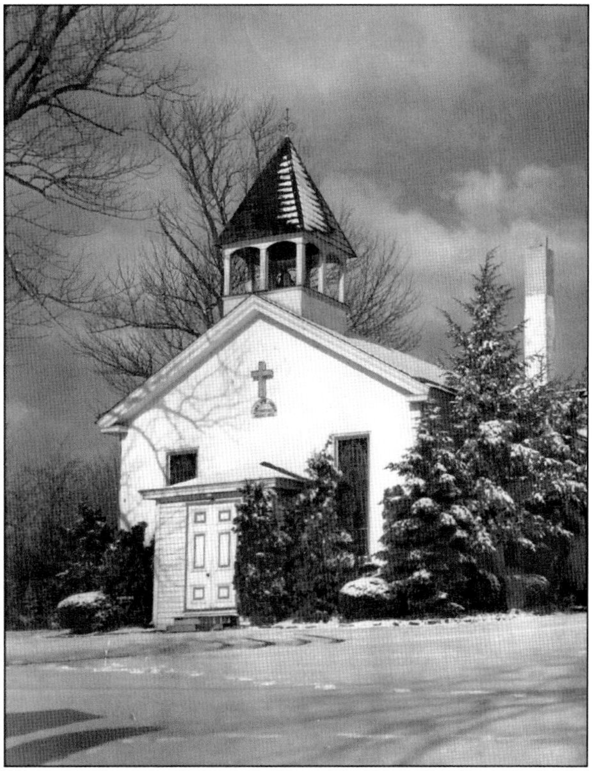

The Lima United Methodist Church, pictured here in 1953, was founded in 1832 in the home of William Fox, located at Pennell and Middletown Roads. The first sanctuary was built in 1835 on the north side of Middletown Road west of Oriole Avenue. Below is the children's choir in 1956. Included in this image are, from left to right, Susan Clower, Jane Kirby, Linda Habbersett, Linda Cox, Robert Clower, Arthur Polishuk, Christine Klepfer, Della Omlor, Jane Hurley, Gary Habbersett, Alma Omlor, Beverly Gould, Nancy Johnson, and Judy Gould. (Right, LUMC; below, Susan Clower Mescanti.)

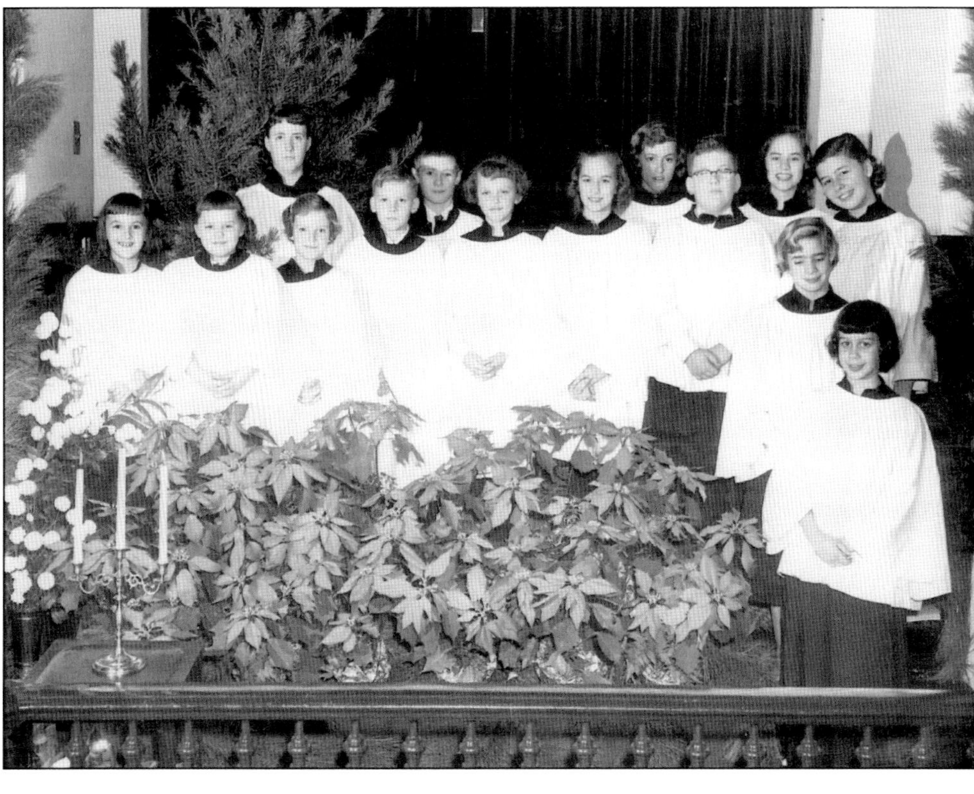

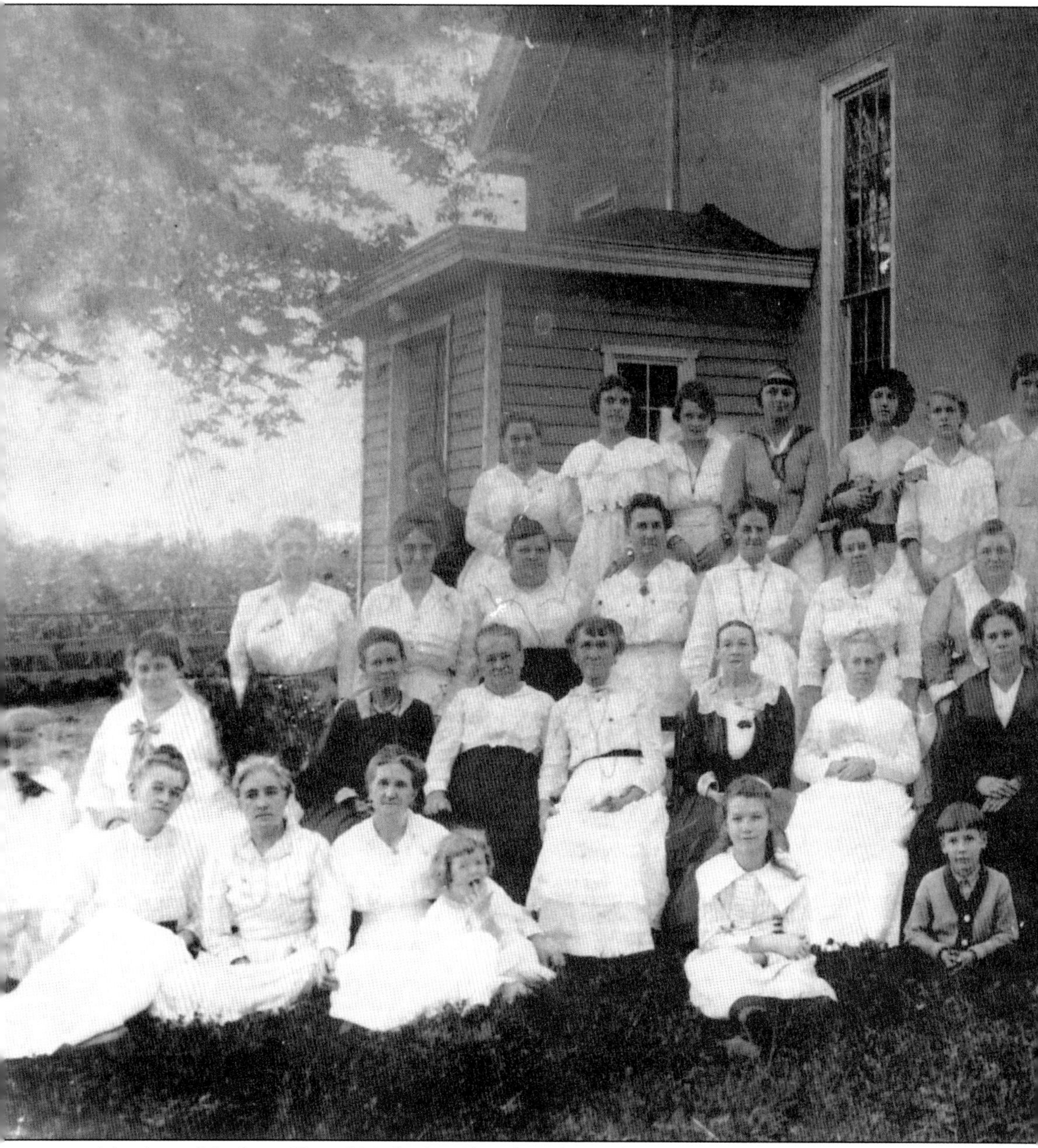

Members of the Lima United Methodist Church Ladies Aid Society gather for their 38th anniversary on September 27, 1917. The members pictured are, from left to right, (first row) Tom Malin, Mrs. Malin, Effie Pierce, Hannah Wood, Beatrice Wood, Elizabeth Graham, Ralph Bowden, Edith Yarnall, Catherine Eves, Clara Ziegenfuss, and Ethel Kramer; (second row) Helen Raezer, Mrs. Richard Baker, Jennie Grant, Barbara Pratt, Mary Gray, Mrs. Powell, Mrs. George Williamson, unidentified, Salome Woodward, Mrs. Baker, Mrs. Amanda Ruffine, Mrs. Edwin Gill, Mrs. W.W. Turner, Miss Gill, Miss Gill, and two unidentified; (third row) Mrs. Howard Mitchner,

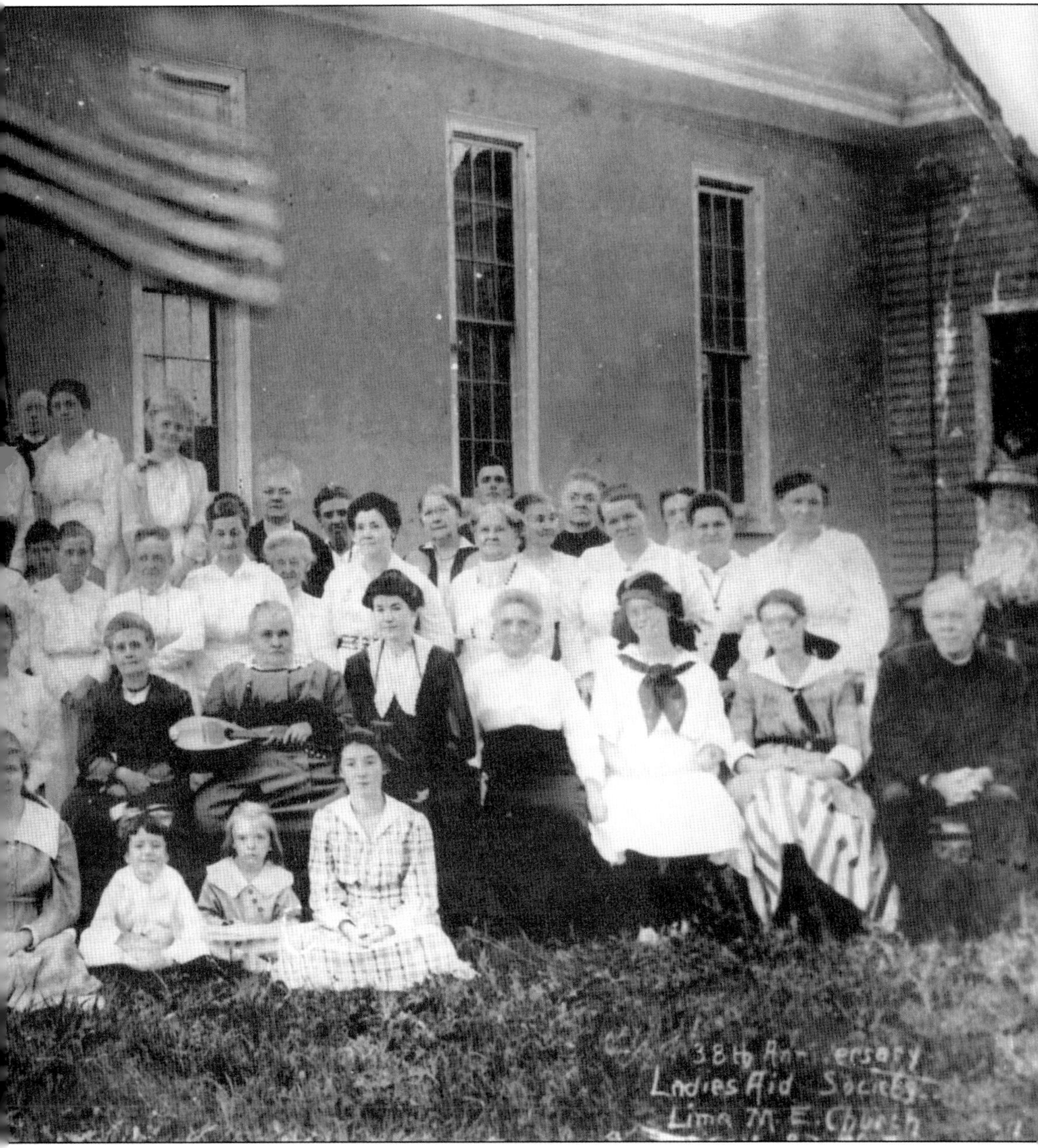

unidentified, Mrs. Newbold, Hannah Smedley, Lydia Eves, Sarah Yarnall, Mrs. Asa Bonsall, Mrs. Mellen, Gladys Williams's son, unidentified, Mrs. Isaac Pennington, Annie Yarnall, Mrs. Altmus, Mary Pyle, Mrs. Frank Thomas, Mrs. Grant Malin, Abbie Miller, Mrs. Rufus Johnson, Edna Young, unidentified, and Mrs. Howard Halton Sr.; (fourth row) Frank Bowden Jr., Clara Pratt, Mrs. Fred Schultz, Alberta Roberts, Letitia Eves, unidentified, Catherine Malin, Clara Agnew, Edith Marshall, Rev. Howard Mitchner, Gladys Williamson, Nan Dutton, unidentified, and Hable Goodman. (LUMC.)

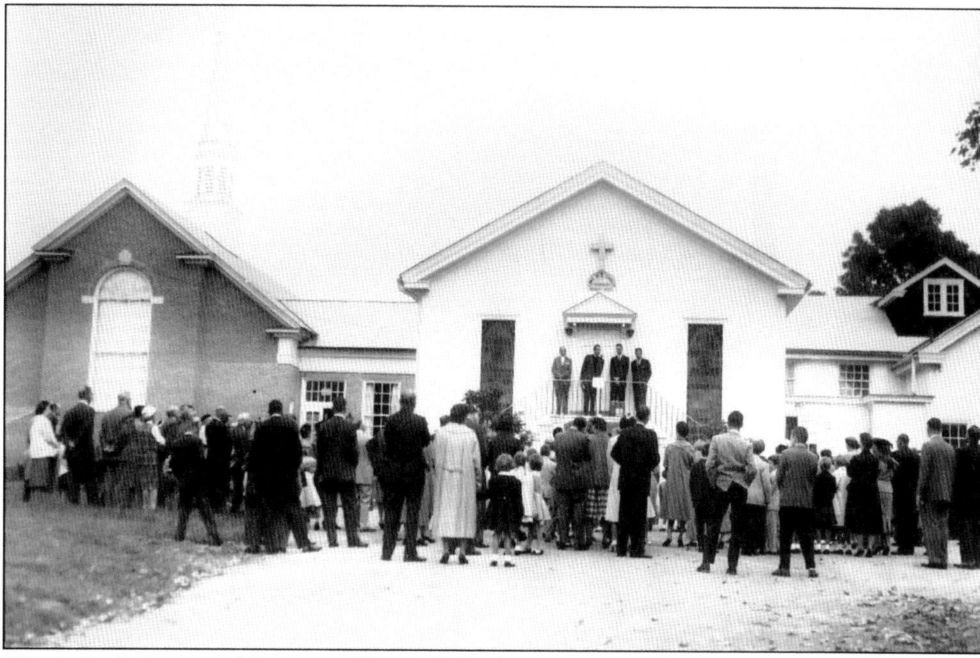

This is the dedication of the original Lima Methodist sanctuary as the Merion Habbersett Memorial in 1966. The new sanctuary, completed in 1960, is to the left. In 1873, the original sanctuary was enlarged. In 1905, the sanctuary was enlarged again, and in 1908 the Sunday school wing (at right) was added. In 1967, an education wing was added to the rear of the new sanctuary. (LUMC.)

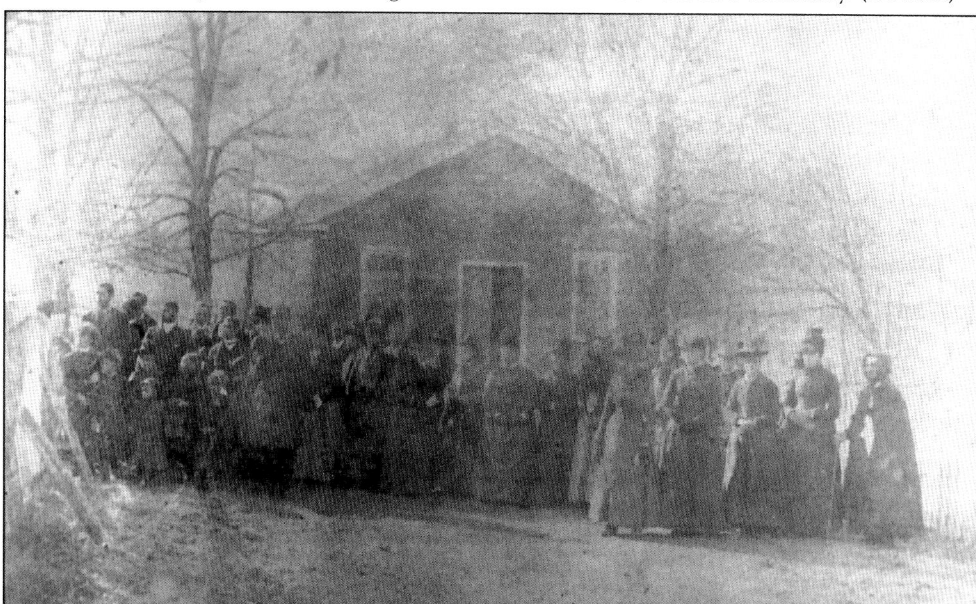

The Honeycomb United African Methodist Episcopal Church was founded in 1852 by James White, Mary White, Rachel Brown, William Sadler, Esther Sadler, Cornelius Barnes, Margaret Brown, and Hannah Ballard. Luke Smith, a local preacher, was made pastor. The church was built in May of that year just off the northwest corner of Barren Road and Van Leer Avenue, behind the Saunders-Winslow-Mason log cabin. (Honeycomb UAME.)

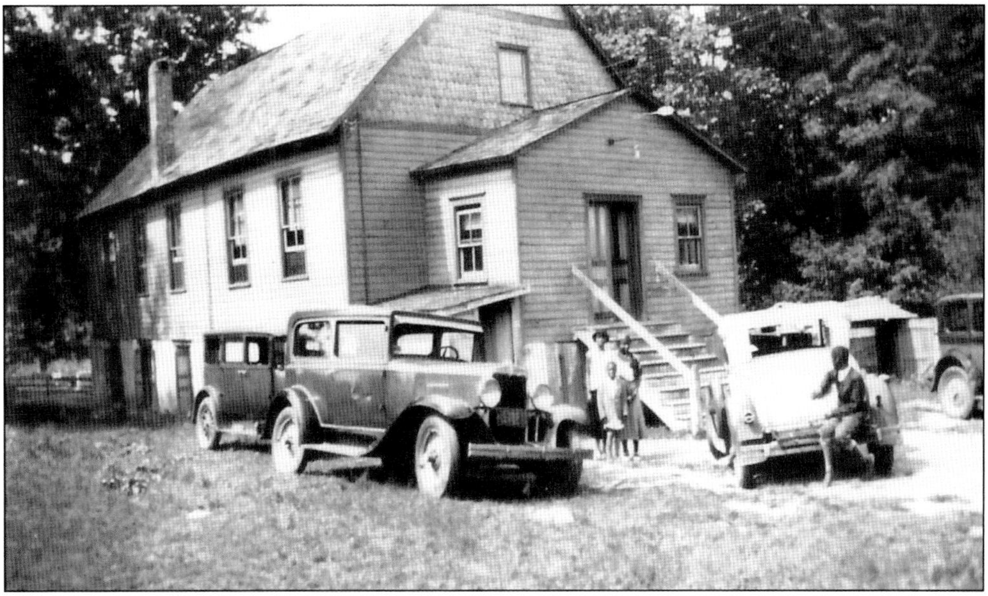

Most of the congregants were local blacks who worked as farmers and laborers. "Honeycomb" comes from the stone with which the church was built. The rich-in-iron pockmarked rocks are usually found in soil around a serpentine district, of which Middletown is plentiful. Barren Road takes its name from the serpentine barren on the hill above Dismal Run west of Painter Road. The iron in honeycomb stone rusts to a golden honey color. The Honeycomb Church, seen above in the 1930s and below in 1978, was a stop on the Underground Railroad before the Civil War. In 1863, when the Confederate army reached Gettysburg, three slaves who served as rebel scouts—William Spradley, George Smith, and John Peters—fled and found their way to Honeycomb. Smith and Peters joined the congregation, and Spradley served as the church's secretary for 60 years. (Honeycomb UAME.)

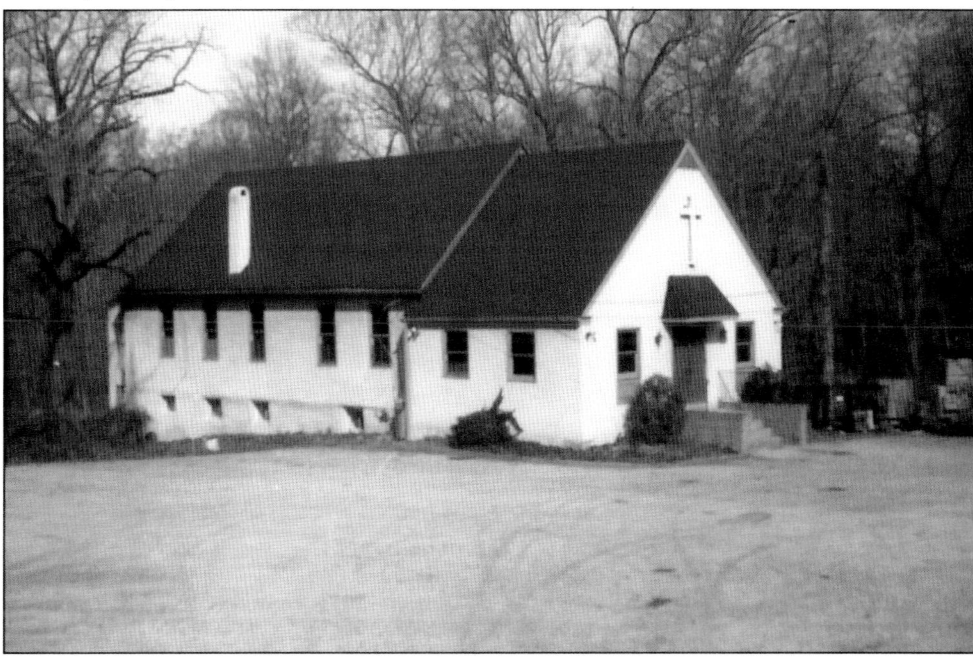

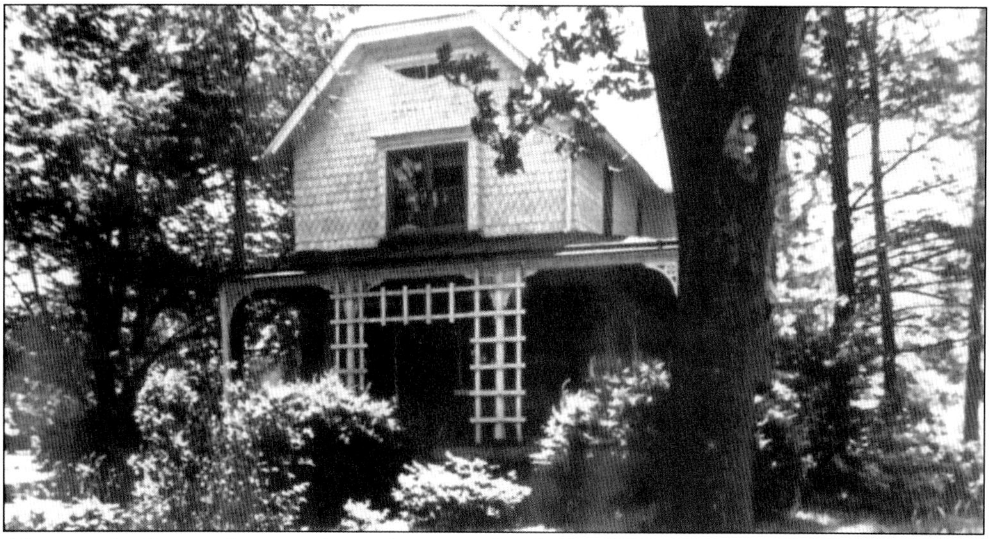

Above is the Queen Anne–style gatehouse to Cumberland Cemetery. Located on the east side of Middletown Road opposite Yearsley Mill Road, the cemetery was opened in 1860 by Thomas Pratt. In 1885, the Cumberland Cemetery Association was incorporated. Members of many old Middletown families are buried there. Below are the graves of Minshall and Jacob Painter. The brothers were members of the Middletown Hicksite Meeting. They wanted to be buried by their mother on the meetinghouse grounds but wanted markers on their graves. The Friends do not allow markers on graves, so the brothers bought a plot at Cumberland on the opposite side of the wall from their mother's grave and were interred there with these ornate monuments. The cemetery is now operated by the Oliver H. Bair Company. Plenty of burial lots are still available at Cumberland. (Below, DCHS.)

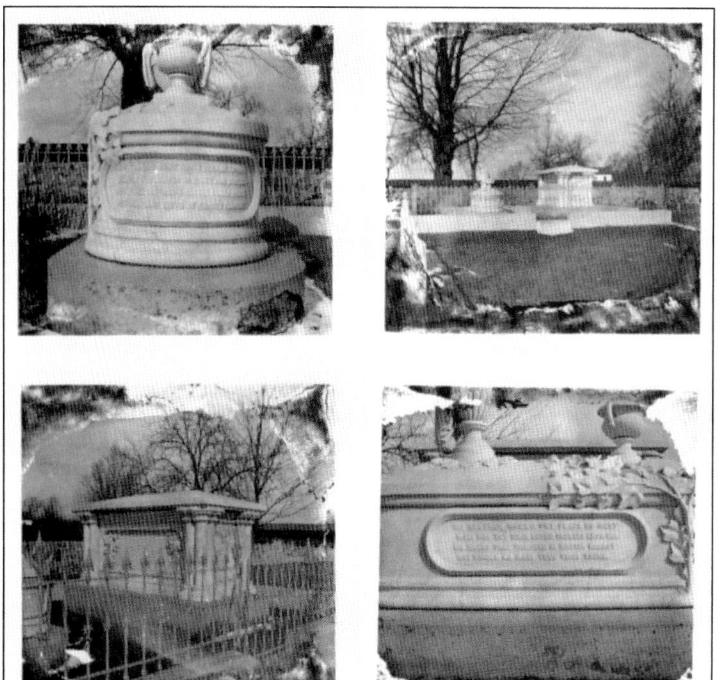

Eight

Schools and Learning

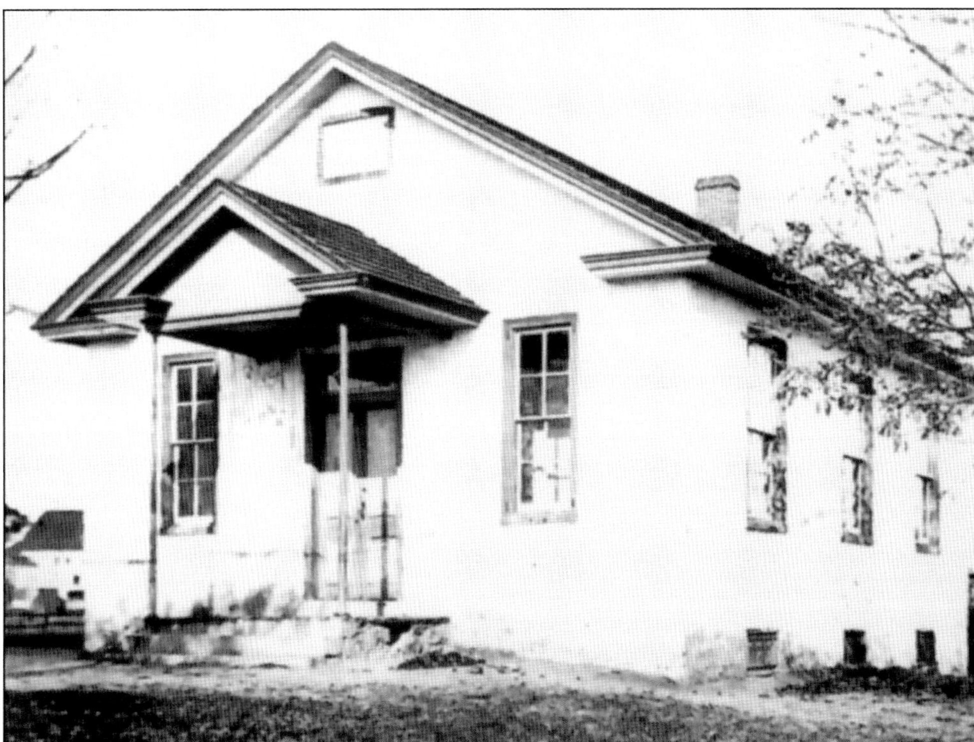

Middletown School No. 1, the Fairlamb School, was built on the northeast corner of Middletown and Knowlton Roads on land purchased from Nicholas Fairlamb. It was opened in 1837 and remodeled in 1866 by William Armstrong at a cost of $670. It was closed in 1922 and sold to E. Harper Habbersett in 1924. Habbersett used some of the school walls as part of his new home, which still stands on the corner. (Keith Lockhart.)

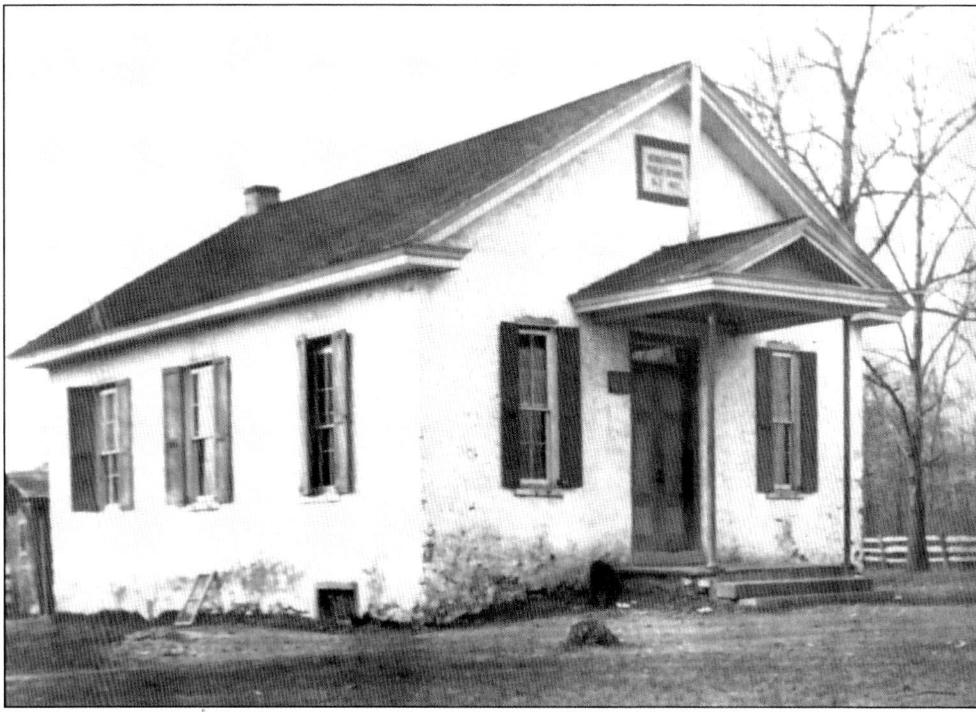

In 1834, the Pennsylvania Free Public School Act was passed. Before then, schools were private concerns organized by civic-minded individuals or affiliated with local churches. By the 1840s, Middletown had five schools. In the 1860s, the township opened several additional schools while remodeling and renumbering the old ones. The second Middletown School No. 2 (above), the Mount Pleasant School, was built in 1867 on the southeast corner of Mount Alverno and Glen Riddle Roads. It is currently a private residence. Middletown School No. 3 and No. 4 (below), which has two numbers because it was built with two stories, opened on November 28, 1861. Known as the Parkmount School, the land on the south side of Parkmount Road was purchased from Samuel Riddle. Additions were made in 1885, 1916, and 1936. It was closed in 1945, and is currently used as a business. (Above, Keith Lockhart.)

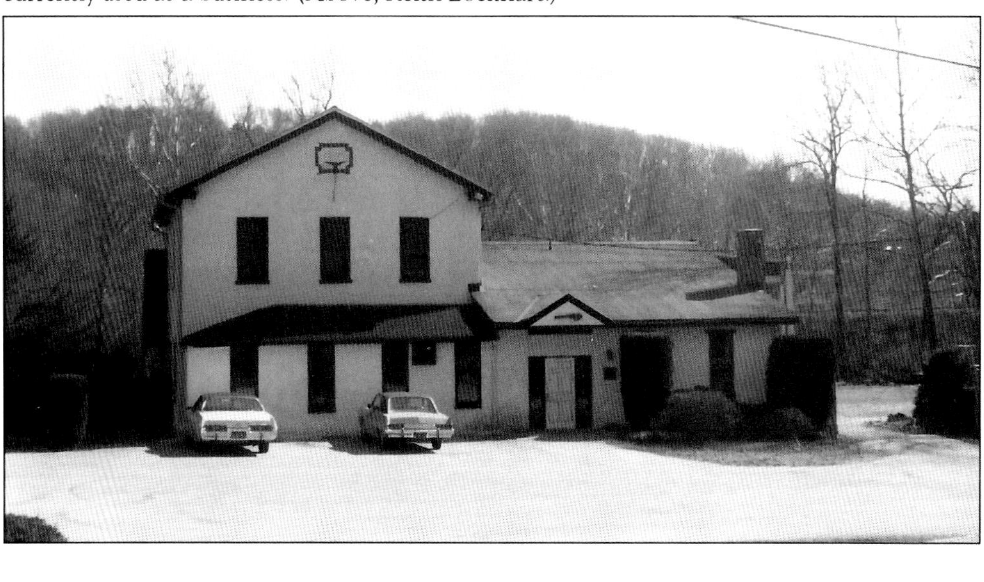

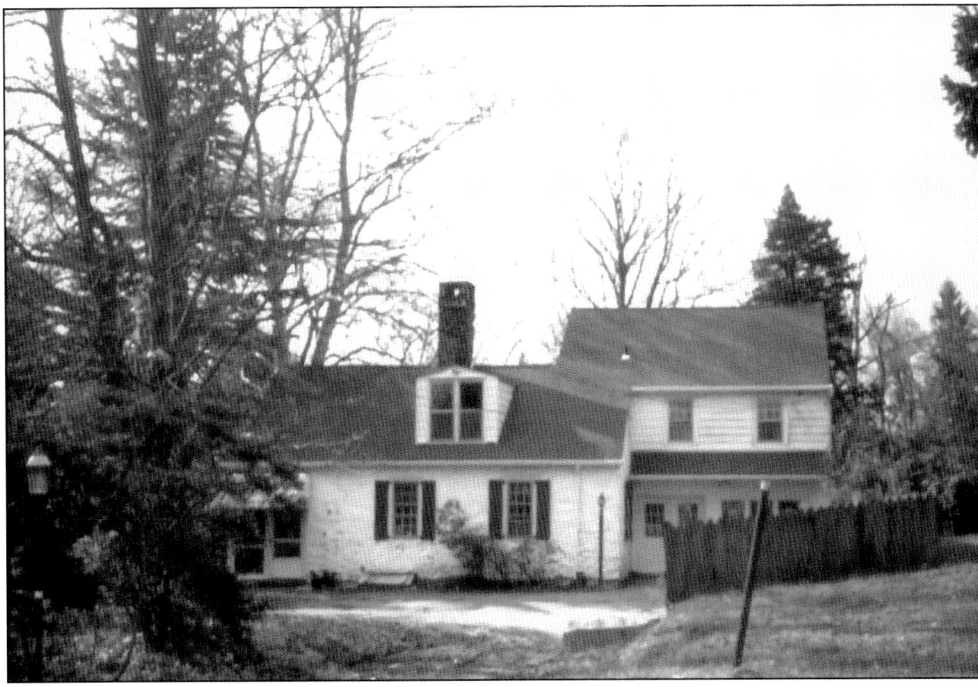

The first Middletown School No. 5 was built by John Eves in 1840. Located on the west side of Middletown Road near Elwyn Road, it was closed and sold in 1868 to Elwood Malin. Since then, it has been a residence with wings added on the north and south sides, but the original stone school, with shuttered windows in this 2004 photograph, is clearly evident. (Keith Lockhart.)

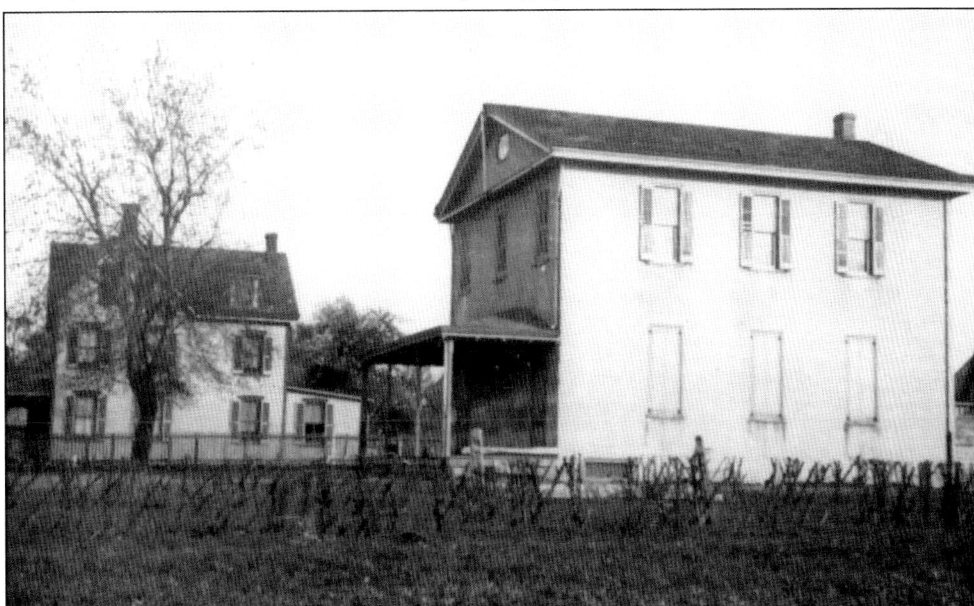

Middletown School No. 6 and No. 7, with two stories, was the Lima School, built by Robert P. Dunn in 1861 at a cost of $1,575. It was on the west side of Middletown Road north of Pennell Road on land purchased from the Delaware County Poor House. In 1915, a two-room addition was added. It was torn down in 1939 after the new Lima School opened on the same site that year.

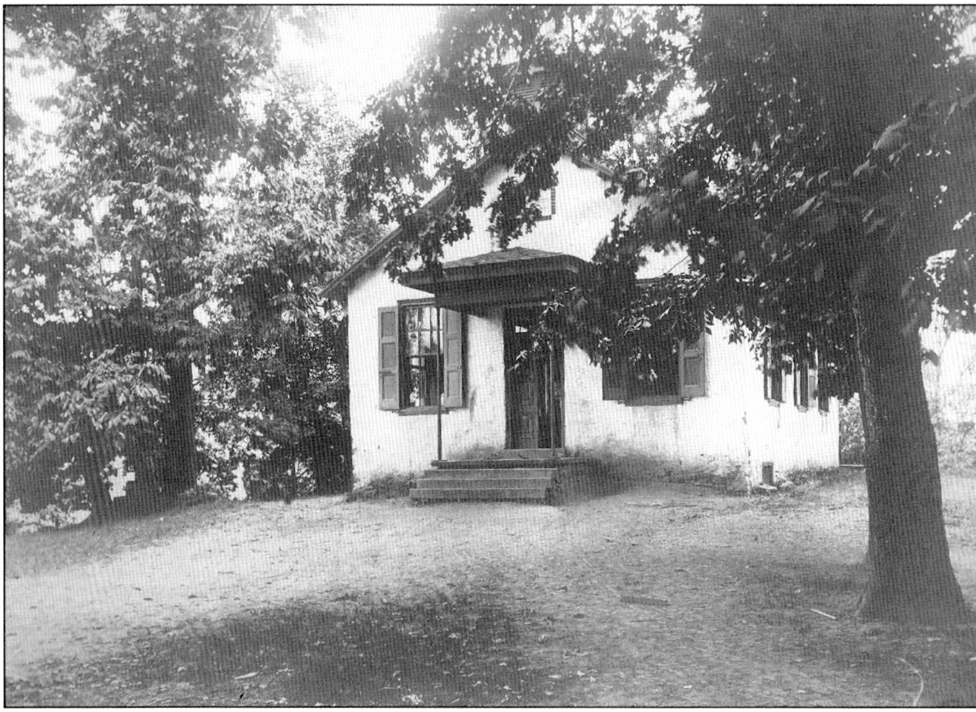

Middletown School No. 8, the Barren School, formerly School No. 2, was built in 1841 by Thomas Rose on land purchased from George Smedley. In 1868, it was substantially remodeled at the cost of $2,139 and renumbered. It was closed in 1914 and sold in 1917 to J. Harry Smart, who sold it to John J. Tyler. It was used as a residence until 1967, when it was torn down. (MHAC.)

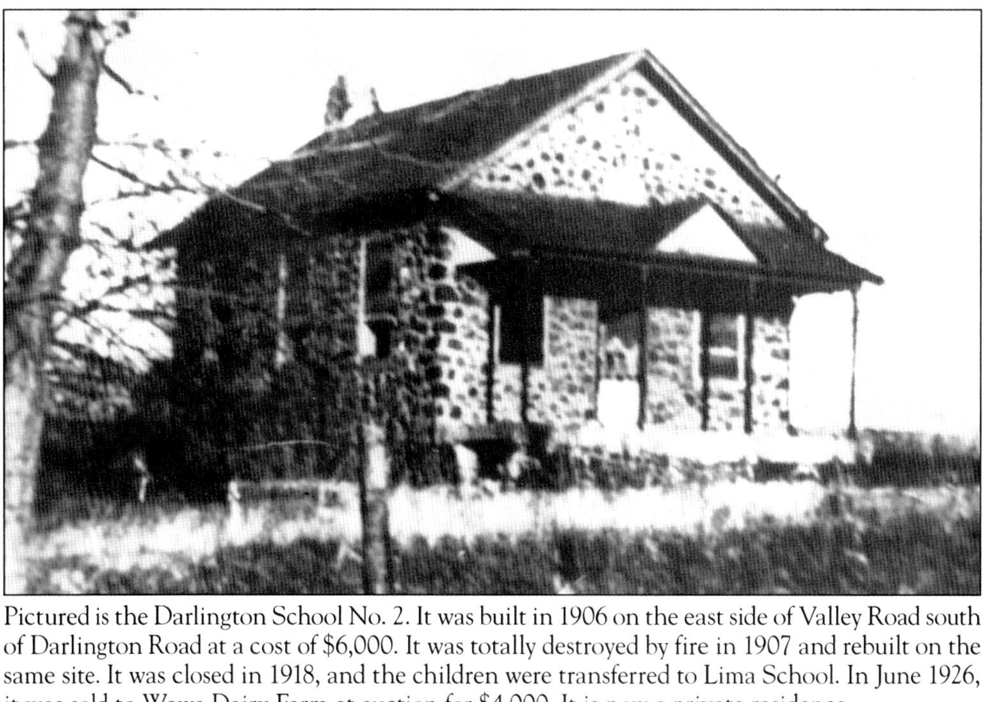

Pictured is the Darlington School No. 2. It was built in 1906 on the east side of Valley Road south of Darlington Road at a cost of $6,000. It was totally destroyed by fire in 1907 and rebuilt on the same site. It was closed in 1918, and the children were transferred to Lima School. In June 1926, it was sold to Wawa Dairy Farm at auction for $4,000. It is now a private residence.

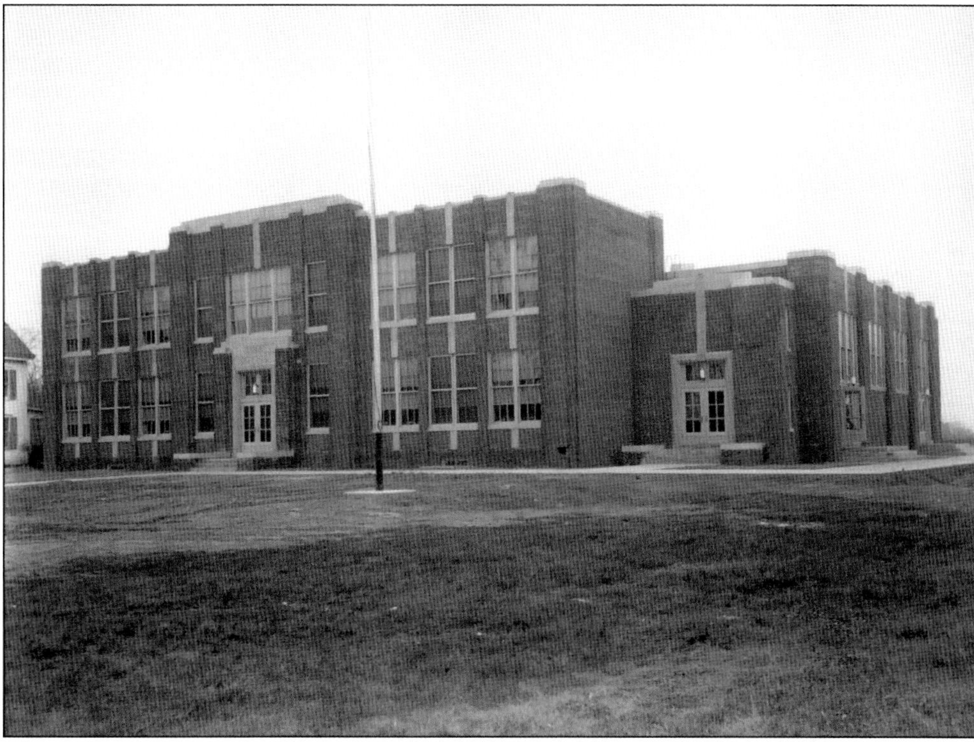

This is the second Lima School. It was built in 1939 on the site of Middletown School No. 6 and No. 7. It was expanded in 1952. In 1978, due to a decrease in the number of elementary school students, Lima School was closed, and the students were transferred to other schools in the Rose Tree Media School District. The building was sold and is still in use as a business. (DCHS.)

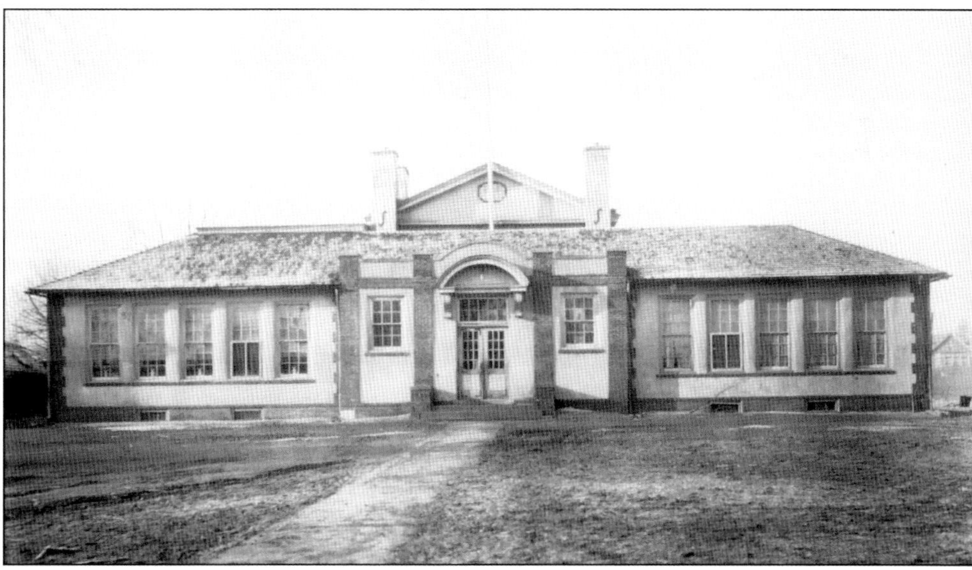

Roosevelt School was built in 1935 on the west side of Old Middletown Road, just south of Bortondale Avenue. It was more than doubled in size in 1952. Continued declining enrollments in the early 1980s led to its closing and sale. It is in use today as an office campus housing a variety of businesses. (DCHS.)

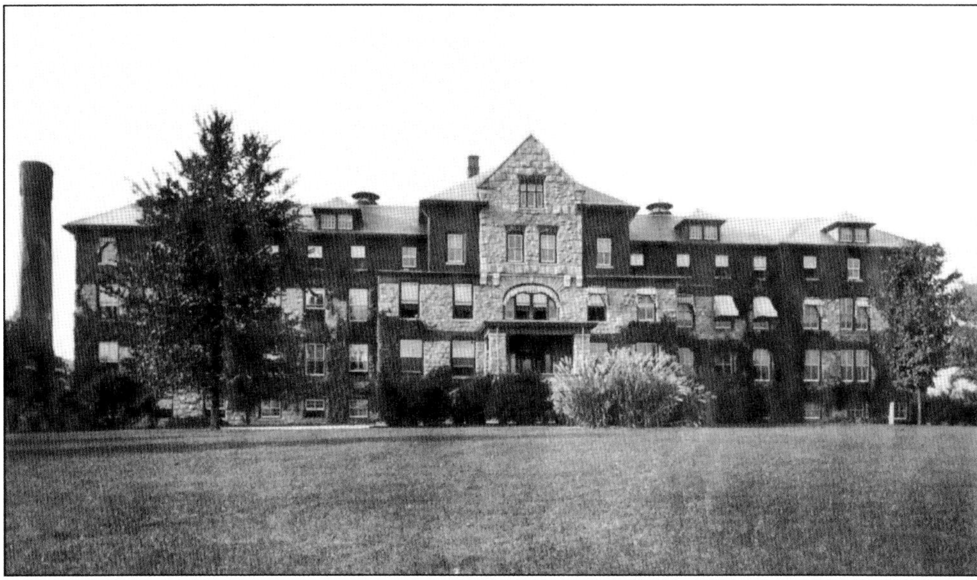

In 1888, Isaiah Williamson, a Philadelphia merchant and philanthropist, founded the Williamson Free School of Mechanical Trades. His purpose was to provide financially disadvantaged young men with the opportunity to become productive and respected members of society. "It was seeing boys, ragged and barefooted, lounging on the streets, growing up with no education, no idea of usefulness, that caused me to think of founding a school where every boy could be taught some trade free of expense." He anonymously gave large sums to favorite charities, hospitals, colleges, and homes for children. The founding of the Williamson Free School with a $2 million endowment was one of his last charitable acts before he died in 1889. The Main Building above is seen in the 1930s. Below is a view of the original Schofield farm buildings on the site. (Above, Williamson Free School; below, Keith Lockhart.)

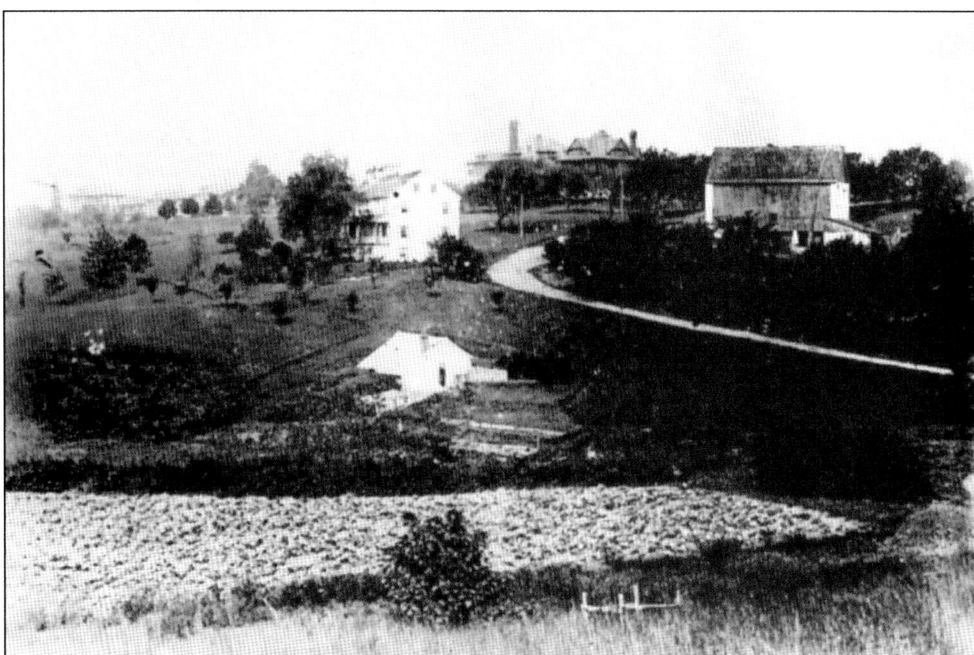

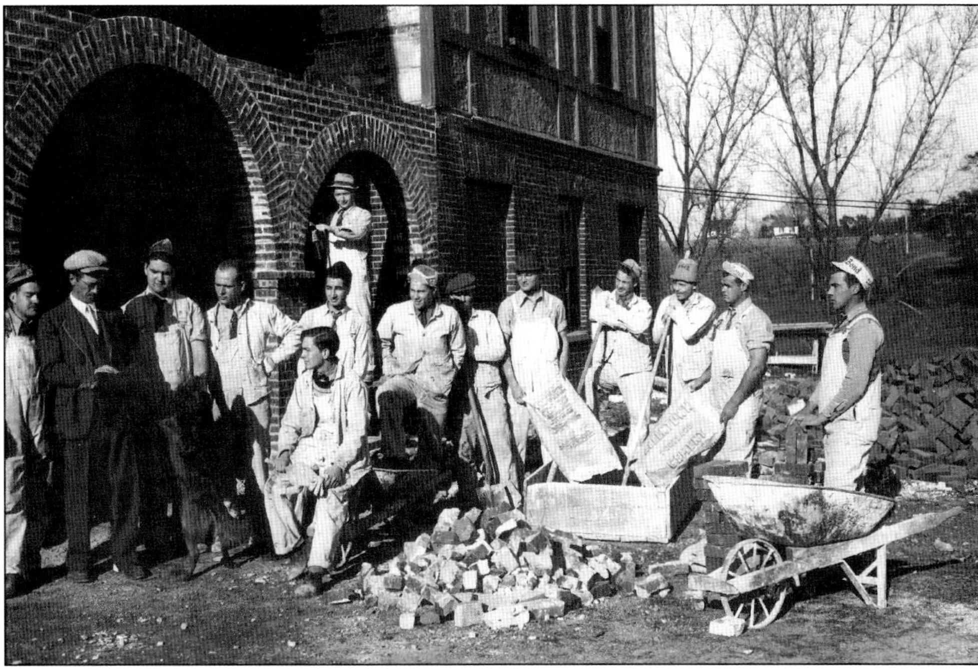

The 220-acre campus on Middletown Road was purchased in 1889. Frank Furness, one of Philadelphia's most prominent architects, was employed to design the buildings. The school opened in 1891 offering three-year programs in bricklaying, carpentry, machine shop, and patternmaking. With the first graduation in 1894, Williamson became a significant pioneer in America's vocational education movement. In 1957, when a fire destroyed all but one of the shop buildings, it looked like Williamson might be forced to close, but it was saved when the trustees entered into agreement with the trustees of the Rodman Wanamaker estate, creating the John Wanamaker Free School of Artisans, now an integral part of Williamson. The agreement funded the construction of four new shop buildings and a general education building and provided an endowment that covered an increase in the number of scholarships offered. (Above, Williamson Free School; below, Keith Lockhart.)

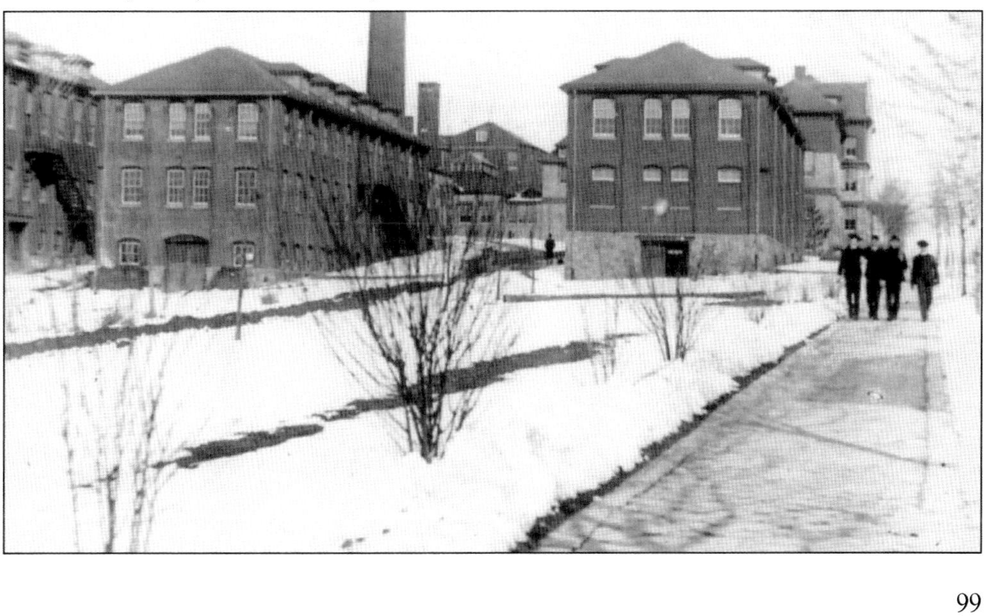

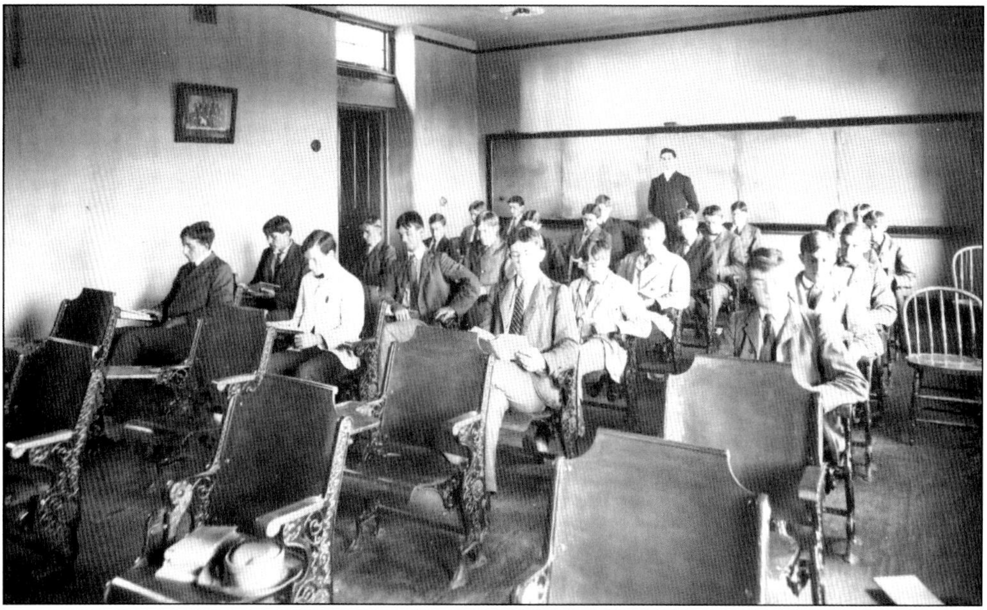

Until 1961, students were of high school age and the school's curriculum emphasized the trades. However, due to the rise of secondary education and the significant advances of technology, the Williamson Board of Trustees decided to convert the school to a postsecondary institution. Programs were upgraded, and in 1972, the Commonwealth of Pennsylvania granted the school the authority to award the Associate in Specialized Technology degree. Williamson now offers Craftsman Diplomas in carpentry and masonry and Associate in Specialized Technology degrees in construction technology (with an emphasis on carpentry or masonry); horticulture, landscaping and turf management; machine tool technology; paint and coatings technology; and power plant technology. (Above, Williamson Free School; below, Keith Lockhart.)

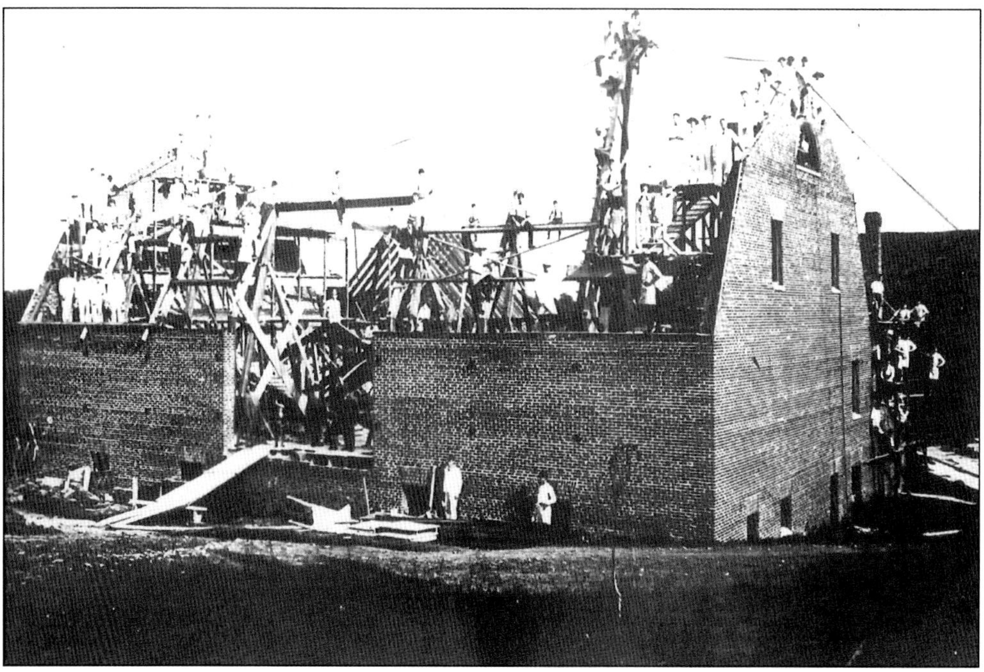

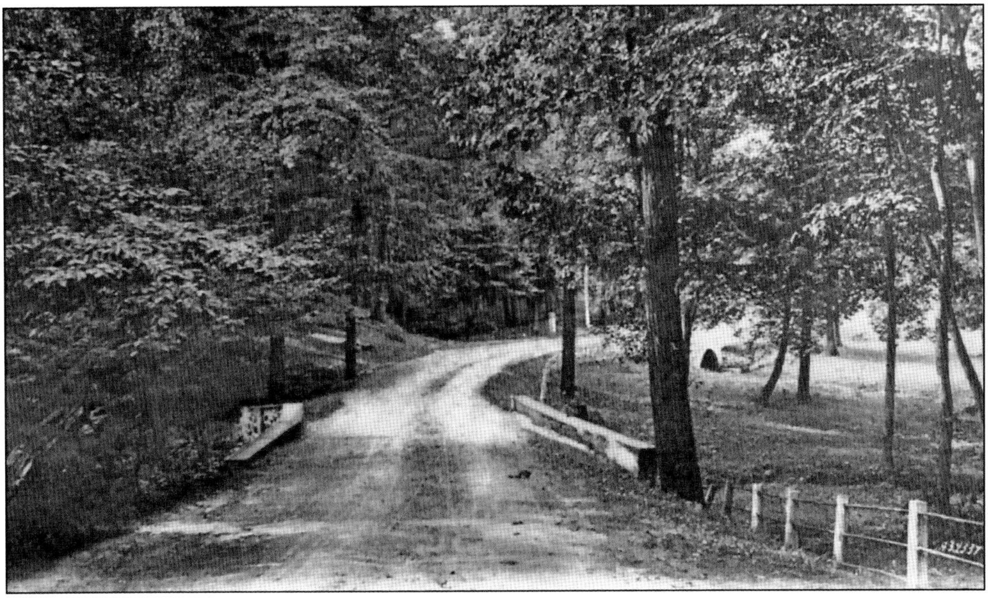

In the 19th century, it was common for the mentally challenged and the mentally ill to be abandoned by their families and to live on the street or to be jailed. In 1852, Dr. Alfred L. Elwyn opened a school in Germantown for children with special needs. In 1853, by special act of the Pennsylvania legislature, the Pennsylvania Training School for Feeble-Minded Children was incorporated. In 1857, with the encouragement of reformer Dorothea Dix, the Pennsylvania legislature funded a grant for the construction of a new, larger school. A 60-acre farm in Middletown was purchased for $10,000. The triangular piece of land was bordered on the north by Baltimore Pike, on the west by Middletown Road, and on the southeast by Elwyn Road. Above is the entrance off Elwyn Road. Below is the schoolhouse building, constructed in 1880 and demolished in 1960. (Below, Elwyn Archives.)

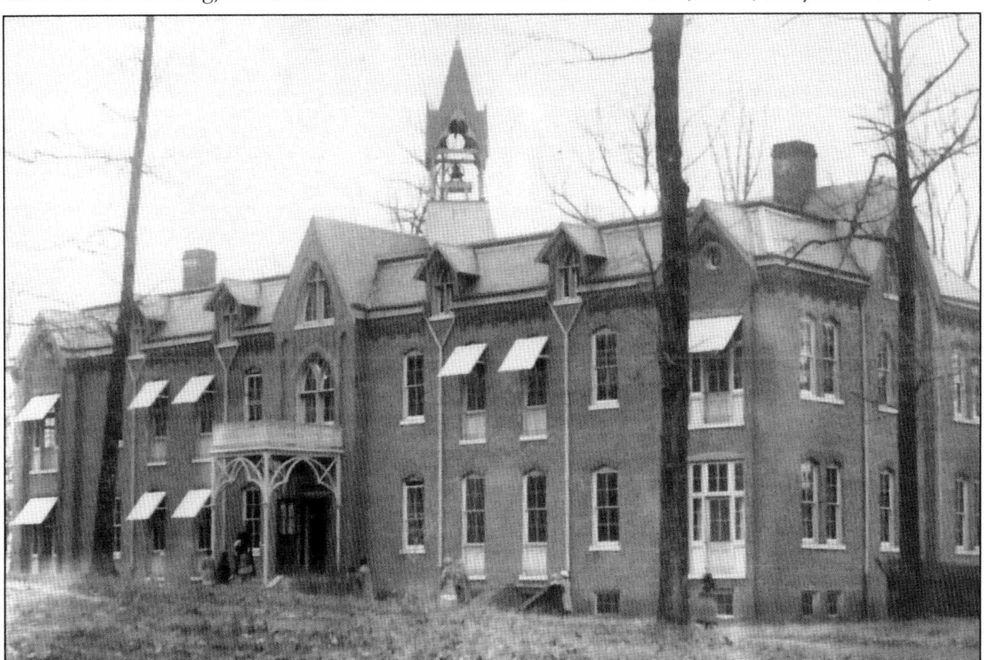

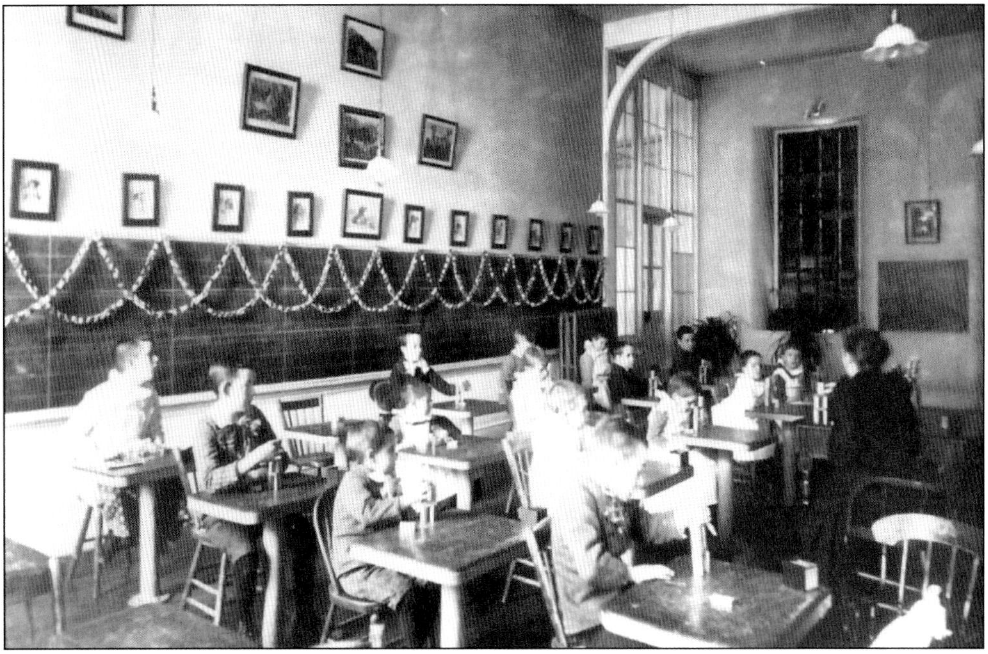

By 1868, there were more than 150 children attending the special-needs school. Children who reached 18 and could not find useful employment in the community or could not return to their families were given jobs in the laundry or farming and stayed on at the school to assist with younger children. In 1870, Dr. Elwyn was elected president of the Training School. In 1871, the term "institution" began to be used to describe the combination of educational and custodial services offered at the school. In early 1876, North Hall, a building for vocational instruction, was built and dedicated, and a nursery for young children was opened. Above, the children are in class; below, they are learning shoe repair in the North Hall cobbler shop. (Both, Elwyn Archives.)

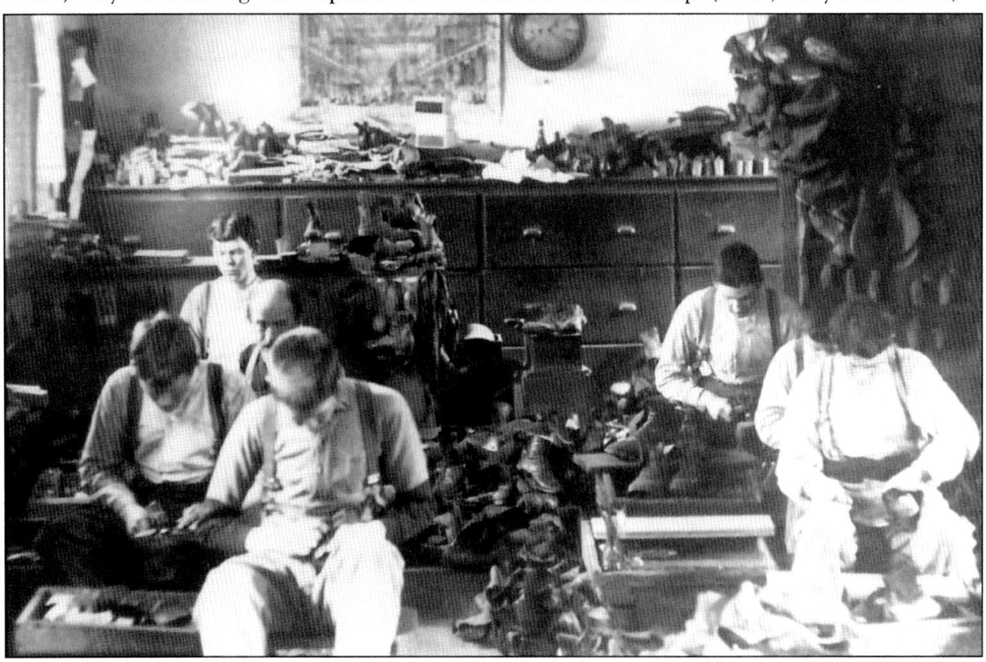

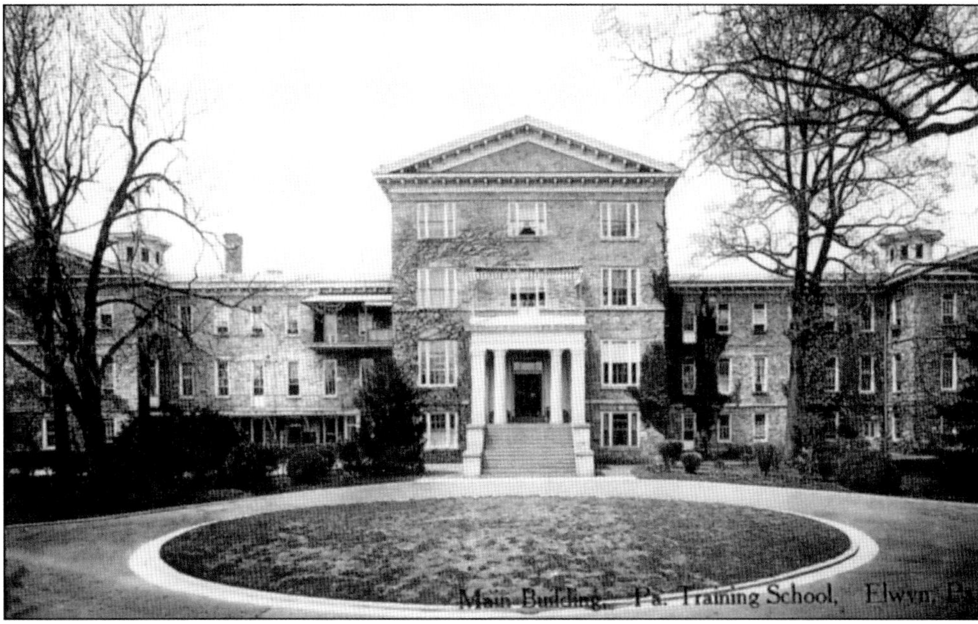

Above, Elwyn's Main Building is pictured around 1910. Built in 1859 and renovated many times, it originally held classrooms and residences for students and teachers. It currently houses Elwyn's corporate headquarters and administrative offices. Today, Elwyn continues its mission by serving over 12,000 people each year, both from the original Middletown campus and at satellite locations throughout Pennsylvania, New Jersey, Delaware, and California. They have more than 80 group homes serving people with mental retardation, and 10 homes for people with mental illness. Elwyn provides early intervention services to more than 2,000 children each year and offers special education to more than 4,000 children. Below, children in the 1910s participate in Elwyn's Field Day or Drill Day. First held in 1905, the students performed drills and calisthenics for families and friends. (Both, Keith Lockhart.)

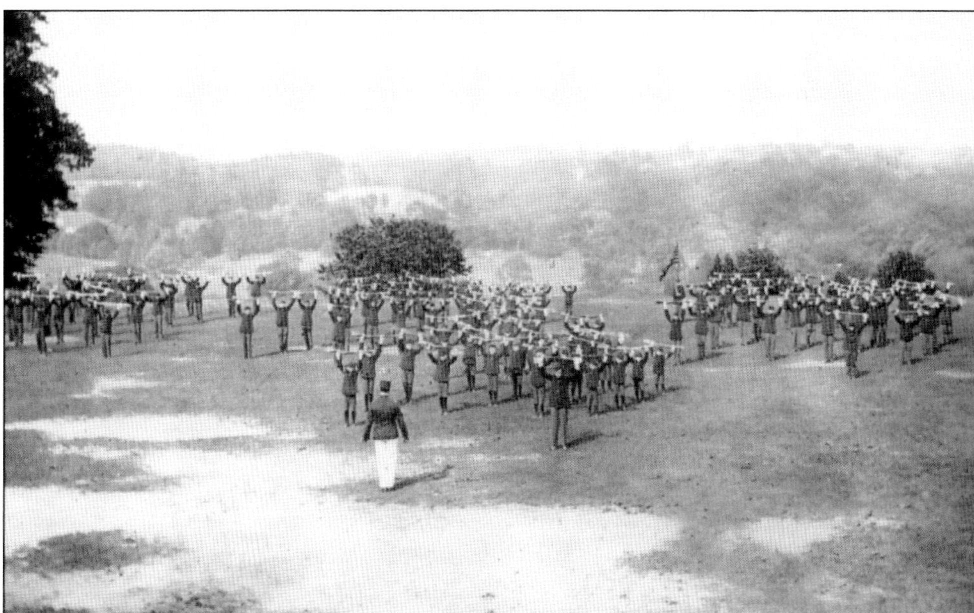

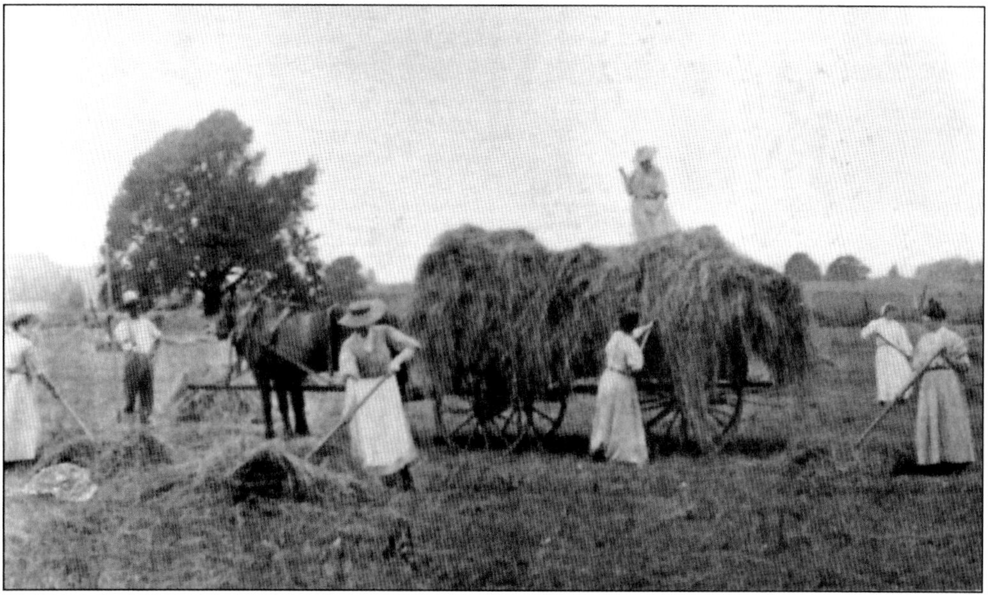

In 1826, the House of Refuge of Philadelphia was founded to provide a place for incarcerated juveniles apart from the adult prison population. In 1910, the House of Refuge moved to Delaware County. The boys were housed at Glen Mills School in Thornbury Township, while the girls lived on the east side of Chester Creek in Middletown Township at Sleighton Farm School for Girls. In 1931, Sleighton Farm School was legally separated from Glen Mills School and incorporated on its own. In 1975, the school became coeducational, changing its name to Sleighton School. In 2001, due to financial difficulties, the school was closed. Middletown is currently developing a part of the former Sleighton campus as a township park. Above, the Sleighton girls are pictured harvesting hay. Pictured below around 1930 is the Lucretia Mott Cottage, a residence hall. (Above, DCHS; below, Keith Lockhart.)

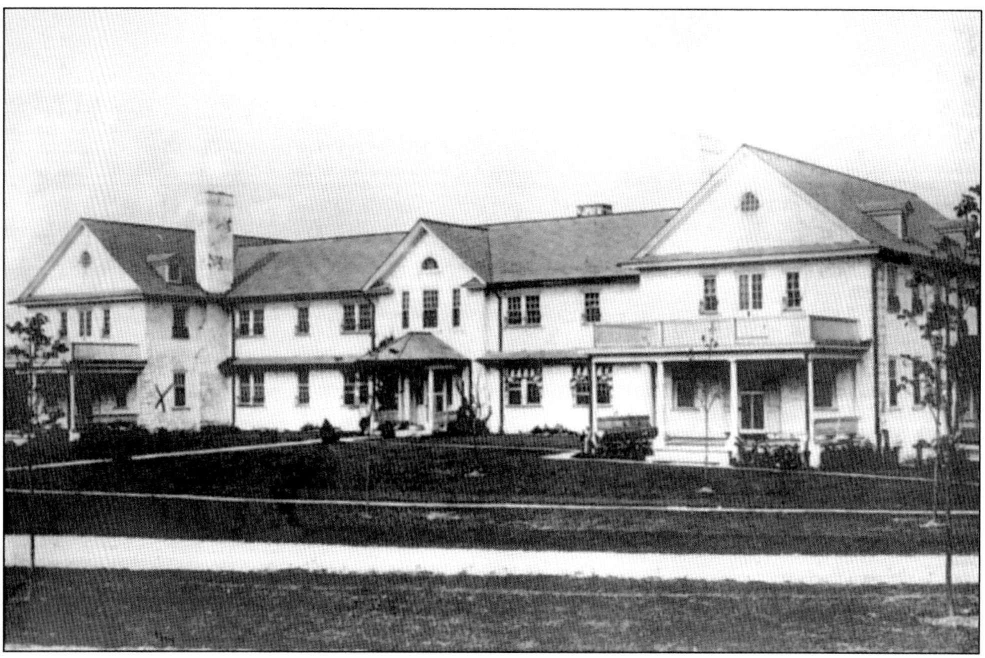

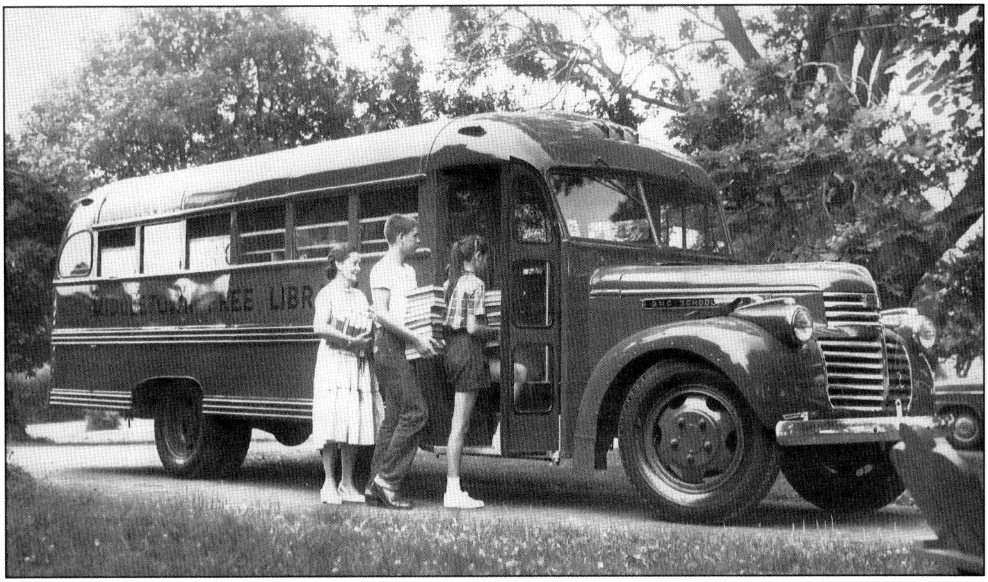

In April 1956, a group of Middletown residents organized the Middletown Free Library Association. Over the next few months, several thousand books were collected from individuals, businesses, and libraries throughout the county. Through a fund drive, an old school bus was purchased and converted to the Bookmobile (above). In August 1956, it made its first run carrying 1,700 books. Staffed by volunteer librarians and drivers, it operated on a weekday schedule, switching to Saturday-only in the fall. Also in the fall of 1956, the library set up temporary quarters at the offices of Naz Mariani on the northeast corner of Baltimore Pike and Black Horse Lane. By 1959, the association had raised enough money to purchase an 1810 house on Pennell Road (below) from the Weathers family. With volunteer help and donations of materials, the Middletown Free Library opened in 1960. (MTFL.)

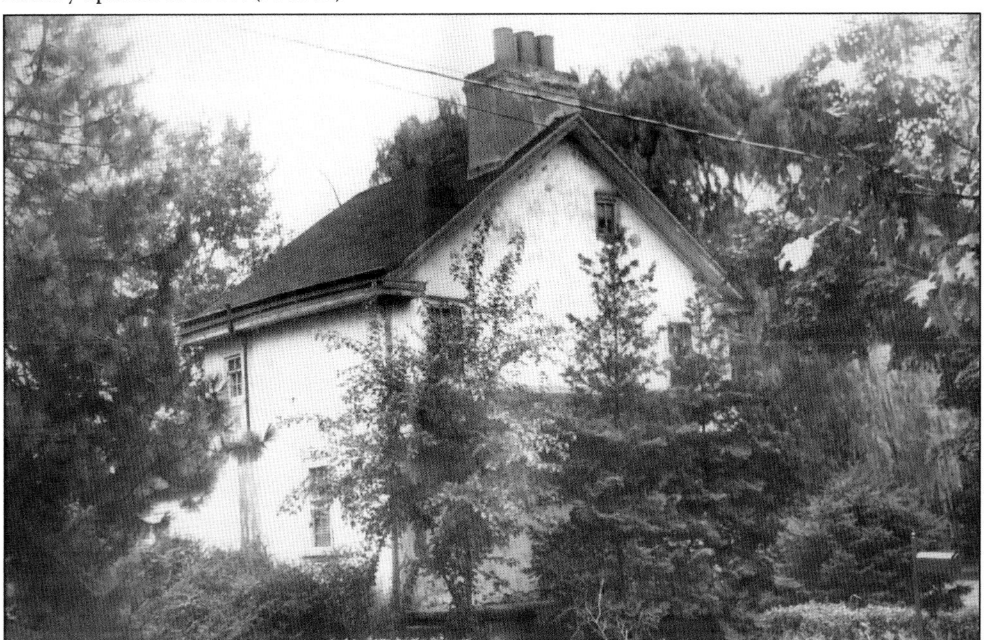

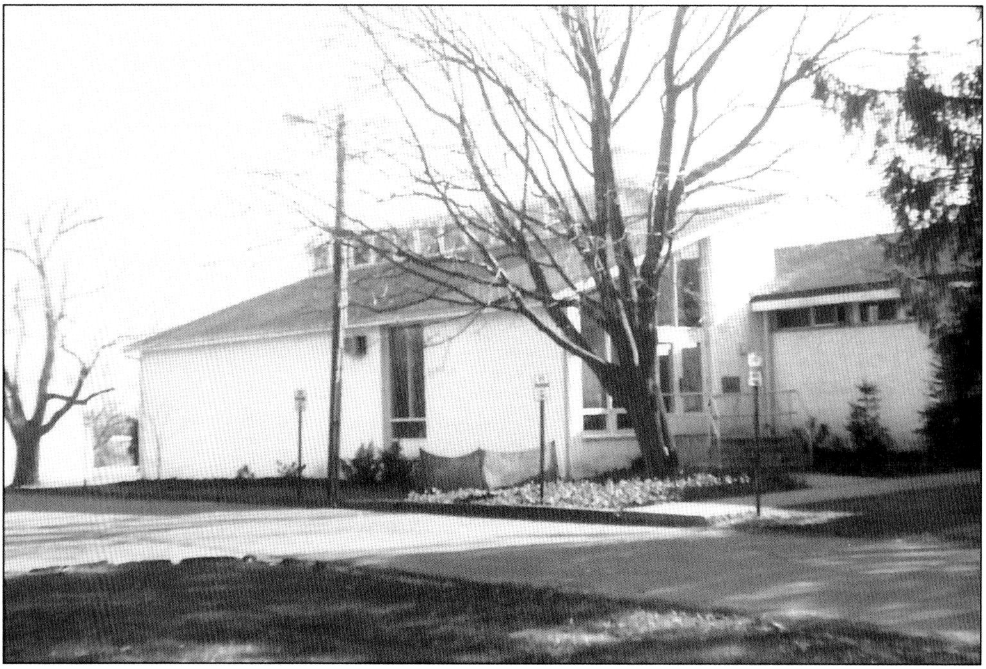

In November 1960, a one mil tax for the library was passed by the township. In 1963, an addition of 1,500 square feet (on the right in the above photograph) was made at a cost of $16,000. A fund drive provided $9,000, and a bank loan furnished the remainder of the money for the addition. A second addition, of 3,000 square feet (on the left, above), was made in 1973 at a cost of $84,000. Of this sum, $35,000 was obtained by a fund drive. Since then, the library has continued to expand and grow thanks to a dedicated staff and devoted volunteers. The library's circulation in June 2009 was 11,154, an all-time high. Shown below is the library as it looks in 2011. (Both, MTFL.)

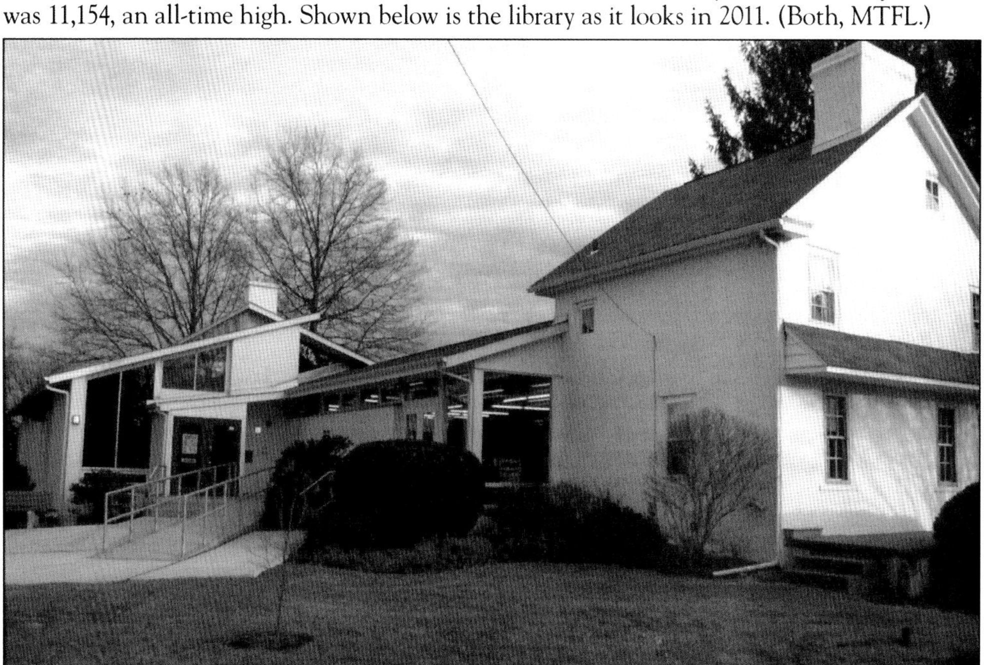

Nine

Sports and Recreation

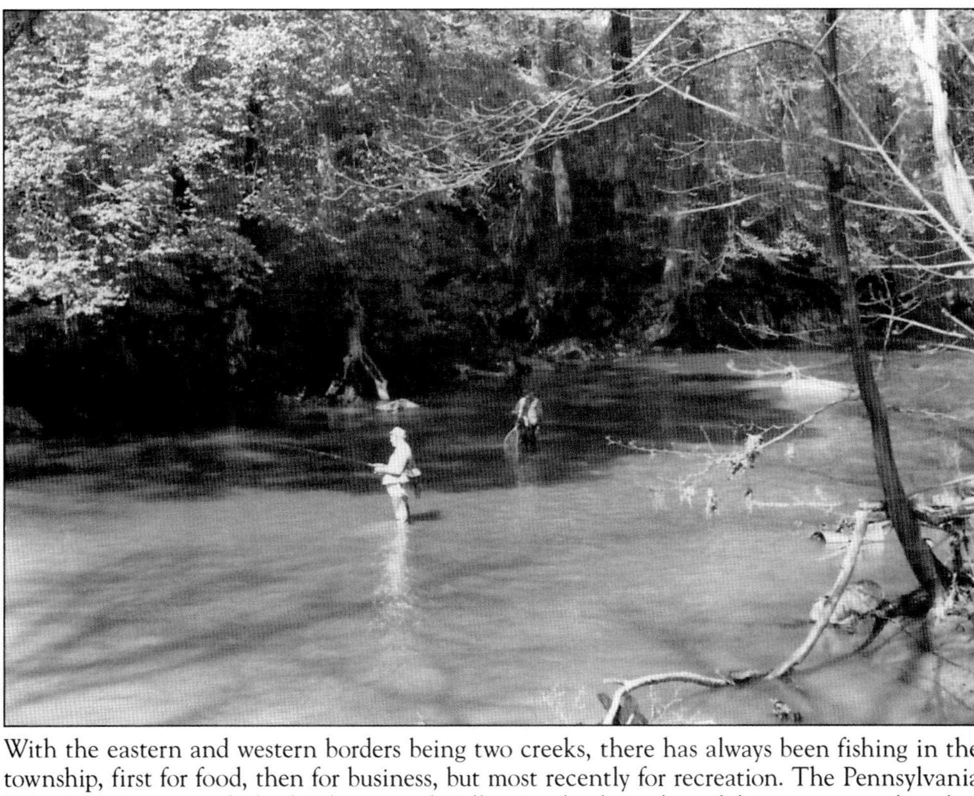

With the eastern and western borders being two creeks, there has always been fishing in the township, first for food, then for business, but most recently for recreation. The Pennsylvania Fish Commission stocks both Chester and Ridley Creeks throughout fishing season and anglers from all over wade into the streams looking for that perfect catch. These people are trying their luck in Chester Creek, just north of Dutton's Mill.

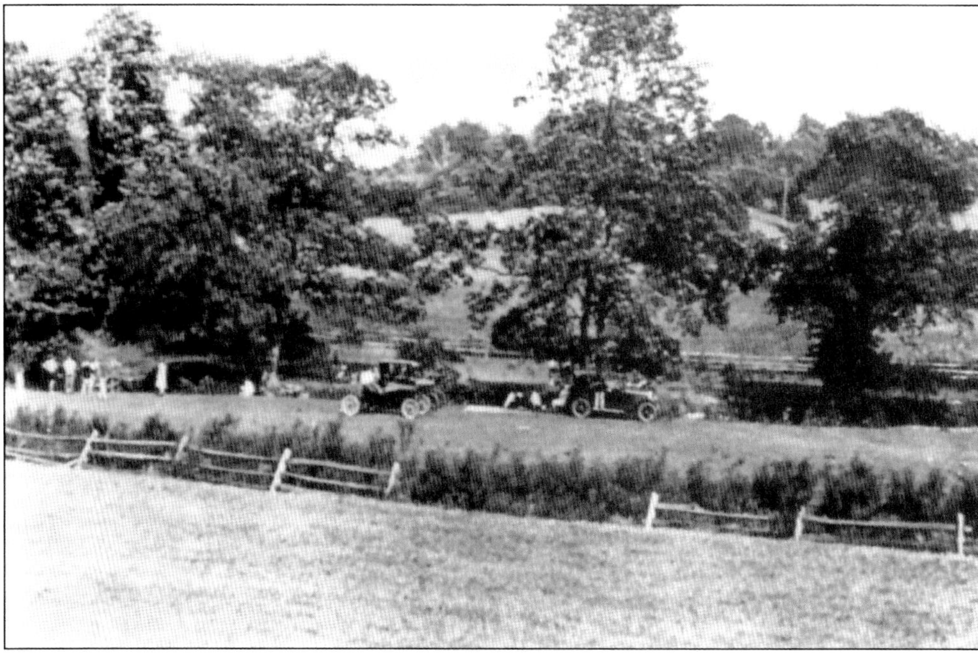

Ridley and Chester Creeks also provided plenty of swimming holes well into the 20th century. Smedley's Meadow, pictured here in the 1920s, was a popular spot for swimming and camping. The meadow is on the west bank of Ridley Creek along Ridley Creek Road at the spot where the creek makes a sharp turn to the west. This is a little north of Red Bridge, where a covered bridge once carried Rose Tree Road over the creek. In the photograph above, swimmers are at the far left preparing to enter the water. Ridley Creek Road runs along the fence on the far bank. Below, campers have set up their tents to use as changing rooms and for sleeping outside on hot summer nights. (Both, MHAC.)

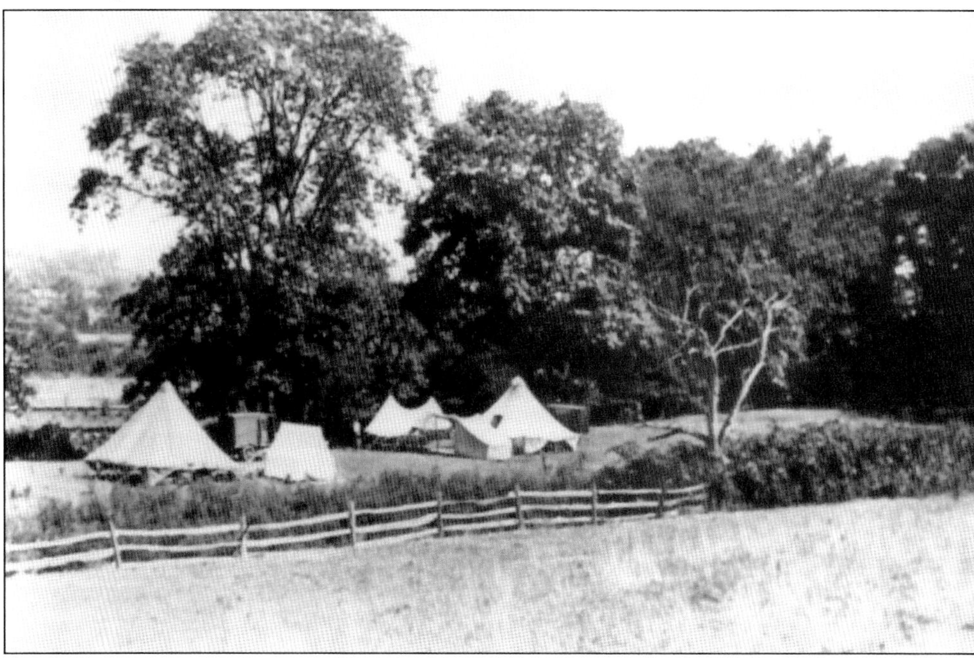

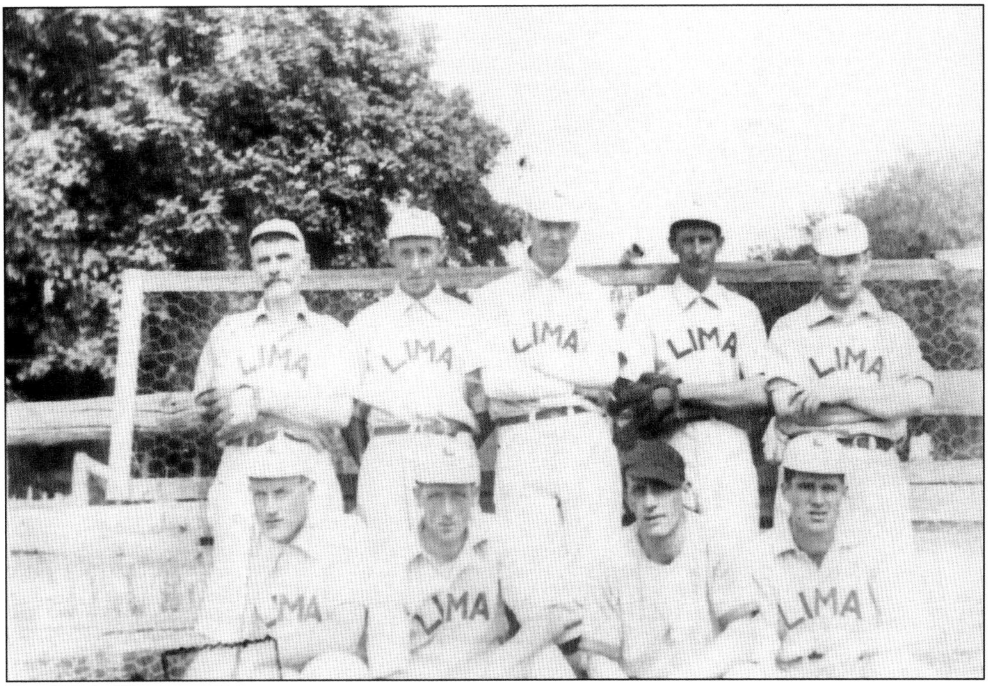

A Lima baseball team of the early 1900s is pictured here in front of their chicken-wire backstop. Included in this image are, from left to right, (first row) Edgar Pennington, George Yarnall, Bill Rosen, and Clarence Pennington; (second row) Bill Garrett, Charles ?, Pearson Turner, Charles Green, and Albert Yarnall.

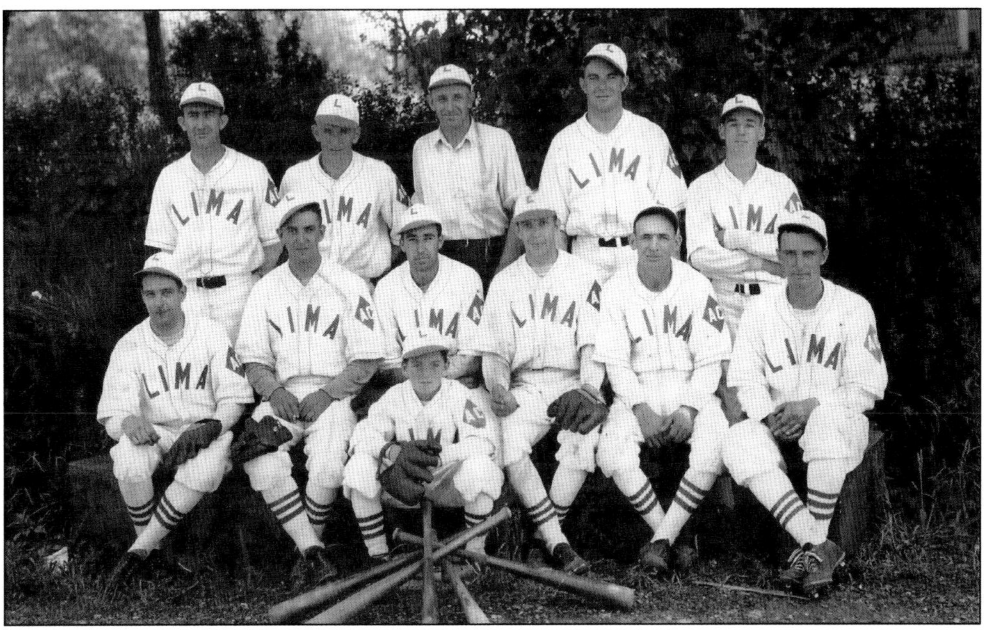

Pictured here is the Lima baseball team of 1934–1935. Included in this image are, from left to right, (first row) Gibby Middleton, Bill Hayes, Puss Johnson, Howard Worrall, J. Crowley (possibly), and William Morrow; (second row) Gerald Matthews, F. Hedge (possibly), Bill Mellen, George Wilson, and Pick McCue. The bat boy is Lefty McDowell.

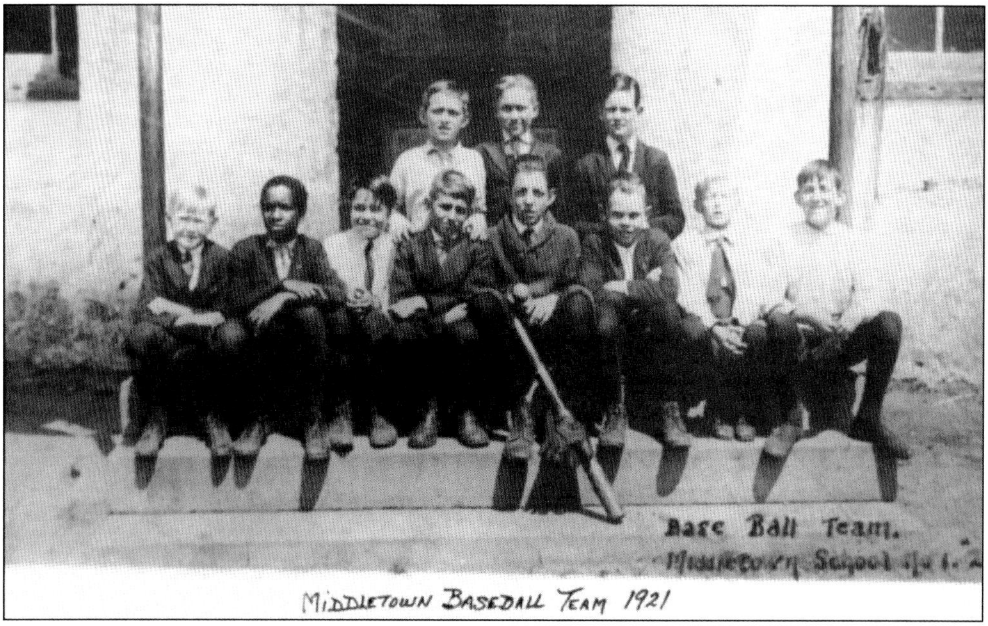

This is the Middletown School baseball team of 1921, possibly at the Parkmount School. Pictured are, from left to right, (first row) Clarence Bonsall, James Carter, Ernest Zerlando, Paul Allam, Charles Thompson, E. Tron, Richard Solomon, and Raymond Pyle; (second row) Charles Moore, Mark Allam, and Ted Scott.

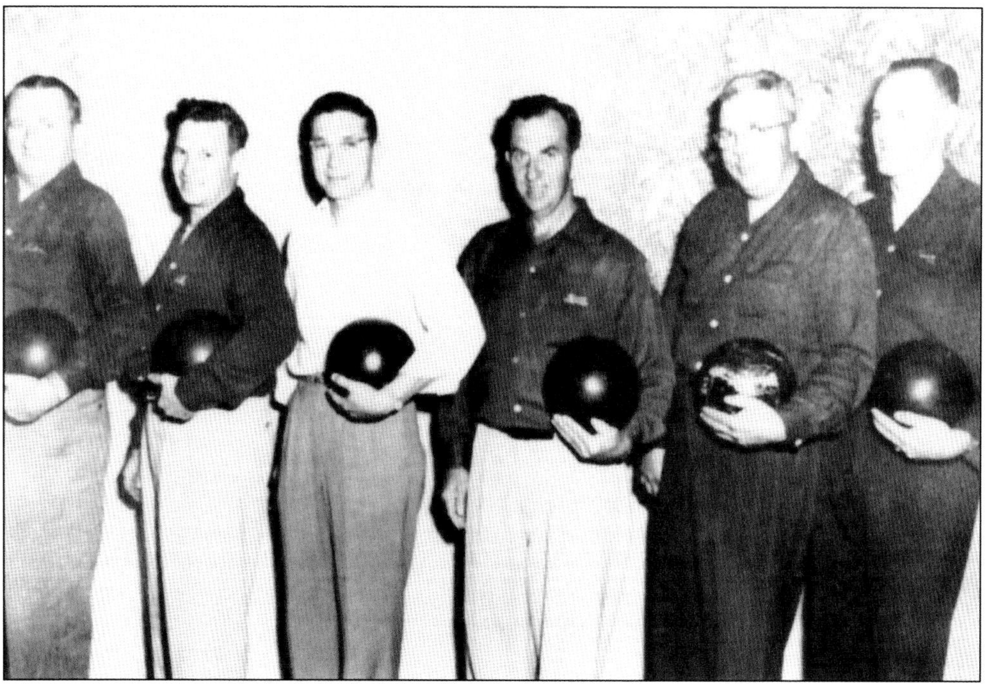

Members of the Lima bowling team of 1938 are, from left to right, John Lank, Richard Darlington, Walt Kearney, Bill Hayes, Dick Hayes, and Mort Kellerman. There was never a bowling alley in Middletown. The consensus among longtime township residents is that the team used bowling lanes in Springfield.

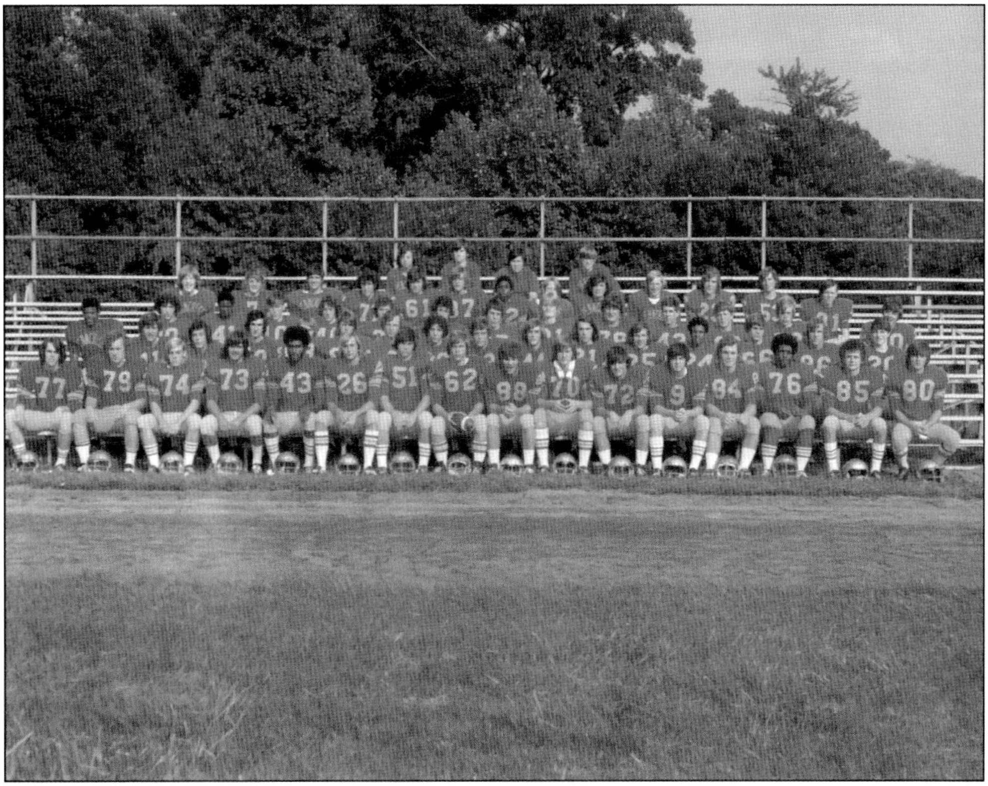

At right, Bill Eves poses in his 1974 Penncrest High School football team uniform. The full team is pictured above. Penncrest was Rose Tree Union School District's first high school. It is on the south side of Barren Road, east of Van Leer Avenue. The land was part of the Smedleys' Penncrest Farm, from which the school takes its name. Prior to its opening in the fall of 1957, most township high school students attended Media High School. The elementary schools in Middletown housed kindergarten through eighth grade until the first junior high, Indian Lane, opened in 1960. In 1966, Rose Tree Union merged with the Media School District; Penncrest, with a second wing of 22 classrooms recently added, became the sole high school in the new Rose Tree Media School District.

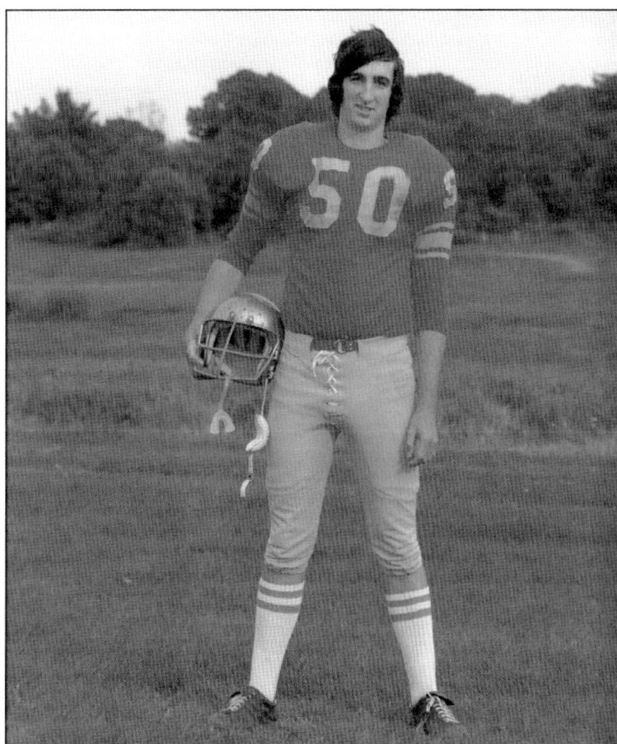

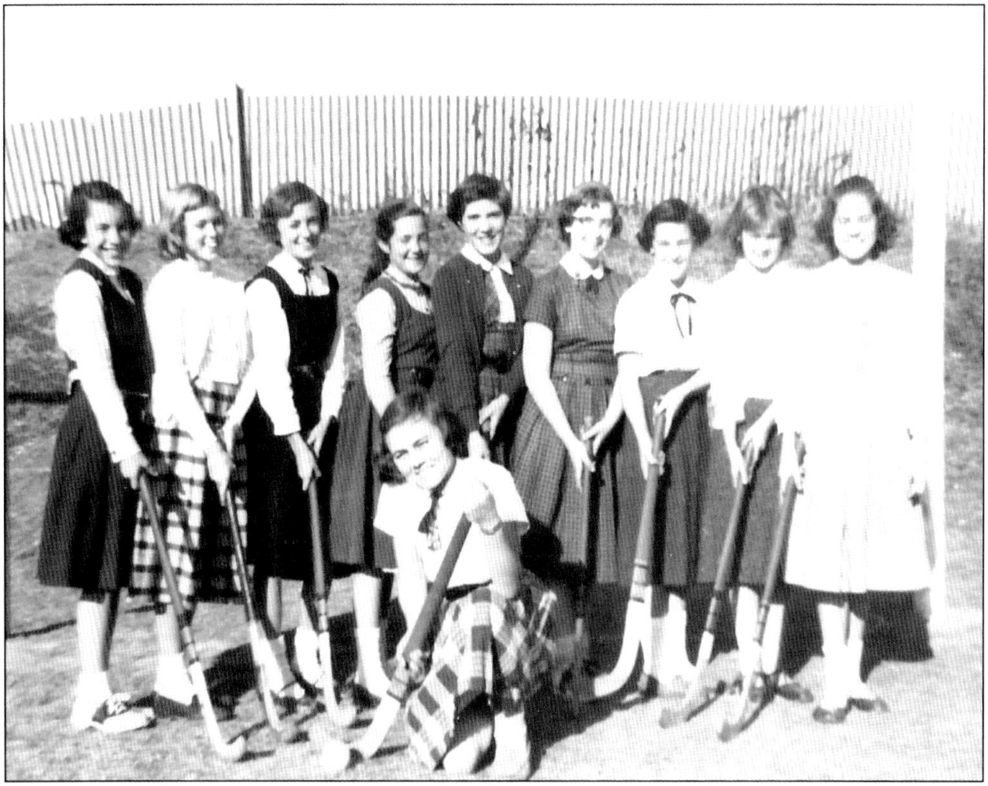

Above are the "Goal Getters," the Penncrest junior varsity field hockey team of 1958. Pictured are, from left to right, Bonnie Strang, Sarah Reed, Patricia Christie, Connie Harbaugh, Hester Goodenough, Helen Smith, Mary Wright, Margaret Fields, and Alma Omlor. Kneeling in front is Helen Allen. Below is the varsity field hockey team in action in the early 1960s. (Above, Barbara Anderson; below, PHSAA.)

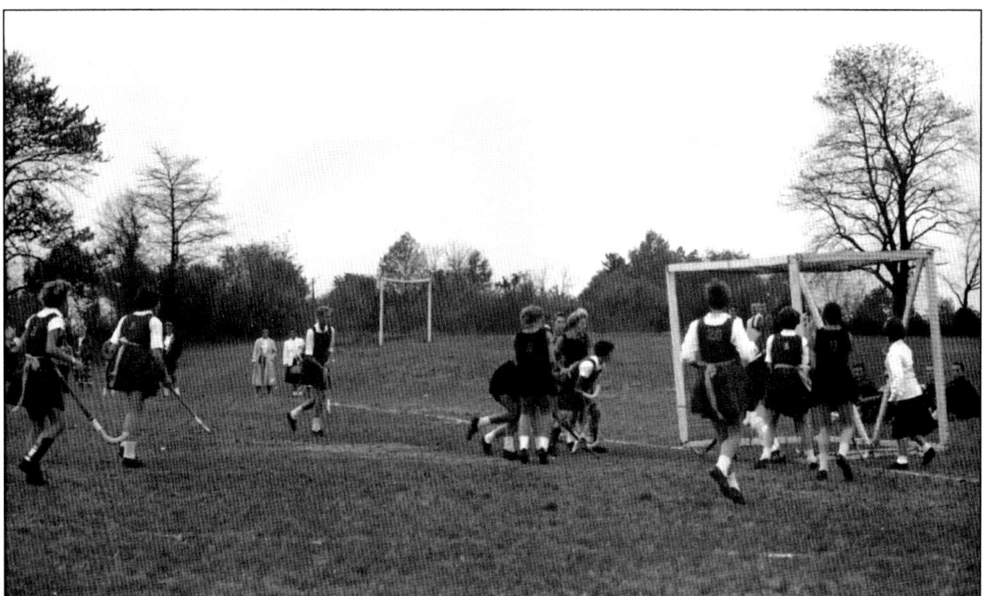

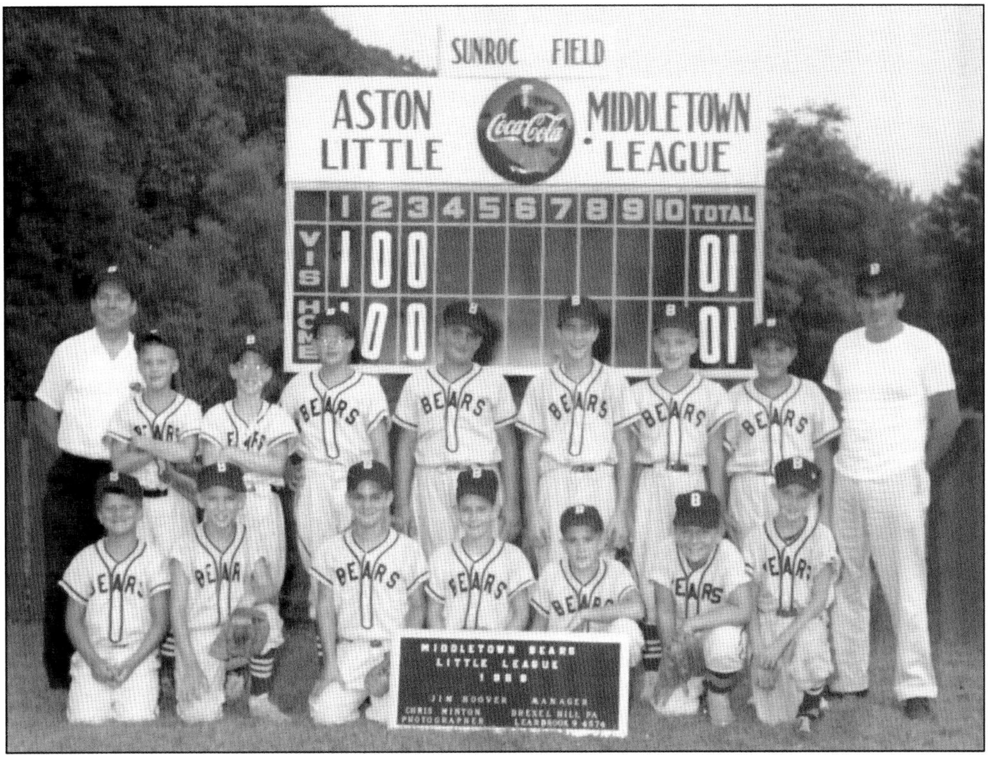

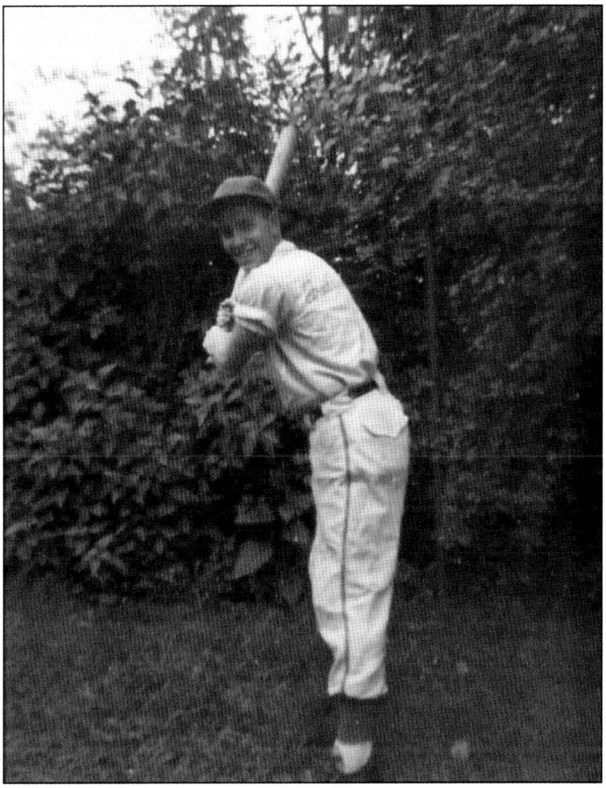

Founded in 1950, the Aston-Middletown Little League has called Sunroc Field home for over 60 years. Nestled in the flood plain between Pennell Road and Chester Creek, this Glen Riddle ballpark is now fielding players whose fathers and grandfathers played here before them. Teams in the first decade included the Aston Lions, the Middletown Bears, the Middletown Tigers, and the Saint Francis Sparrows. Above, the Middletown Bears of 1956 and their managers are, from left to right, (first row) unidentified, Eugene Rydell, Miles Lull, Bob Barrow, Chuck Longbottom, and two unidentified; (second row) manager Jim Hoover, Bill Wilkinson, Tony Sheeky, Ken Johnson, Pat Sheeky Jr., John Hoover, unidentified, Hank ?, and assistant manager Pat Sheeky Sr. At right, J. Karl Thomas plays for the Lenni Athletic Club in 1951.

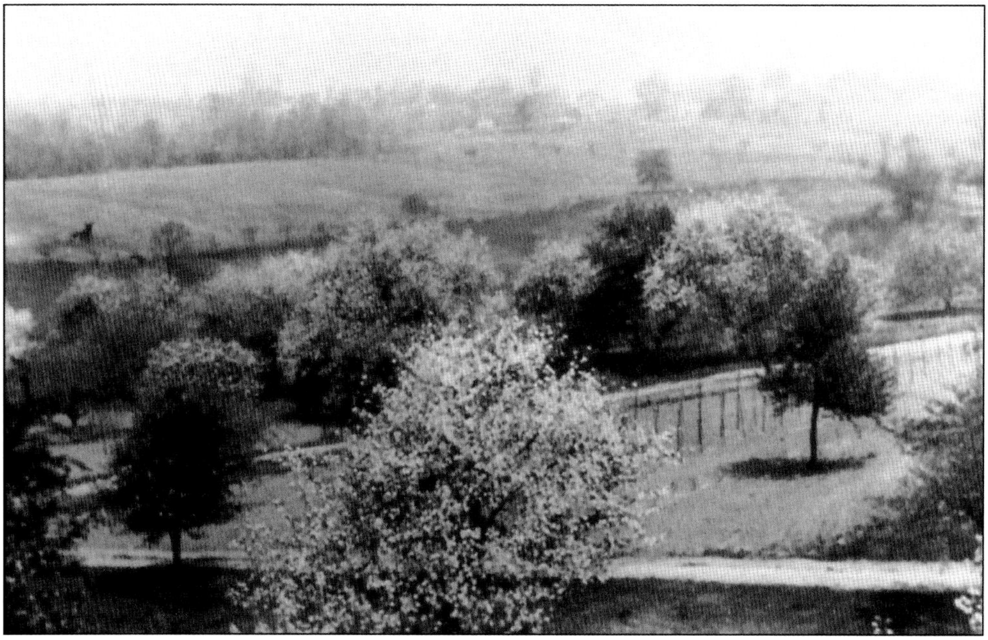

In 1932, Herman and Edith Cope made part of their farm and orchard, on the west side of Middletown Road at Copes Lane, available to the Girl Scouts of Delaware County. Camp Indian Orchards was used as a day camp for the Scouts and a training area for leaders. In 1952, the Girl Scouts purchased the 33-acre site from the Cope family, adding an additional three acres in 1955. Through the summer of 1978, four camps lasting two weeks each were held, with a total of 800 day campers participating. In 1979, the Girl Scouts decided to close the camp and sell the land. Above is a view of Cope's orchard in the 1940s, below is the main shelter at Camp Indian Orchards in 1979.

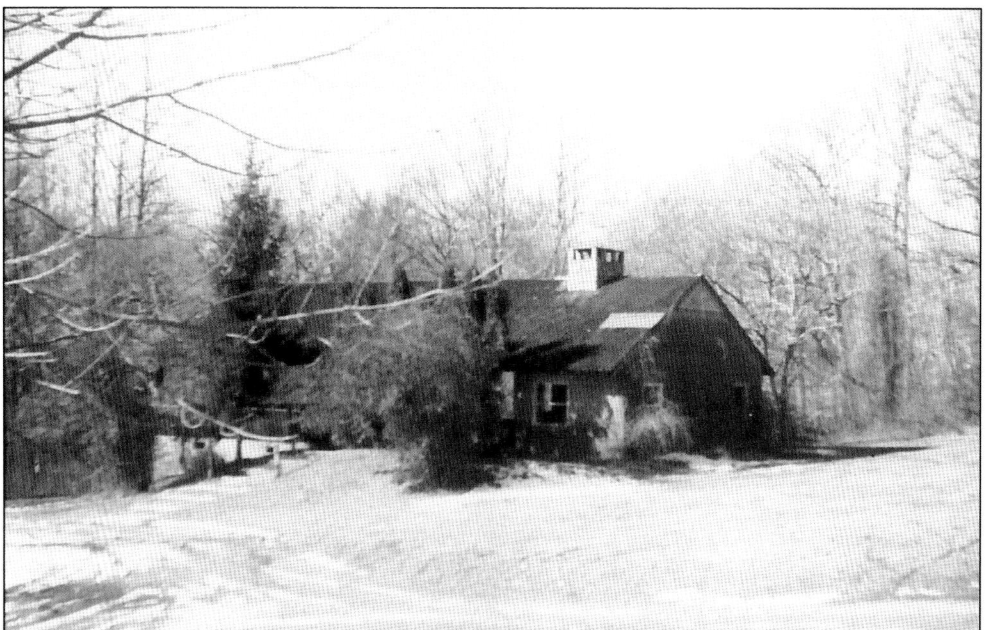

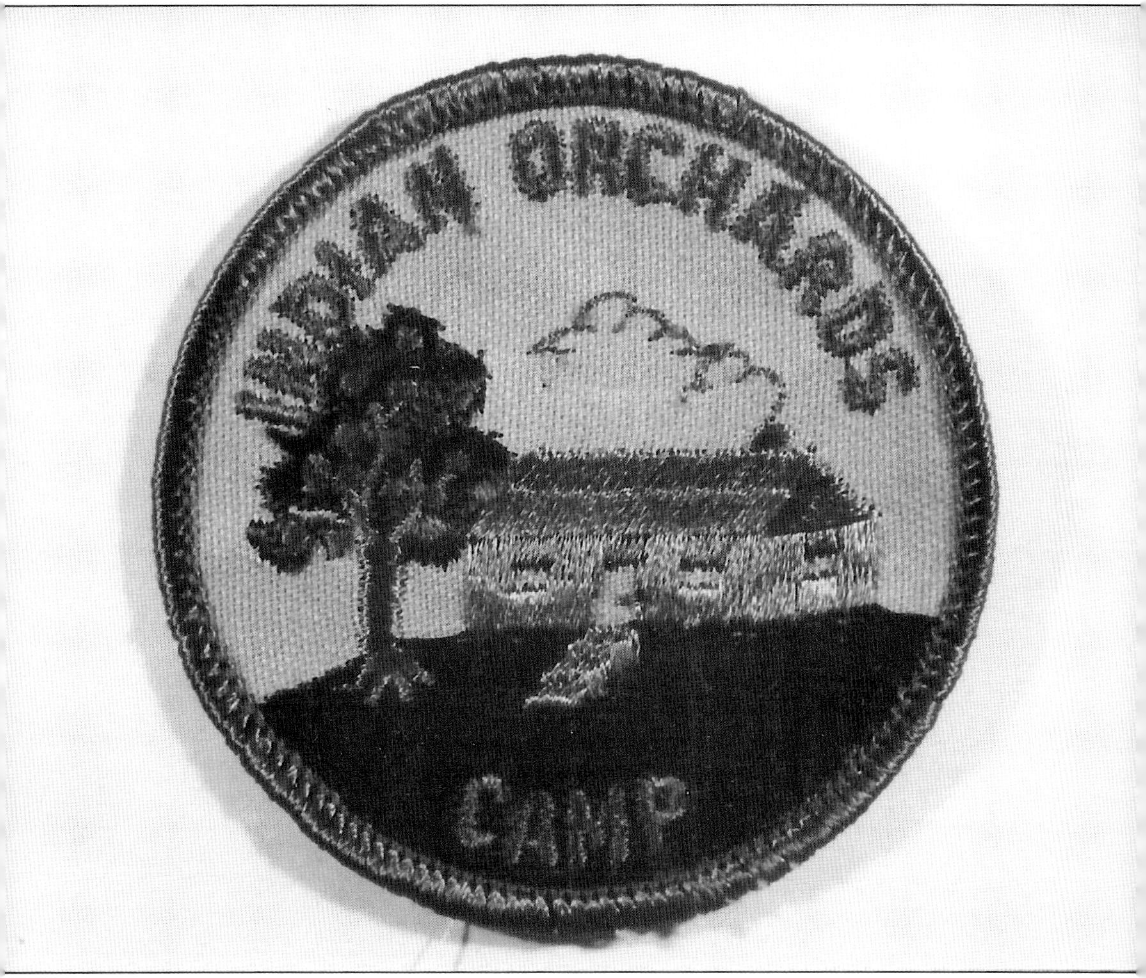

The Middletown Township Land Conservancy (MTLC) was formed in 1981 when a group of neighbors joined together to preserve Camp Indian Orchards from being developed. This natural area was one of the few available undeveloped large tracts of land in a sea of houses and included 100- to 200-year-old trees, three streams that are part of the Chester Creek watershed, and a rich habitat for small animals and numerous migratory and nesting birds. MTLC launched a campaign to persuade the township to purchase the land for a passive recreational park. The township was awarded a grant of $75,000 from the federal government, while MTLC conducted a fundraising drive to make up the rest of the approximate $225,000 purchase price. Indian Orchard Park was officially dedicated by township officials on September 21, 1985. In 1995, David Lansdale, a charter member of MTLC, conveyed 4.7 acres of his land adjoining Indian Orchards Park to the township. The walking trails of the park were extended through this additional acreage, which became known as Lansdale's Glen. Since its founding, MTLC has played a major role in changing attitudes about open space preservation in Middletown Township. In 1987, a special binding referendum won overwhelming approval from Middletown voters, allowing the township to acquire over 300 acres of farmland owned by the Linvill family in the eastern part of the township and by the Darlington family on the township's western border.

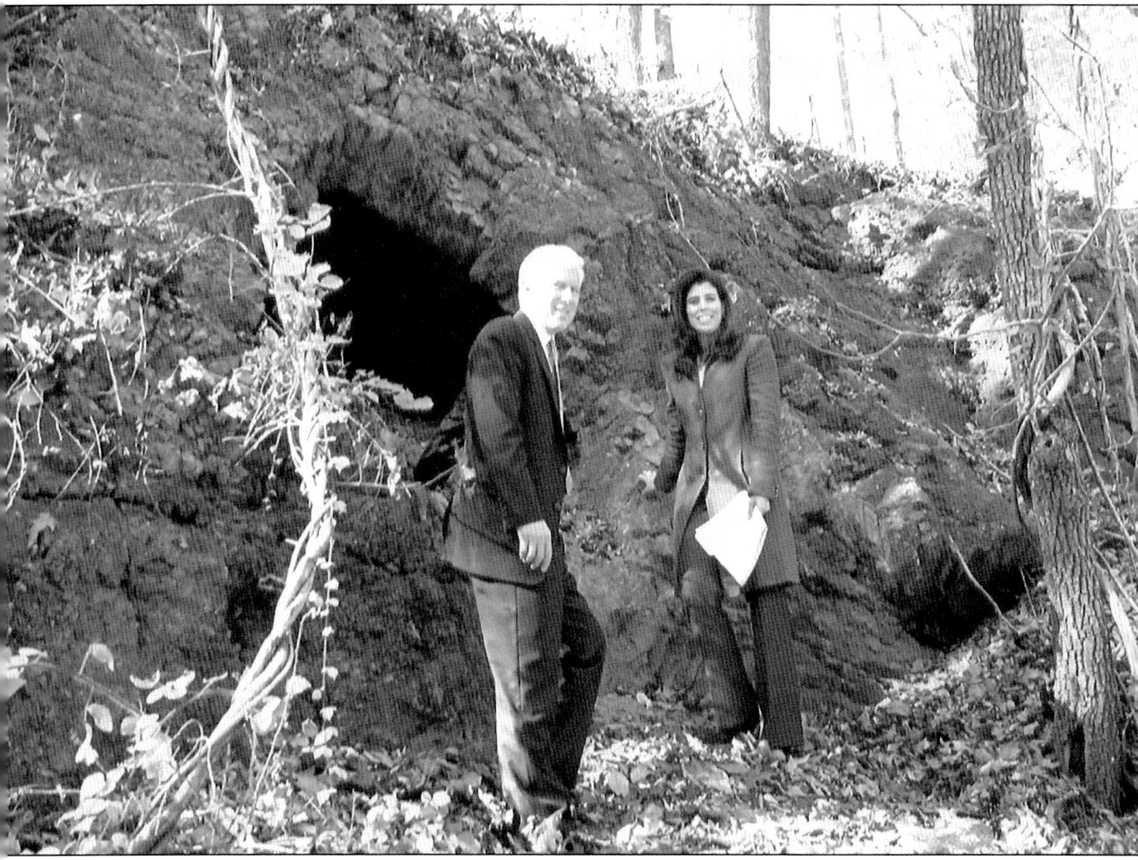

In November 2010, Delaware County dedicated Mineral Hill as a new park. Local efforts to protect this property, on the north side of Baltimore Pike rising west from Ridley Creek, began in 1994. Under the direction of county council vice chair Christine Fizzano Canon (above, at the former Crumps' Quarry site on Mineral Hill with Councilman Andy Lewis), the county, the township, the Natural Lands Trust, and MTLC were among the many groups working toward saving Mineral Hill. J. Roger Mitchell, from the Delaware County Institute of Science, said, "Not many people realize that Mineral Hill is famous among rock buffs, nor do they know that the land's most unusual natural resources are underground and in stream beds. Science museums all over the world have minerals from Mineral Hill."

Ten

Elsewhere in the Township

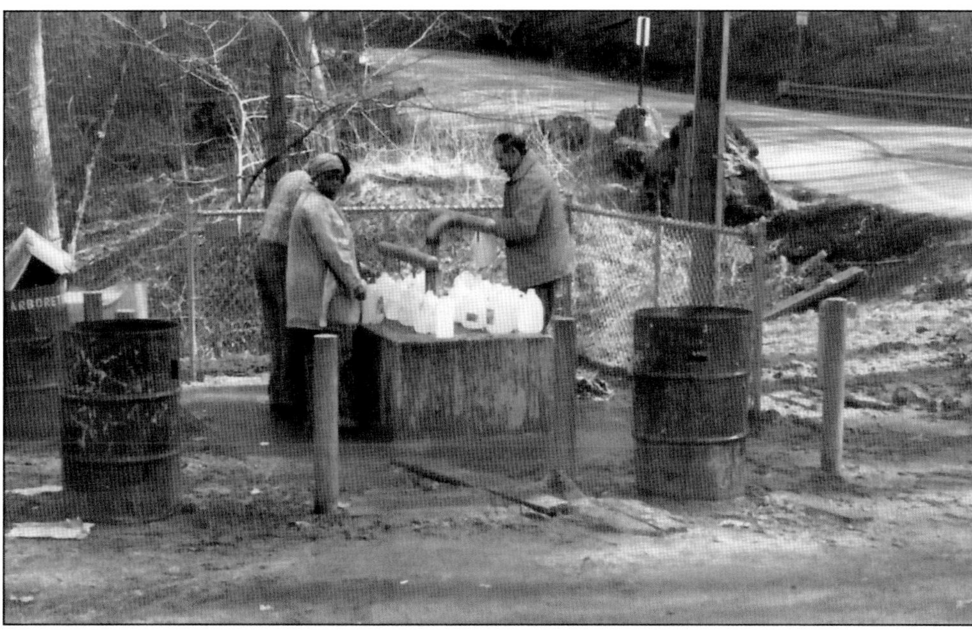

This is Black Hawk or the Barren Spring. It was on the south side of Barren Road, about 2,000 feet east of Sycamore Mills. Since 1928, residents from all over the county had come to bottle water from this natural aquifer. In 1977, Tyler Arboretum assumed responsibility for water testing on a regular basis. In October 1997, no longer able to afford the expense of testing, Tyler closed the spring permanently.

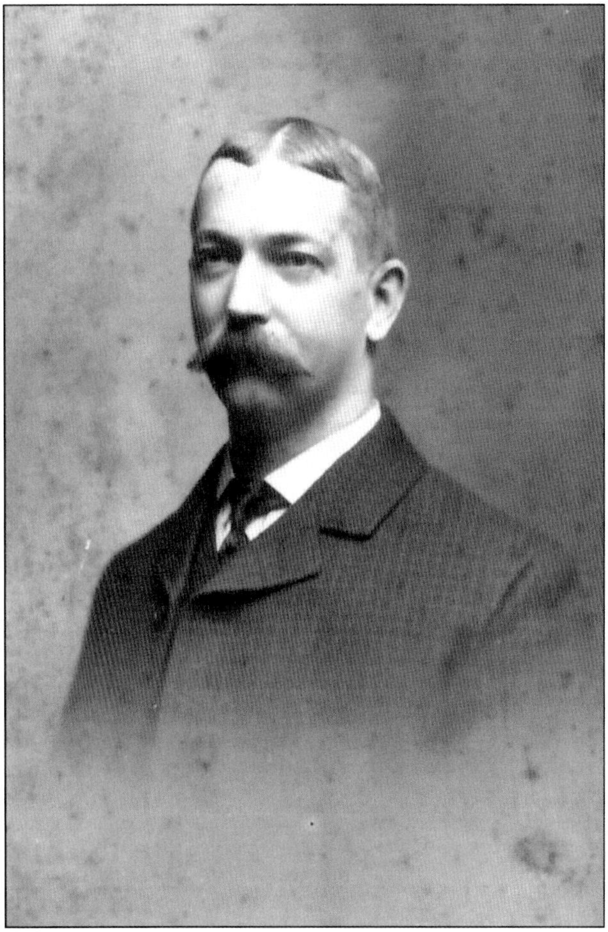

Bortondale was built by William R. (left) and Martha Borton from 1905 to 1915. It was the first housing development in the township, a group of homes without the usual mill, crossroads, or business associated with them. It was originally called Wellscrest, because Bortondale Road was first a trolley right-of-way across Samuel Wells's farm. In the early 1900s, the homes had water rights to be served with gravity-fed water from a spring located north of Bortondale. The view below is from the 1920s. (Left, MHAC.)

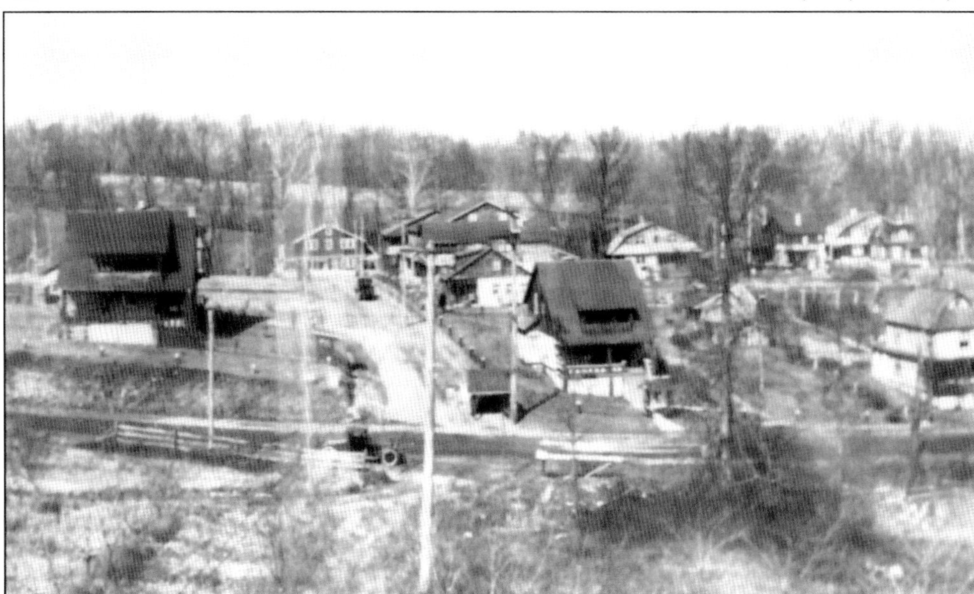

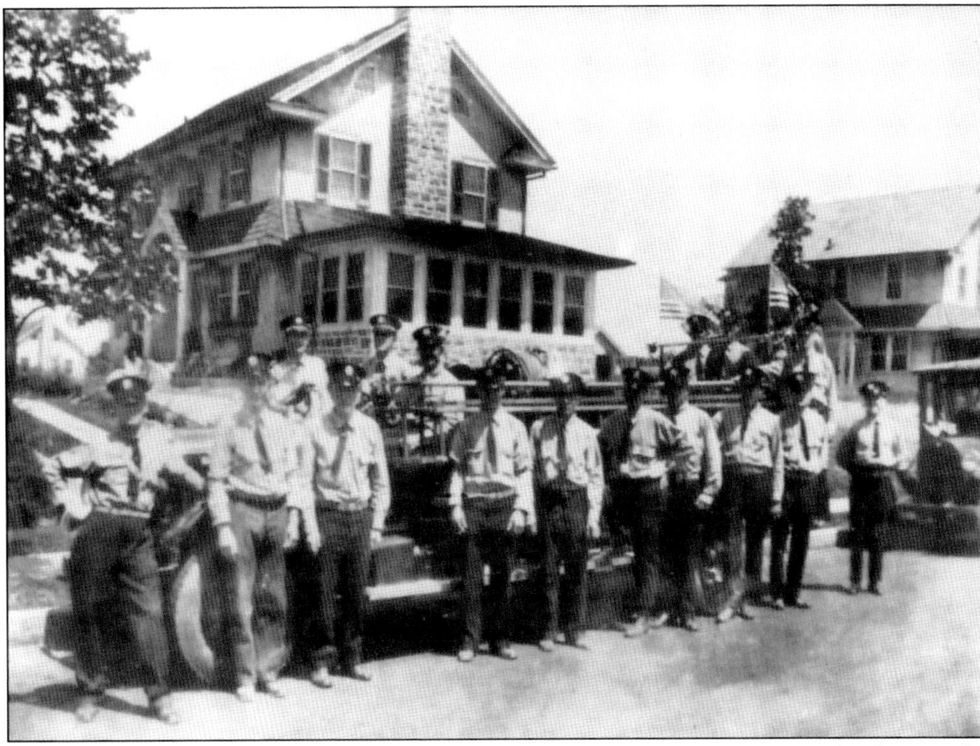

Chartered in 1922, the all-volunteer Middletown Fire Company No. 1 was the first in the township. They began in Bortondale with 12 buckets and a two-wheeled hand-pulled hose cart. William Borton constructed a small building on Howarth Street to hold the equipment. In 1922, the company purchased a used 1919 Ford fire truck (above), and work began on a firehouse at Bortondale Road and Oak (now Levis) Avenue. With the volunteers working in shifts, the structure was completed in 1925. From 1962 to 1964, a new station (below) was built on the site of the former station. In 1996, the company moved to a much larger, state-of-the art station on the east side of Middletown Road behind Roosevelt School, with access to Old Middletown Road via the PennDOT facility.

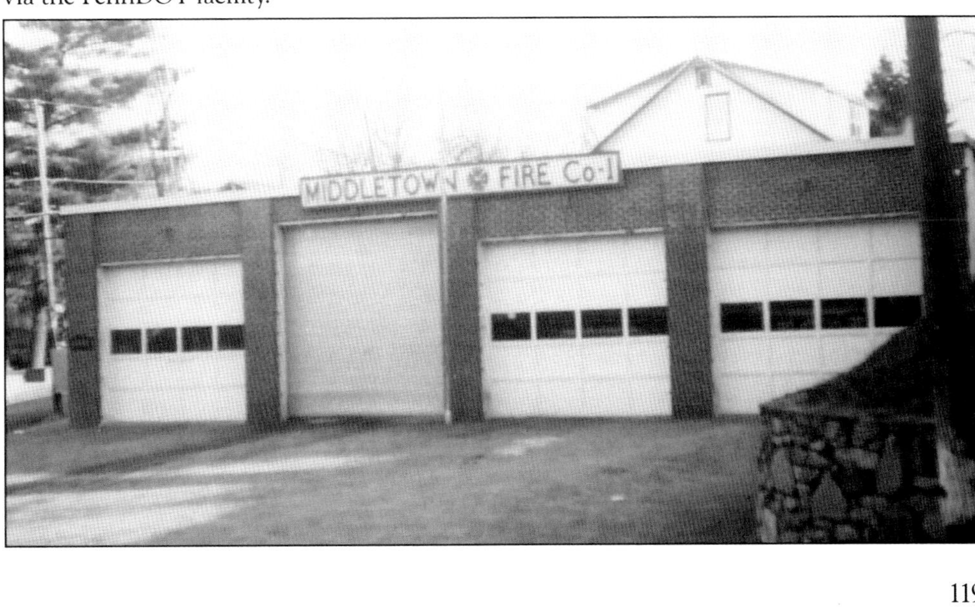

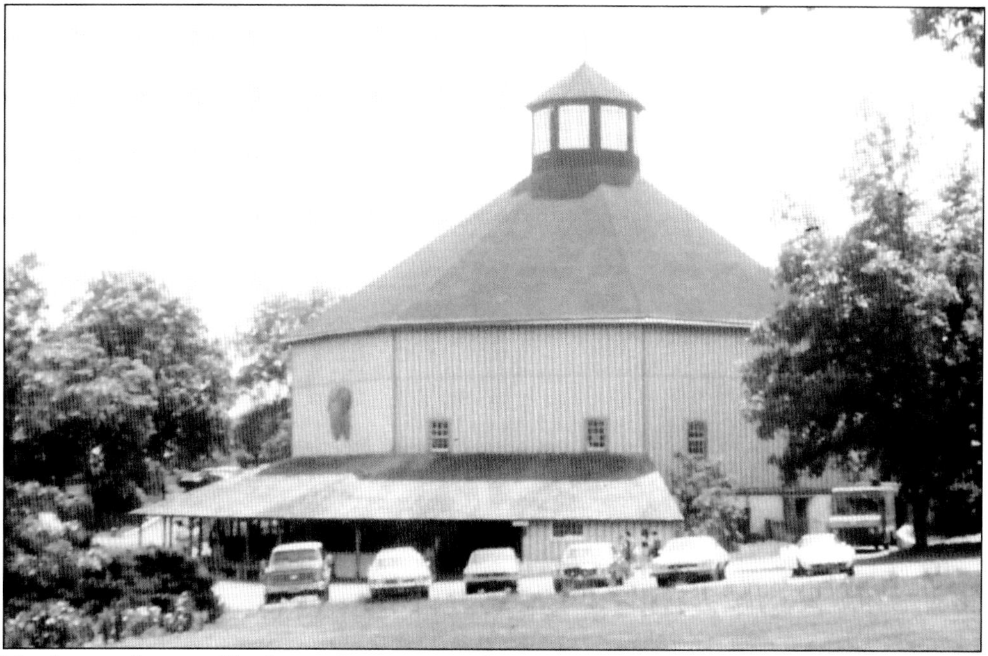

Until it was destroyed by fire in August 2002, this 80-foot octagonal barn, seen in 1979, was the symbol of Linvilla Orchards. Located on the north side of Knowlton Road, it was built as a cattle barn in 1889. The unique inverted funnel shape provided air circulation for the livestock. Arthur Linvill purchased the farm in 1914 and planted a peach orchard. By 1918, he was selling peaches from the porch of his house, which is still in the Linvill family. The house is pictured below in 1984. From peaches, the family expanded to a wide range of fruits and vegetables over the past 100-plus years, turning the barn into their farm market. The barn was not rebuilt after the fire, but the market continues in two other buildings on the property. Today, the orchard offers quality fresh and prepared foods, pick-your-own crops, hayrides, and other seasonal events.

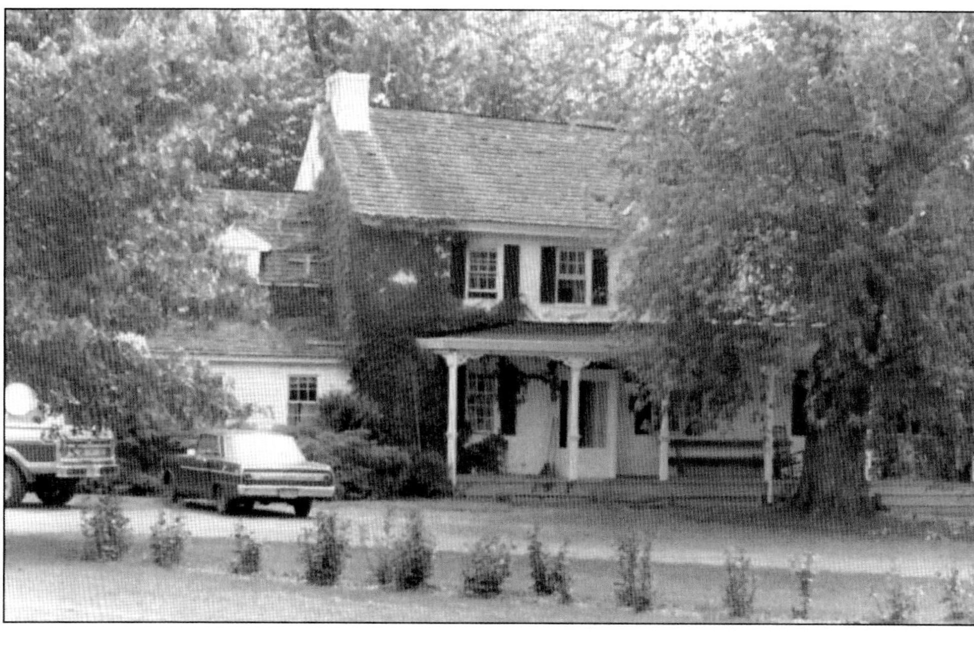

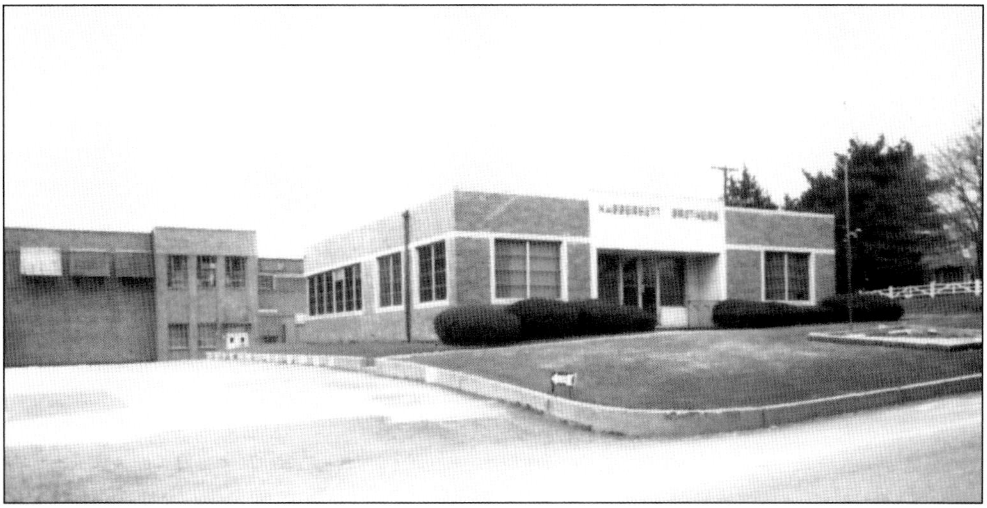

Isaac Habbersett started to make and sell fine quality sausage and scrapple in 1863 at his farm along Middletown Road north of Knowlton Road. As the farm prospered, Isaac's sons, Isaac Jr. and E. Harper Habbersett, took over the business as Habbersett Brothers. In 1914, they built a pork processing plant on the north side of Knowlton Road west of Middletown Road. The plant was enlarged in 1941. By 1988, the fourth generation of Habbersetts was running the business. Facing the prospect of vastly upgrading the aging facility, they elected to sell the brand to Jones Dairy Farm of Fort Atkinson, Wisconsin. Today, Habbersetts is still "Philadelphia's Favorite," even though it is no longer manufactured in Middletown. Above is the plant in 1979, and below is one of Isaac Habbersett's delivery wagons in Media's 1950 centennial parade.

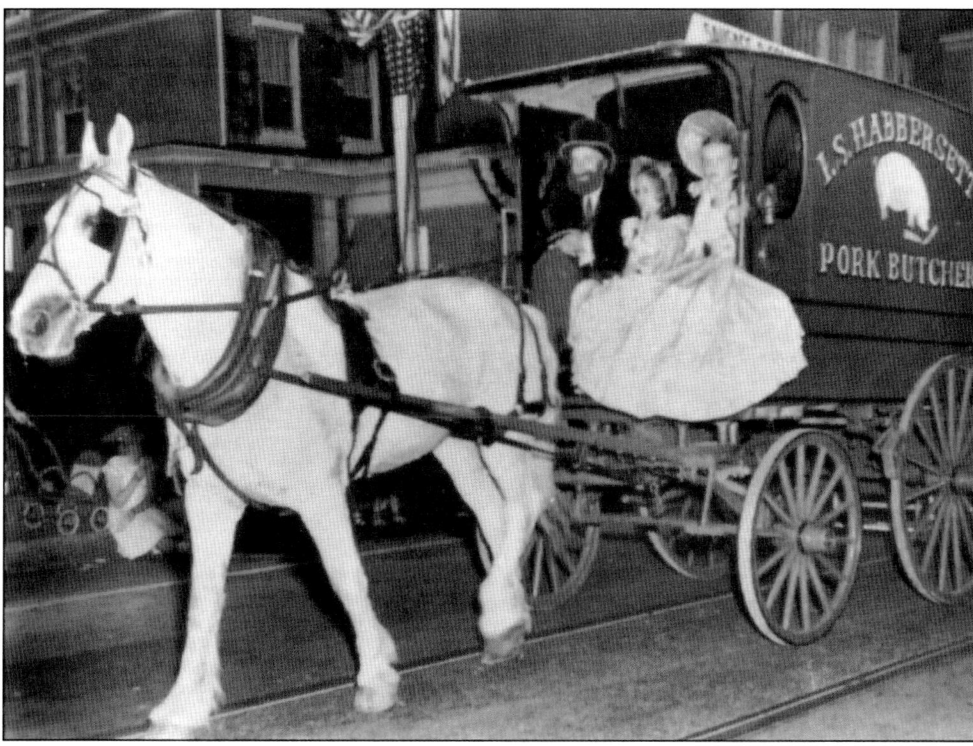

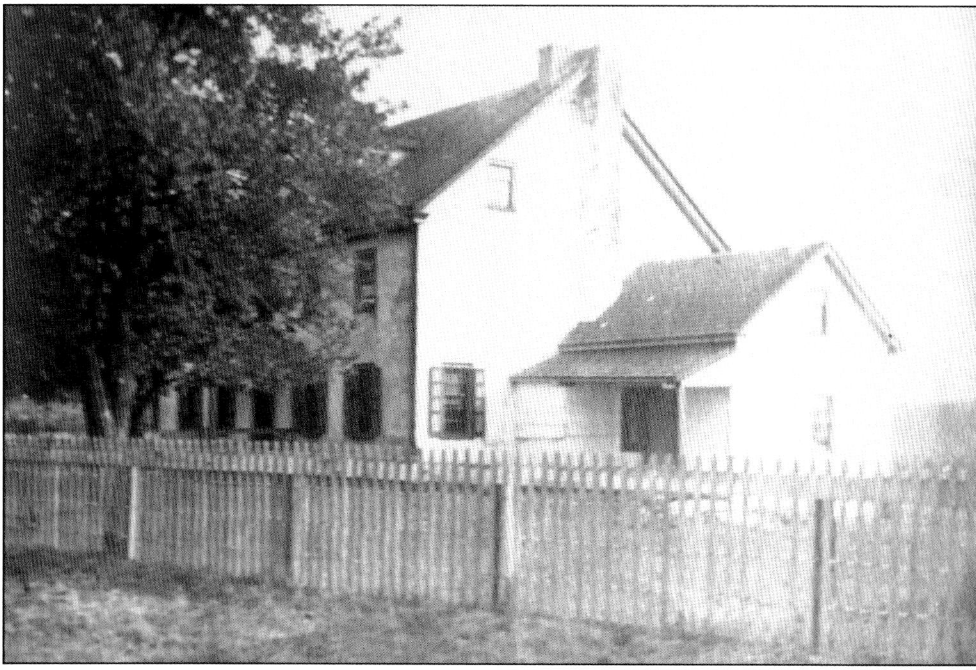

The Ogden-Pennell House, pictured above in 1912, is on the northwest corner of Middletown Road and Old Forge Road. Since 1856, it has been part of Fair Acres Geriatric Center. A small part of this house may remain from the home built here by David Ogden in 1681, but most of the house is from the 18th and 19th centuries. By 1856, it was the residence of Abraham Pennell. This may also have been the Polly Hill Tavern beginning in 1731, when Jonathan Hunter applied to keep a "house of entertainment" on the "Great Road from Chester to the Valley." The license was transferred to other owners until 1788, when it ceased to be a tavern. In the 1979 photograph below, the 13-story Geriatric Building at Fair Acres is just visible on the left. (Above, DCHS.)

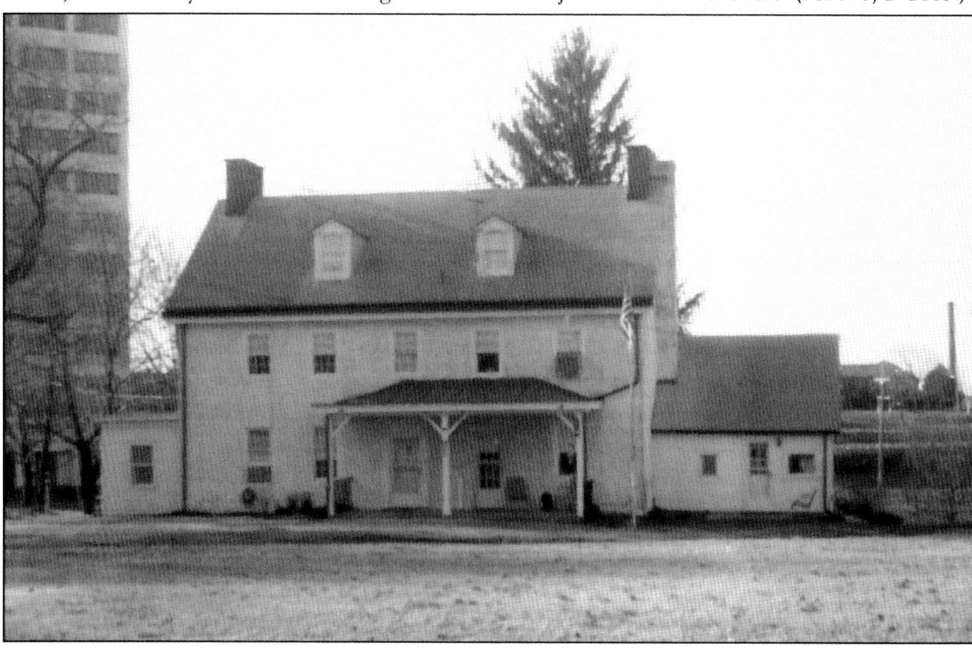

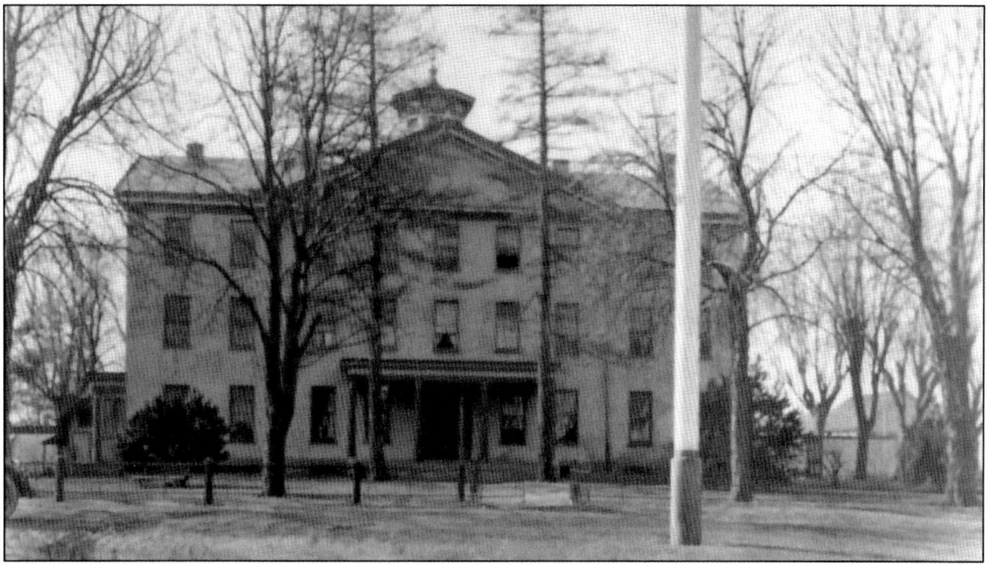

The act creating the Delaware County House of Employment, also known as the county poor farm or county almshouse, was passed on February 13, 1804. A 137-acre farm in Upper Providence Township was purchased that year, and by 1807, a poorhouse had been built on the grounds. In May 1856, the Directors of the Poor purchased a farm from Abraham Pennell on the west side of Middletown Road. A new residence/administration building (pictured above in 1907) was opened in May 1857. Over time, dozens of new buildings were added to the campus, often replacing older, out-of-date facilities. Still operated by Delaware County, over the past 200 years Fair Acres has evolved from a working farm where residents who were able worked in the fields to earn their keep to a full-scale geriatric care center. Middletown Road runs across the top of the c. 1970 view below. (Above, DCHS.)

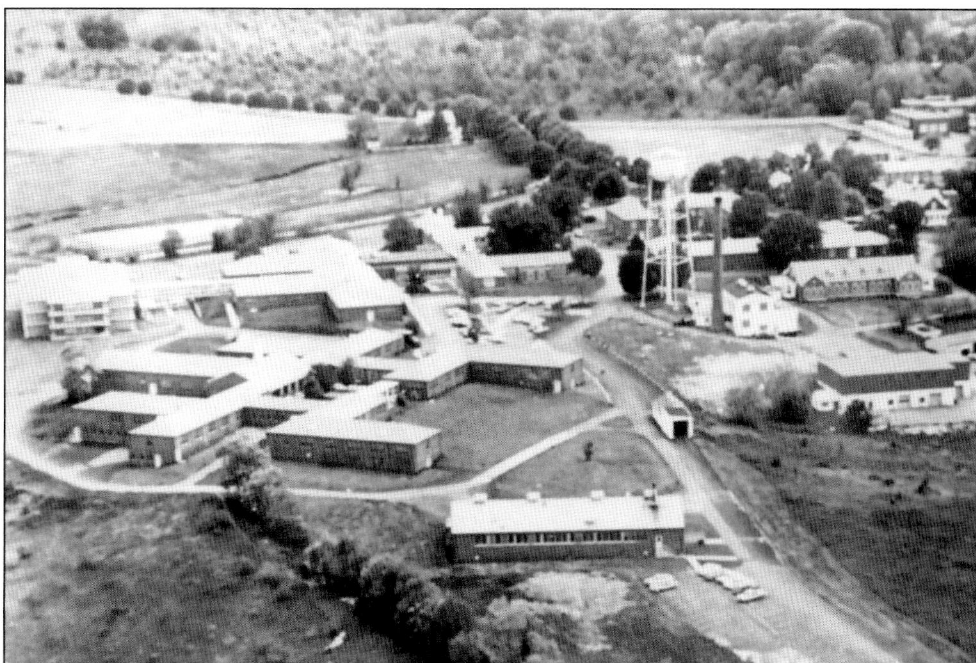

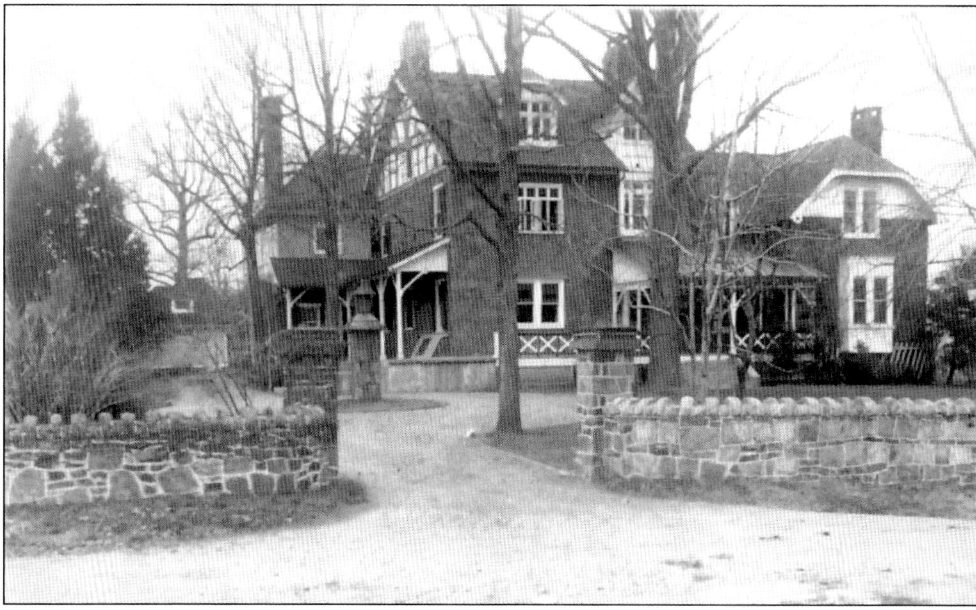

This house, built in the 1880s, stands on the north side of Rose Tree Road at the top of the hill between Painter and Ridley Creek Roads. It is seen above in a 1900s postcard and below in 1979. It originally had 17 rooms. The house was the setting for the 1978 ghost story *Night Stalks the Mansion* by Constance Westbie and Harold Cameron. In the book, Rose Tree Road was changed to Plum Tree Lane in the fictional Philadelphia suburb of Wynne. The Camerons lived there for about 18 months in the late 1940s. No other residents have reported any supernatural occurrences. The house had been unoccupied and boarded up for several years when it was destroyed by arson in June 1987. Only the stone walls remained when a new residence was built within the old walls.

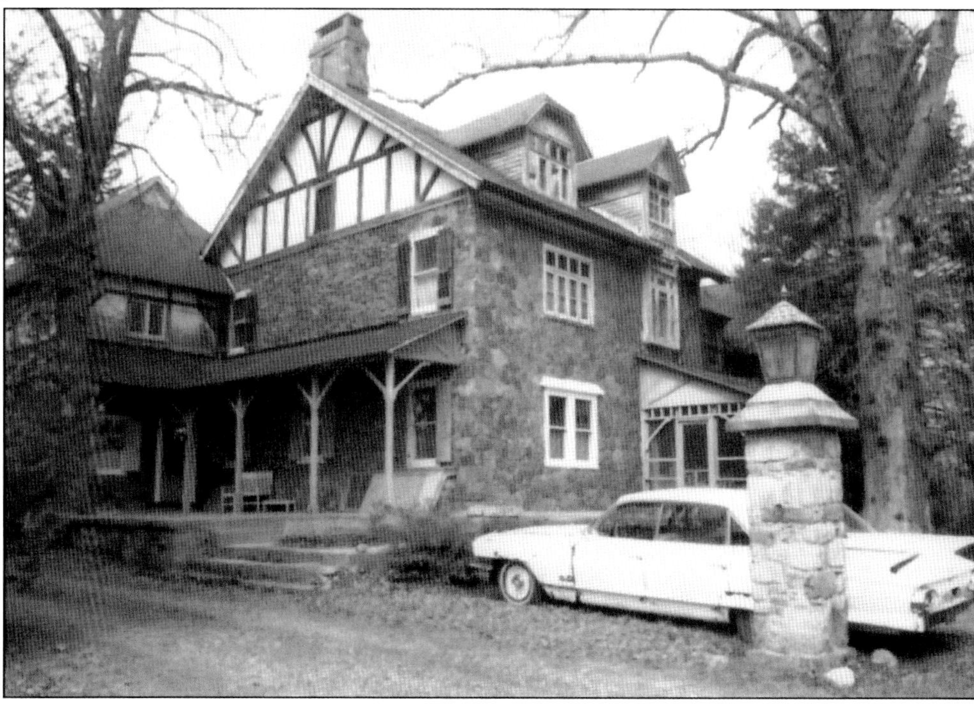

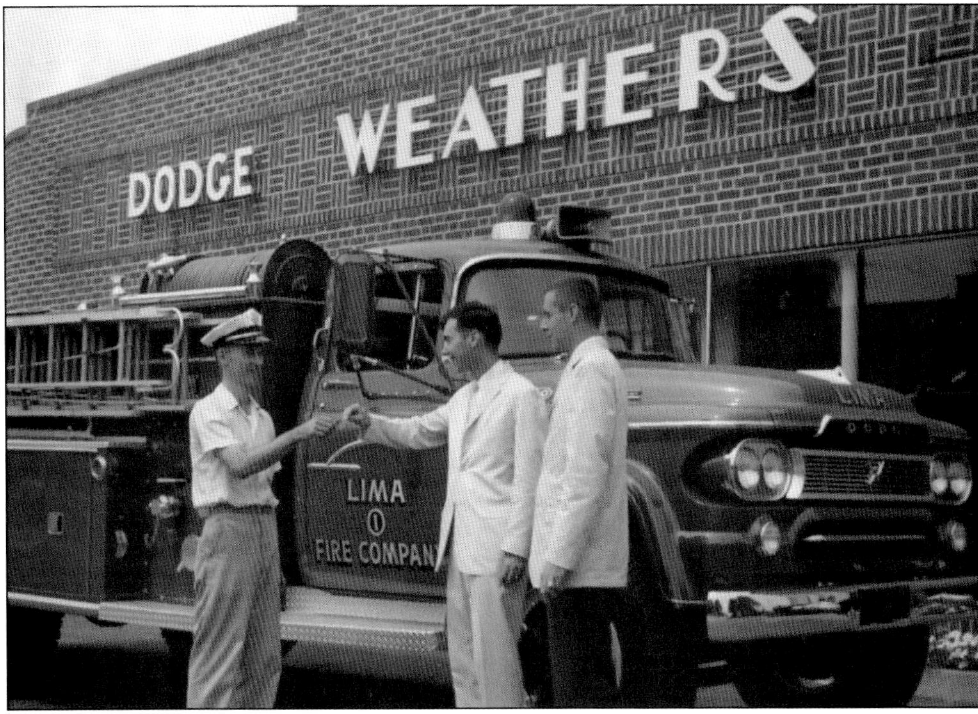

Above, Capt. Tommy Morris of the Lima Fire Company No. 1 receives the keys to a new 1960 Dodge fire truck from Dick Weathers and Larry Weathers Jr. of Weathers Dodge. The new firefighting apparatus is fully equipped and was custom built to designs created by members of the fire company. The company was happy to be able to serve the residents of Lima and the rest of Middletown Township with this new equipment. Below, the fire company responds to the October 1967 fire at the Clover Leaf Inn. (Both, MHAC.)

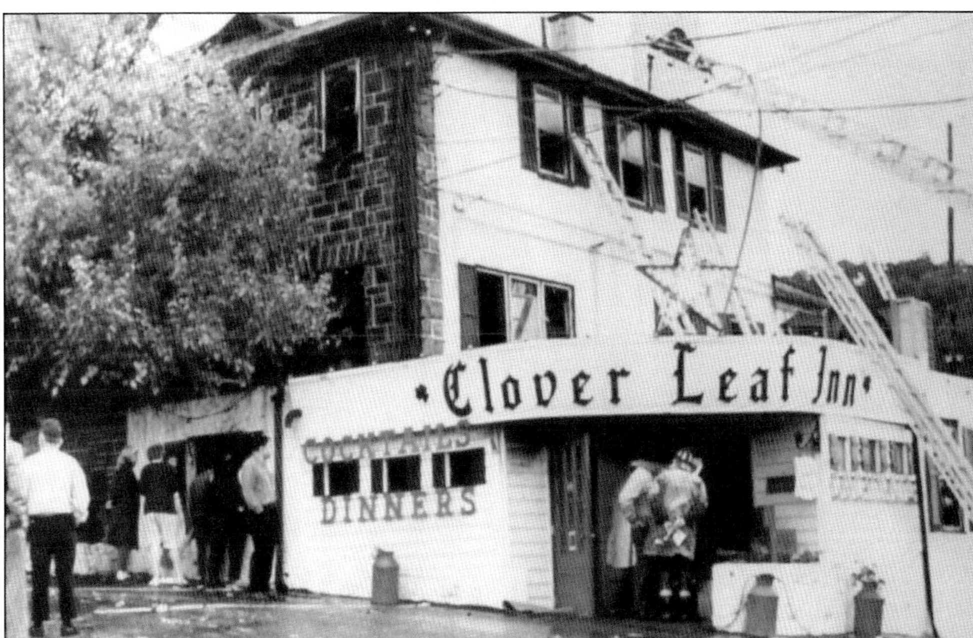

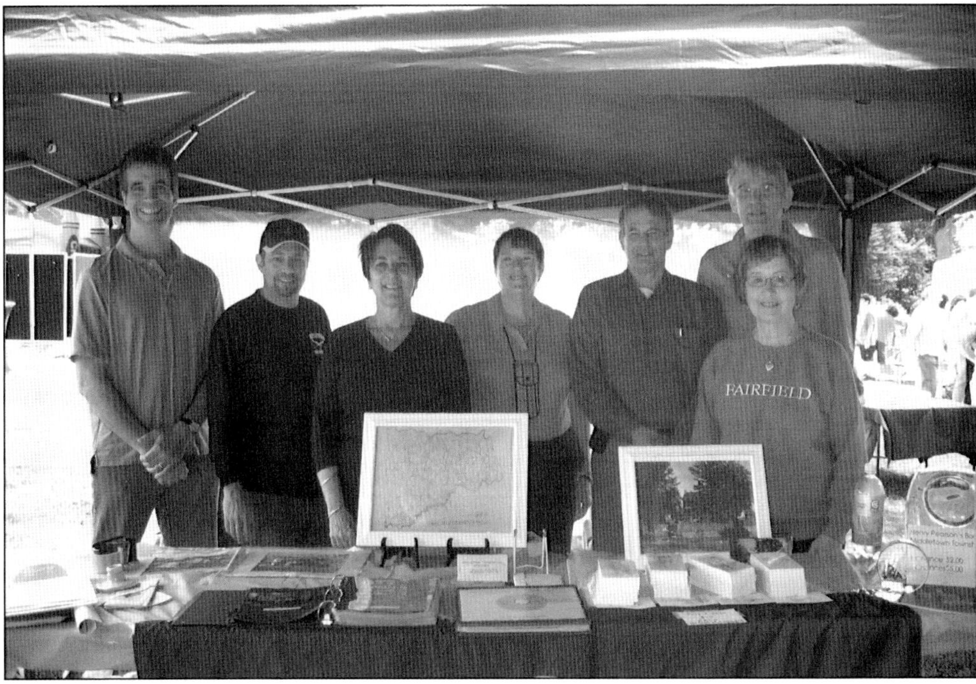

Above, the Middletown Township Historical Society participates in Middletown Township Pride Day in May 2010 at Williamson School. Included in the photograph are, from left to right, Chris Biordi, website chair; Anthony Ieradi, membership chair; Susan Mescanti, president; Mary Anne Eves, vice president; Michael Benson, secretary; Gary Grove, board member; and Suzanne Davis, board member. Below, at the society's Veteran's Day ceremony in November 2010, cosponsored by and held at Cumberland Cemetery, are, from left to right, Katherine Herman, Stephanie Herman, Michael Benson, Mary Anne Eves, Susan Mescanti, Gary Grove, and John Laskas.

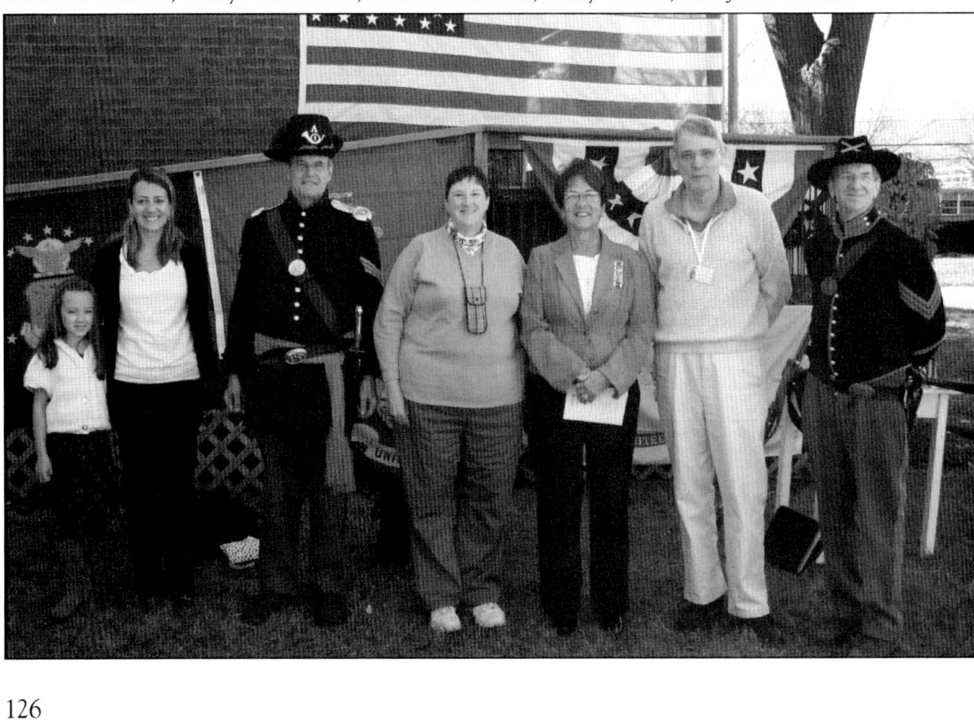

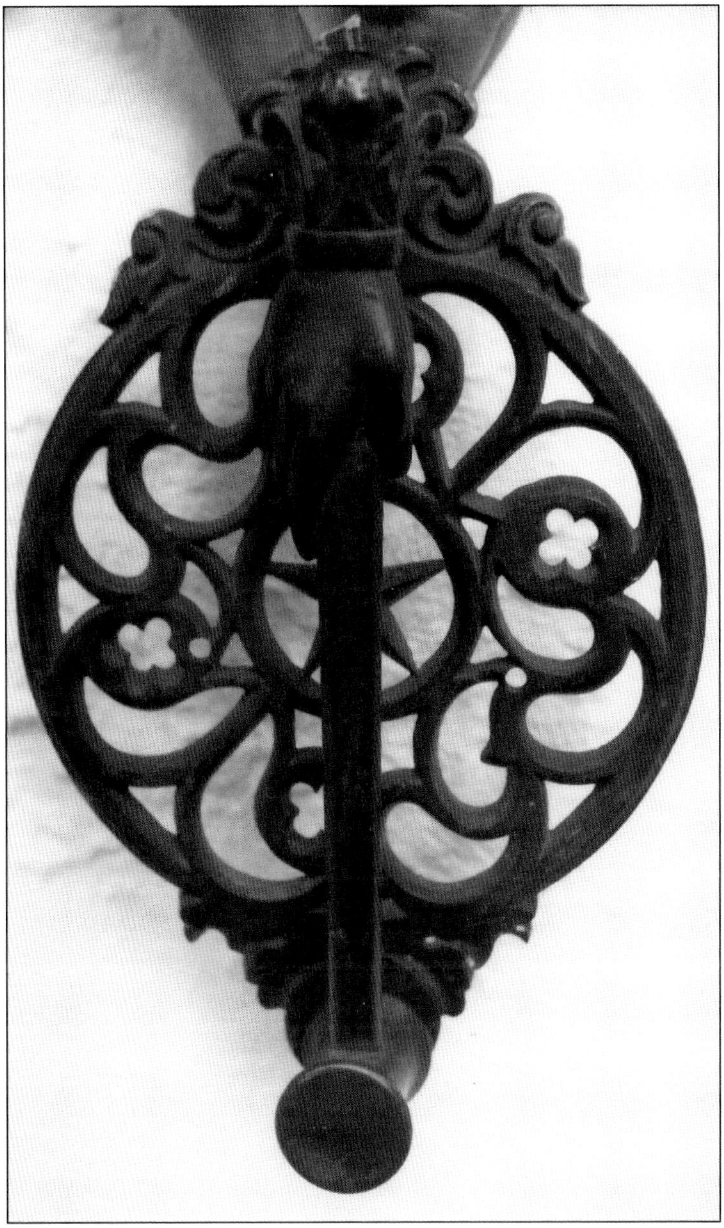

The Middletown Township Historical Society was organized in 1982 to celebrate Middletown Township's 300th anniversary in 1986. It was disbanded in the early 1990s but reformed in April 2009 in anticipation of the township's 325th anniversary in 2011. In 2009, we chose the doorknocker of the Black Horse Hotel as our logo because it symbolizes our mission, "opening the door to our past." The doorknocker was rescued from the old hotel in 1939 just before the building was demolished. We want to gather, catalog, preserve, and make available the history of Middletown Township for future generations of residents. We see this book as a first step toward that goal. If you have photographs of your family, residence, or business in Middletown Township that you would be willing to allow us to scan for our archives, please contact us at 610-316-5620; info@mthsdelco.org; or PO Box 203, Lima, Pennsylvania, 19037. If you have questions about membership or our programs please call, e-mail, or visit our website at www.mthsdelco.org.